DEVELOPING COUNTRIES AND THE GLOBAL
TRADING SYSTEM

Volume 1   Thematic Studies from a Ford Foundation
Project

STUDIES IN INTERNATIONAL TRADE POLICY

Studies in International Trade Policy includes works dealing with the theory, empirical analysis, political, economic, legal relations, and evaluations of international trade policies and institutions.

General Editor: Robert H. Stern

John H. Jackson and Edwin A. Vermulst, Editors. *Antidumping Law and Practice: A Comparative Study*

John Whalley, Editor. *Developing Countries and the Global Trading System*, Volumes 1 and 2

John Whalley, Coordinator. *The Uruguay Round and Beyond: The Final Report from the Ford Foundation Project on Developing Countries and the Global Trading System*

Developing Countries and the Global Trading System

Volume 1   Thematic Studies from a Ford
             Foundation Project

Edited by
John Whalley

Ann Arbor

The University of Michigan Press

Published in the United States of America by
The University of Michigan Press

1992   1991   1990   1989   4   3   2   1

ISBN 0–472–10148–X

Library of Congress Cataloging-in-Publication Data
Developing countries and the global trading system / edited by John Whalley.
     p.   cm.   —   (Studies in international trade)
    Contents: v. 1. Thematic studies from a Ford Foundation project   v. 2. Country
    studies from a Ford Foundation project.
    ISBN 0–472–10148–X (v. 1)—ISBN 0–472–10149–8 (v. 2)
    1. Developing countries—Commerce.   2. International trade.
    I. Whalley, John.
    HF4055.D485   1989
    382'.091724—dc20
                                                89–5203
                                                 CIP

Contents

List of Tables

List of Abbreviations

ACP	African, Caribbean and Pacific (countries)
AD	Anti-dumping
ASEAN	Association of South-East Asian Nations
BOP	Balance of payments
CACM	Central American Common Market
CAP	Common Agricultural Policy
CARICOM	Caribbean Community
CFC	Common Fund for Commodities
CSIER	Centre for the Study of International Economic Relations
CVD	Countervailing duty
ECDC	Economic Cooperation among Developing Countries
ECLA	Economic Commission for Latin America
ECOSOC	Economic and Social Council (UN)
ESCAP	Economic and Social Commission for Asia and the Pacific
G-5	Group of Five (France, Japan, West Germany, UK, USA)
G-77	Group of 77 developing countries
GATT	General Agreement on Tariffs and Trade
GDP	Gross domestic product
GNP	Gross national product
GSP	Generalized System of Preferences
GSTP	Global System of Trade Preferences
IATA	International Air Transport Association
IBRD	International Bank for Reconstruction and Development
ICA	International Commodity Agreement
ICCICA	Interim Coordinating Committee for International Commodity Agreements (UN)
IDA	International Development Association
IFPRI	International Food Policy Research Institute
IIE	Institute for International Economics
IMF	International Monetary Fund
IPC	Integrated Programme for Commodities

ITO	International Trade Organization
ITU	International Telecommunications Union
LDC	Less developed country
LDDC	Least-developed-developing country
LFV	Less than fair value
MFA	Multifibre Arrangement
MFN	Most favoured nation
MTN	Multilateral trade negotiations
NBER	National Bureau of Economic Research
NIC	Newly industrializing country
NIEO	New International Economic Order
NST	North–South trade
NTB	Non-tariff barrier
ODC	Overseas Development Council
OECD	Organization for Economic Cooperation and Development
OMA	Orderly Marketing Agreement
OPEC	Organization of Petroleum Exporting Countries
OTC	Organization for Trade Cooperation
PSE	Producer Subsidy Equivalent
PTO	Production and Trade Organization
QRs	Quantitative restrictions
RBP	Restrictive business practice
S&D	Special and differential (treatment)
SAF	Structural Adjustment Facility
SDR	Special drawing right (currency unit of the IMF)
SITC	Standard Industrial Trade Classification
SST	South–South trade
STABEX	Stabilization System for Export Earnings (Lomé Convention)
TPRC	Trade Policy Research Centre
UNCTAD	UN Conference on Trade and Development
UNDP	UN Development Programme
VER	Voluntary export restraint
WIDER	World Institute for Development Economic Research
WTO	World Trade Organization

Preface and Acknowledgements

This is the first of two volumes of studies which have resulted from a project on 'Trade Policy and the Developing World' supported by the Ford Foundation. This project was initiated in 1985 with three objectives in mind. The first was to organize a group of scholars from developing countries to work on the participation of developing countries in the trading system, with scholars to be chosen on the basis of their scholarly credentials as well as their degree of involvement in policy-related activities in their own countries. Having assembled this group, commissioned studies from each were to be used to draw together experience on global trade issues from these countries. Finally, the hope was that through the activities of this group it might be possible to produce a final project report which would present some fresh ideas for a policy audience on how developing countries should participate more broadly in the current GATT system, and more concretely in the Uruguay Round.

Project activities began with an initial conference held in Oaxaca, Mexico, in July 1986. Participants in the project presented papers which summarized the structure of their own countries' protection, how this had been changing, and what their countries' objectives seemed to be in global trade policy reform, including negotiations in GATT. Papers from this conference appeared in 1987, published by CSIER, University of Western Ontario, London, Canada, in *Dealing with the North*. This contained eleven papers on different countries as well as a thematic overview, and summarized many of the countries' experiences which are taken further in the present two volumes.

Work on the project continued with a series of project meetings in both developed and developing countries including Mexico, Costa Rica, Brazil, Kenya, Tanzania, Canada and Switzerland. At all of these meetings, paper presentations were made and revisions followed. In addition, project participants interacted extensively with staff from international organizations such as GATT, UNCTAD, the World Bank and others. The chapters included in this volume are the result.

They show a freshness and novelty, which reflects both the widely varying backgrounds of the authors and the grass-roots nature of the project. Along with the final report from the project, which is published together with these two volumes, they form the written output from the project.

All the participants are grateful to the Ford Foundation in New York and its officers, not only for the financial support without which the project could not have been undertaken, but also for their ongoing interest in the intellectual support for our efforts. In addition, the time devoted to project support by officials of a large number of agencies (GATT, the World Bank, UNCTAD, IMF, various directorate-generals of the EEC, and officials in departments and agencies of the US and Canadian governments) has been far beyond the call of duty. Many of them have attended project meetings, and participants have always found a warm and sympathetic welcome upon visiting these agencies. Also, the strong support for the project by a number of research institutes, such as the IIE in Washington and the TPRC in London, have added greatly to the project. In addition, there are a large number of academics and private researchers who have given generously of their time in support of our efforts. To all, we are indebted.

At the University of Western Ontario, Connie Nevill has provided the guiding hand that has helped the project run smoothly from which these papers result and Debbie Fretz has done an outstanding job in overseeing the editorial process of these volumes. Lucy Steffler and Rich Jones also provided invaluable assistance in seeing the contributions through to their final form.

JOHN WHALLEY

Notes on the Contributors

Marcelo de Paiva Abreu is Associate Professor at the Department of Economics, Catholic University of Rio de Janeiro. He studied at the Catholic University of Rio de Janeiro, the Federal University of Rio de Janeiro, the London School of Economics and the University of Cambridge. His publications in Brazil and overseas include books and articles in academic journals and collected volumes, mainly on contemporary and historical aspects of links between Brazil and the world economy.

Manmohan Agarwal is a Professor of Economics in the Trade and Development Division, School of International Studies at Jawaharlal Nehru University. After receiving his MA in Economics in 1966 at the Delhi School of Economics, he worked as an economist at the World Bank from 1971 to 1979. He received his PhD in economics in 1979 from the Massachusetts Institute of Technology in Cambridge, MA. In 1983, he was a Senior Consultant in the International Economics Division of the Planning Commission for the Government of India. He has written and published papers on Indian agriculture, India's exports and non-alignment.

Ramon L. Clarete works in the Office of the Secretary, Department of Agriculture in the Republic of the Philippines. He received his MA in economics from the University of the Philippines in 1980 and his PhD in economics from the University of Hawaii in 1984. He was a consultant for the Asian Development Bank in 1985 and for US AID in 1986. He was a Research Fellow at the East-West Centre in Honolulu in 1986 (summer) as well as Visiting Assistant Professor at the University of Western Ontario from 1985 to 1988. His areas of specialization are economic and agricultural development, applied general equilibrium analysis, international economics and trade policy, and econometrics.

Winston Fritsch is Associate Professor of Economics at the Catholic University of Rio de Janeiro in Brazil. He studied at the Federal University of Rio de Janeiro and the University of Cambridge and

has been Director of the Faculty of Economics and Administration
of the Federal University of Rio de Janeiro. He is currently Dean
of the Faculty of Social Sciences at the Catholic University of
Rio de Janeiro. He has published extensively on the history of
Brazilian economic policy and on current issues in international
political economy in academic and collected volumes in Brazil and
overseas.

B.H. Gunasekera is a Principal Research Officer in the Australian
Bureau of Agricultural and Research Economics. He holds an
honours degree in agriculture from the University of Sri Lanka
and postgraduate degrees in economics from the Australian National
University. Dr Gunasekera's recent research has focused on general
equilibrium analyses of Korean trade policy under imperfect competition and scale economics, intra-industry trade between Asian
newly industrialising countries and major industrial economies, and
international agricultural trade issues.

Colleen Hamilton is a research associate in the Department of
Economics at the University of Western Ontario. Previously she
worked with John Whalley studying Canadian trade policies and
the world economy and has also been a consultant to the Institute
for Research on Public Policy, Ottawa, on Africa and the global
trading system.

Robert E. Hudec is Melvin C. Steen Professor of Law at the
University of Minnesota. He is a graduate of Kenyon College
and of Jesus College, Cambridge. He obtained his law degree
from the Yale Law School, where he was Editor-in-Chief of the
Yale Law Review. Professor Hudec has published three books and
numerous articles on the law of international trade, specializing in
the law of GATT. In the 1960s he served on the staff of the US
Trade Representative. In recent years he has been a consultant to
the GATT Secretariat, and has served as a member of two GATT
dispute settlement panels.

Miles Kahler is a Professor in the Graduate School of International
Relations and Pacific Studies, at the University of California, San
Diego (UCSD). He received his PhD in political science from
Harvard University. Professor Kahler taught at Yale University and
the Woodrow Wilson School at Princeton University before coming

to UCSD in 1986. His recent publications include *The Politics of International Debt* (editor), *Decolonization in Britain and France, The Domestic Consequences of International Relations*, and numerous articles on comparative politics and international relations. Professor Kahler is chairman of the Committee on Foreign Policy Studies of the Social Science Research Council. He has been awarded fellowships by the Rockefeller Foundation and the National Science Foundation, and was a Council on Foreign Relations fellow at the International Monetary Fund in 1983–4.

Michael G. Kirby, is Assistant Director, Economic and Policy Analysis Branch, of the Australian Bureau of Agricultural and Resource Economics, and is responsible for macroeconomic analysis and major international trade research within the Bureau. Prior to joining the Bureau he worked in the Treasury and at the Australian National University. Dr Kirby holds an honours degree in economics from the University of Sydney and postgraduate degrees in economics from the Australian National University.

Janette Mark is an International Economic Relations Officer with the Canadian Federal Ministry of Finance. She contributed to this volume while working as a Researcher at the North–South Institute, Ottawa. She has a Masters of Public Administration from Carleton University and a BA from Guelph University. She has written a number of papers on Canada's trade with developing countries, and, with Professor G.K. Helleiner, she co-authored *Trade in Services, The Negotiating Concerns of the Developing Countries*, published by North–South Institute in December 1988.

John McMillan received his PhD in economics from the University of New South Wales. Professor McMillan was on the faculty at the University of Western Ontario before joining the Graduate School of International Relations and Pacific Studies, University of California, San Diego, in 1987. His publications include *Game Theory in International Economics, Incentives in Government Contracting* and numerous articles. His main area of research is microeconomic theory, in particular the modelling of strategic decisions under imperfect information. He has also researched Japanese business practices, economic reform in China, and international trade negotiations, and has been a consultant for the Canadian government and the Rand Corporation. Professor McMillan is a native of New Zealand

and was educated in Australia. He has received fellowships from the Social Sciences and Humanities Research Council of Canada and the National Science Foundation.

John Odell is Associate Professor at the School of International Relations, University of Southern California, USA. Formerly he was a professor at Harvard University, a visiting fellow at the Institute for International Economics in Washington, and a staff officer with the US Trade Representative. He received his PhD in political science from the University of Wisconsin in 1976. His publications include: *US International Monetary Policy: Markets, Power, and Ideas as Sources of Change* (1982) and *Anti-Protection: Changing Forces in US Trade Politics* (with I.M. Destler, 1987).

Ademola Oyejide is a Professor of Economics and former Chairman of the Department at the University of Ibadan in Nigeria. He has a BA (1968) from the University of Ibadan, MSc (1969) from the London School of Economics and a MA (1970) and PhD (1972) from Princeton University. He has written extensively on trade policy and other issues and has spent time at the Institute for International Economic Studies at the University of Stockholm as well as at the World Bank. He has also been involved in projects with the International Food Policy Research Institute (IFPRI) in Washington, DC, and the International Development Research Council (IDRC), Canada.

David Parsons is the Executive Director of the Pacific Economic Cooperation Conference's Minerals and Energy Forum and is based at the Australian National University in Canberra. He was previously a Senior Research Officer with the Australian Bureau of Agricultural and Resource Economics, where his research focused on agricultural trade and protection issues. He has an honours degree in economics from the University of Adelaide.

Gary Sampson was educated at Melbourne University and Monash University, where he obtained a DPhil in economics. He was appointed Senior Lecturer in 1973 in the Department of Economics at Monash University. Subsequently, he worked in various divisions at UNCTAD in Geneva. From 1984 to 1986 he held the joint positions of Senior Fellow in Economic Policy with the Reserve Bank of Australia and Professorial Fellow at the Centre of Policy Studies, Monash University. During this period of time he also held various advisory positions with the Australian Government. In 1987, he joined GATT in Geneva, where he is currently Director of the Group of Negotiations on Services Division.

Ann Weston is Director of the Trade and Adjustment Program at the North–South Institute, Ottawa. After receiving a BA in economics from the University of Sussex and a MSc in economics from the University of London she worked as a Research Officer at the Overseas Development Institute and then as a Senior Economics Officer in the Economic Affairs Division of the Commonwealth Secretariat in the UK. She has co-authored a number of books, including *The Commerce of Culture; The Experience of Indian Handicrafts* (1988 with Vincent Cable and L.C. Jaim), and *The EEC's Generalised System of Preferences* (1980, with Vincent Cable and Adrian Hewitt) and written several articles on various aspects of international trade.

John Whalley is William G. Davis Professor of International Trade and the Director of the Centre for the Study of International Economic Relations, in the Department of Economics, University of Western Ontario, London, Canada. He is also a Research Associate of the National Bureau of Economic Research in Cambridge, MA. He received his MA in economics from the University of Essex in 1969 and his MPhil and PhD in economics from Yale University in 1973. His fields of specialization include, international trade, general equilibrium analysis and policy issues in Canada.

Participants in the Ford Foundation Project

AUTHORS

Professor Marcelo de Paiva Abreu
Department of Economics
Pontificia Universidade Catolica do
    Rio de Janeiro
Rua Marques de São Vicente 225
Gavea, CEP 22453
Rio de Janeiro, Brazil

Dr Manmohan Lal Agarwal
Centre for Studies in Diplomacy
International Law and Economics
School of International Studies
Jawaharlal Nehru University
New Delhi – 110 067 India

Professor Nisso Bucay
El Colegio de Mexico, AC
Camino al Ajusco No. 20
Codigo Postal 01000
Mexico, DF
Mexico

Professor Eui Tae Chang
Department of Economics
Kyung-Hee University
1, Hwoiggi-Dong
Dongdaemoon-Ku
Seoul 131, Korea

Mr Guo Chong Dao
International Trade Research
    Institute
Ministry of Foreign Economic
    Relations and Trade
28 Donghouxiang,
Andingmenwai Street
Beijing
The People's Republic of China

Professor Felix Cirio
Advisor to the Director-General
Inter-American Institute for
    Cooperation on Agriculture
PO Box 55
22200 – Coronado
San José, Costa Rica

Professor Ramon Clarete
Department of Economics
University of Western Ontario
Social Science Centre
London, Ontario N6A 5C2
Canada

Professor Winston Fritsch
Department of Economics
Pontificia Universidad Catolica
    do Rio de Janeiro
Rua Marques de São Vicente 225
Gavea CEP 22453
Rio de Janeiro, Brazil

Professor Juan Alberto Fuentes
United Nations Development
    Programme
4ta. Entrada los Yoses
100 Metros al Sur
Apartado Postal 4540
San José, Costa Rica

Mr H. Don B.H. Gunasekera
Economic and Policy Analysis
    Branch
Bureau of Agricultural Economics
MacArthur House
GPO Box 1563
Canberra ACT 2601
Australia

Mrs Colleen Hamilton
Department of Economics
University of Western Ontario
London, Ontario N6A 5C2
Canada

Professor Robert E. Hudec
Law School
University of Minnesota, Twin Cities
285 Law Center
229-19th Avenue South
Minneapolic, MN 55455 USA

Professor G.K. Ikiara
Department of Economics
University of Nairobi
PO Box 30197
Nairobi, Kenya

Professor Miles Kahler
Graduate School of International
    Relations and Pacific Studies
University of California
La Jolla, CA 92093 USA

Dr Michael G. Kirby
Economic and Policy Analysis
    Branch
Bureau of Agricultural Economics
MacArthur House
GPO Box 1563
Canberra ACT 2601
Australia

Professor Nguyuru H.I. Lipumba
Department of Economics
University of Dar es Salaam
PO Box 35045
Dar es Salaam, Tanzania

Ms Janette Mark
North–South Institute
55 Murray Street, Suite 200
Ottawa, Ontario K1N 5M3
Canada

Professor John McMillan
Graduate School of International
    Relations and Pacific Studies
University of California – San Diego
Q-O62
La Jolla, CA 92093 USA

Professor John S. Odell
School of International Relations
University of Southern California
University Park – MC 0043
Los Angeles, CA 90089-0043
USA

Mr Manuel Otero
Embassy of the Argentine
    Republic
1600 New Hampshire Avenue, NW
Washington, DC 20009 USA

Professor T. Ademola Oyejide
Department of Economics
Faculty of Social Science
University of Ibadan
Ibadan, Nigeria

Mr David Parsons
Economic and Policy Analysis
    Branch
Bureau of Agricultural Economics
MacArthur House
GPO Box 1563
Canberra ACT 2601
Australia

Professor Eduardo Perez Motta
El Colegio de Mexico, AC
Camino Al Ajusco No. 20
Codigo Postal 01000
Mexico, DF
Mexico

Professor Gary Sampson
Deputy Director General's Office
GATT
Centre William Rappard
154 rue de Lausanne
Geneva, 21 Switzerland

Ms Ann Weston
North–South Institute
55 Murray Street, Suite 200
Ottawa, Ontario K1N 5M3
Canada

Professor John Whalley
Department of Economics
University of Western Ontario
Social Science Centre
London, Ontario N6A 5C2
Canada

ATTENDERS AT PROJECT MEETINGS AND CONTRIBUTORS TO THE PROJECT

Dr Robert Baldwin
Department of Economics
University of Wisconsin
Madison, WI 53706 USA

Dr Thomas Bayard
International Institute of Economics
11 Dupont Circle
Washington, DC 20036 USA

Dr Richard Blackhurst
GATT
Centre William Rappard
154 rue de Lausanne
Geneva, 21
Switzerland

Professor Ake Blomqvist
Department of Economics
University of Western Ontario
Social Science Centre
London, Ontario N6A 5C2
Canada

Dr Salih Booker
Assistant Program Officer
The Ford Foundation
PO Box 41081
Silopark House
Nairobi, Kenya

Professor Primo Braga
Department of Economics
University of Sao Paolo
Saõ Paolo, Brazil

Professor Drusilla Brown
Department of Economics
Tufts University
Medford, MA 02155 USA

Professor Gerardo Bueno
Centro de Estudios Internacionaies
El Colegio de Mexico
Camino al Ajusco No. 20
10740 Mexico, DF
Mexico

Lic. Rafael Castol
SRIA. de Comercio Y Fomento
   Industrial
Alfonso Reyes No. 30
06140 Mexico, DF
Mexico

Dr Jose Cordoba
Director General de Politica
   Economica Y Social
SRIA. de Hacienda Y Cred. Publica
Palacio Nal. Patio Central
4T0 Pisa,
06066 Mexico, DF
Mexico

Dr John Cuddy
UNCTAD
Palais de Nations
Geneva 10,
Switzerland

Lic. Fernando de Mateo
Asesor Del. C. Srio. De Comercio
SRIA. De Comercio Y Fomento
   Industrial
Alfonso Reyes No. 30
12 Piso,
06140 Mexico, DF
Mexico

Dr Dean A. DeRosa
Economics Office
Asian Development Bank
2330 Roxas Boulevard
Metro Manila, PO Box 789
Manila, 2900
The Philippines

Professor Ashok Desai
The Delhi School of Economics
University of Delhi
Delhi 110007 India

Lic. Francisco Gil Diaz
Director de Investigacion
  Economica
Banco de Mexico
Condesa 5, Piso 4TO
06059 Mexico, DF
Mexico

Professor Raul Fabella
School of Economics
University of Philippines
Diliman, Quezon City 3004
The Philippines

Dr Jeffrey Fine
Program Director, Regional Con-
  sortium for Economic Research
International Development
  Research Centre
Nairobi, Kenya

Dr Catherine Gwin
The Rockfeller Foundation
1133 Avenue of the Americas
New York, NY 10036 USA

Dr Michael Hart
Trade Negotiations Office
50 O'Connor Street, 17th Floor
Ottawa, Ontario K1A 1J1
Canada

Professor Carl Hamilton
Institute for International Economic
  Studies
University of Stockholm
Universitetsvagen 10A, 8th Floor
Stockholm, Sweden

Minister Clodoaldo Hugueney Filho
Department of Foreign Relations
Rio de Janeiro, Brazil

Dr Michel Kostecki
GATT
Centre William Rappard
154 rue de Lausanne
Geneva 21
Switzerland

Dr Sam Laird
The World Bank
Room S8-044, S Building
1818 H Street, NW
Washington, DC 20433 USA

Dr David Lee
Trade Negotiations Office
50 O'Connor Street, 17th Floor
Ottawa, Ontario K1A 1J1
Canada

Dr Ken Lewis
Trade Negotiations Office
50 O'Connor Street, 17th Floor
Ottawa, Ontario K1A 1J1
Canada

Professor Peter Lloyd
Department of Economics
Faculty of Economics and
  Commerce
The University of Melbourne
Parkville, Victoria 3052
Australia

Dr Patrick Low
c/o Gloria Sagarra
ACNUR
Apartado Postal 6-719
06600 Mexico, DF
Mexico

Professor Fidelis Mtatifikolo
Department of Economics
University of Dar es Salaam
PO Box Dar es Salaam, Tanzania

Dr Chong-Hyun Nam
The World Bank
1818 H Street, NW
Washington, DC 20433 USA

Dr Benno J. Ndulu
Head, Department of Economics
University of Dar es Salaam
PO Box 35045
Dar es Salaam, Tanzania

Dr Julio Nogues
DRDIE
The World Bank
1818 H Street, NW
Room 18-133
Washington, DC 20433 USA

Lic. Jesus Ortiz
SRIA. De Comercia Y Fomento
  Industrial
Alfonso Reyes No. 30
12 Piso
06140 Mexico, DF
Mexico

Dr Alfred Reifman
Senior Specialist in International
  Economics
Economics Division
Congressional Research Service
Library of Congress
Washington, DC 20540 USA

Professor Tom Rutherford
Department of Economics
University of Western Ontario
Social Science Centre
London, Ontario N6A 5C2
Canada

Professor Jaime Serra-Puche
El Colegio de Mexico SA
Mexico, DF
Mexico

Dr Shekhar Shah
Program Officer
International Economics
The Ford Foundation
55 Lodi Estate
New Delhi 110003 India

Dr Eckhard Siggel
Kenya Long Range Planning
  Program
Institute for Research on Public
  Policy
275 Slater Street, 5th Floor
Ottawa, Ontario K1P 5H9
Canada

Dr Murray Smith
Director, International Economics
  Program
Institue for Research on Public
  Policy
275 Slater Street, 5th Floor
Ottawa, Ontario K1P 5H9
Canada

Dr Frank Stone
Institute for Research on Public
  Policy
275 Slater Street, 5th Floor
Ottawa, Ontario K1P 5H9
Canada

Lic Miguel Angel Toro
Secretaria de Hacienda Y Cred.
  Publico
Palacio Nal.1 Patio Marian
4T) Piso OFNA/4038
06066 Mexico, DF
Mexico

Dr Christopher Welna
Asesor de Programs en Mexico
  Y Centroamerica
Fundacion Ford
A. Dumas 42
Col. Planco
11560 Mexico, DF
Mexico

Per Magnus Wijkman
Research Secretariat
Kommerskollegium
National Board of Trade
Box 1209
N-111 82 Stockholm
Sweden

Dr Martin Wolf
Chief Economic Leader Writer
Financial Times
Bracken House
Cannon Street
London EC4P 4BY
England

Dr Frank Wolter
GATT
Centre William Rappard
154 Rue de Lausanne
Geneva 21
Switzerland

Dr Roger Young
North–South Institute
55 Murray Street, Suite 200
Ottawa, Ontario K1N 5M3
Canada

Dr Soogil Young
Senior Fellow
Korea Development Institute
PO Box 113
Chungryang
Seoul, Korea

Part I

Designing the System

1 Introduction[1]

Colleen Hamilton and John Whalley

INTRODUCTION

This first of two volumes contains eleven wide-ranging thematic studies from a multi-country Ford Foundation project on Developing Countries and the Global Trading System.[2] How developing countries should approach their participation in the global trading system defines their subject matter. They outline some of their broad strategic options[3] along with what seem to be the directions being taken on global trade issues in the various project countries.[4] The chapters which follow evaluate the negotiating options for developing countries within the existing multilateral trade policy framework, including GATT and the Uruguay Round. They also ask what they might seek in terms of restructuring global arrangements so as to accommodate issues of concern to them.

Their options include keeping to a bloc-wide approach as in UNCTAD in the past; stressing broad principles in GATT, such as S & D status; negotiating reciprocally with developed countries in the GATT; pursuing issue-specific negotiations either inside or outside GATT through smaller subgroups of countries; forming coalitions with developed countries on issues of joint interest; or pursuing individual country interests on a go-it-alone basis. Broader issues have also been raised in the project, such as how important is improved market access compared to the contribution domestic policy reform would make in improving export performance; and whether developing countries should accept the current structure of global institutions as given and enter negotiations under existing rules, or instead focus on changes in institutional arrangements.

Substantial attention has been given in the project to the bloc-wide options for developing countries, despite the fact that some seem either disinterested in global negotiations, or have trade issues that are moving them toward regional rather than bloc-wide negotiating approaches. In previous GATT negotiations, developing countries adopted a passive approach to reciprocal bargaining, focusing on S & D status. They have sought recognition from developed countries that their trade problems are special, emphasizing that balance-of-payments difficulties prevent liberalization and domestic protection is needed by them to achieve their own developmental objectives. This is essentially a statement that developing countries cannot undertake any international discipline over their own trade policies and that, as a result, no reciprocity should be expected from them in trade negotiations. They have also argued that they should be granted preferential access to developed country markets to offset what they have seen as their own poor export prospects. Among the issues raised by the project are how significant the benefits achieved by developing countries using this approach have been, and whether the bloc-wide coalition of all developing countries on which this strategy has relied is sustainable in the long run.

The project also stresses how a number of issues which are central to developing countries are not adequately captured by the institutional framework under which trade policy bargaining currently takes place. Nine of the eleven countries in the project have major debt problems, but no negotiating framework currently exists within which firmer debt service guarantees by debtor countries can be negotiated against improved market access in order to provide export earnings to service the debt. Furthermore, several of the participating countries are major exporters of commodities, and for them stability of export earnings and their terms of trade are the central issues, neither of which is a negotiable issue within the current GATT structure. Also, most of the participating countries have at various times been recipients of IMF loans, which through the 1970s and 1980s have come with varying degrees of conditionality attached, including commitments to devaluation and trade liberalization. Such liberalization is not the result of a reciprocal bargaining process in the usual GATT sense, and how to treat such arrangements in negotiations is an issue.

The project has also reviewed the Uruguay Round negotiating agenda, (which was dominated by agriculture, services, intellectual property, and trade-related investment issues) and portrays it as offering relatively little of direct interest to developing countries. Indeed, when seen against a multilateral GATT–IMF institutional structure whose design (from the 1940s) is a reflection of developed rather than developing country concerns, the difficulties for developing countries in using the existing global institutional structure to negotiate changes in the trading system become clearer. As a result of these and other factors, there seems to be a lack of interest in either GATT-based or institution-changing negotiations in many of the project countries. This in part reflects the limited leverage and small economic size of developing countries both individually and as a group, and is reinforced by their belief that they can have little influence on the outcome of negotiations.

Despite adhering to a common position on principles with respect to multilateral negotiations, such as S & D status, individual developing countries typically use whatever is available to them when it comes to more narrowly focused trade issues which affect their own self-interest. For smaller countries this frequently involves using geo-political leverage, and exploiting the strategic interests of the developed powers. As a result, it is mainly the higher income and larger developing countries which are more interested in the broad spectrum of issues in the current multilateral negotiations. Some are in open conflict with developed countries on key issues, others are joining with the smaller developed countries on issues of importance to them. As the Round progresses, more distinct coalitions might form, and beyond the Round coalition-based strategies on a range of issues (including those outside GATT) seem possible. How all of this might develop over the next few years has been a major concern of the project.

DEVELOPING COUNTRIES AND THE GLOBAL TRADING SYSTEM

Our use of the term 'global trading system' encompasses both domestic policies in developed and developing countries which affect international trade flows and payments, and the various international arrangements and institutions which set the rules governing how these policies may or may not be used. Included are domestic trade and payments policies in both the developed and developing world, GATT arrangements, the activities of the IMF, the World Bank, UNCTAD, ICAs and regional trade arrangements (such as the Lomé Convention and the Caribbean Basin Initiative).

GATT[5]

Over the post-war years, trade has grown rapidly in the major developed countries, with trade as a fraction of GNP roughly doubling over a 30-year period in many (if not most) of these countries.[6] This growth in trade, in part, reflects reductions in tariff barriers on manufactured products by developed countries resulting from seven rounds of trade negotiations in GATT. The early GATT agreements set the levels at which tariffs on manufactured goods could operate in developed countries. They were then reduced through subsequent sectoral negotiations and general formula cuts in the Kennedy and Tokyo Rounds. These negotiations have also produced varying degrees of discipline over other trade-distorting practices, such as subsidies, domestic taxes and quotas. The net result has been mutually-agreed limits on the use of a range of trade-distorting policies (both trade-restricting and trade-promoting), although these largely apply to developed rather than developing countries, and have many gaps in coverage.

Developing countries are widely believed to have benefited from these tariff cuts, even though they have been concentrated on manufactures, since under the MFN principle they receive improved access to developed country markets when developed countries negotiate tariff cuts with one another. But along with tariff reductions under GATT has come a series of adjustment-resisting trade measures in developed countries which affect developing countries adversely.[7] These include voluntary restraint agreements covering 'import sensitive' industries such as textiles, steel, vehicles and consumer electronics; and 'contingent protection' (safeguards, AD and CVDs). The latter is largely protection triggered by imports which cause injury and/or are subsidized.

The aim of these trade restrictions is to limit adjustment costs for workers in trade-impacted industries in developed countries, but these measures have affected a number of developing countries which are now major exporters of manufactured items. These include Korea, Taiwan, Singapore, Hong Kong and Brazil, together with China and India to a lesser extent. These developing countries often refer to these measures as derogations from GATT (that is, violations of the agreements entered into by developed countries in the GATT). They have been particularly forceful in stating their position that these forms of protection should be removed. Some developing countries see these measures as targeted on their manufactured exports to developed countries, making development doubly difficult, since successful export promotion will produce further restrictions on their market access. Trade restrictions against textiles under the MFA have been the most contentious issue, although more recently similar forms of trade restrictions in steel have also been a source of complaint.[8]

In the various rounds of GATT negotiations developing countries have agreed to almost no discipline over their own trade policies. Most continue to use both high tariffs and quotas to restrain imports,[9] and have fixed exchange rates and foreign exchange rationing which operate as further trade-restricting measures.[10] The need for these high levels of protection was argued in the 1950s and 1960s by Prebisch (1962, 1964) on the grounds that developing countries needed protectionist policies to allow them to pursue industrialization policies (which were seen as development-promoting), and that chronic balance-of-payments problems and export pessimism prevented them from removing their trade restrictions. Both of these arguments were behind the call by developing countries through UNCTAD in the 1960s for S & D status which led to Part IV of GATT in 1965, in effect granting developing countries the special status they sought, although with no concrete benefits attached.

The developing countries expected such benefits would follow, while at the same time maintaining that their special status prevented any significant liberalization on their part and that preferential access for them was merited. The major benefit achieved thus far has been preferential tariff schemes in developed countries under the GSP. These are concessional schemes entered into unilaterally by developed countries which grant preferential access to a range of developing country imports. Since developed countries generally have only small (or no) tariffs on raw materials and commodities, GSP has largely benefited exporters of manufactures such as Korea and Brazil. Furthermore, benefits are not the result of any reciprocal bargaining, but are unilaterally bestowed by each participating developed country. The GSP is thus non-binding, and can be changed at any time without prior consultation with affected developing countries. In the case of the US, threats of withdrawal of GSP benefits are now being used to coerce beneficiaries to adhere to certain US demands such as labour standards and intellectual property protection. Also, higher income developing countries are increasingly being 'graduated' from preferences.[11]

The IMF and the World Bank

Also central to the interests of developing countries are the IMF
and the World Bank. These are the agencies through which credits
have been extended to developing countries with major balance-of-
payments problems, and which have taken on the role of providing
developmental assistance. Lending by these agencies to developing
countries first accelerated in the mid-1970s following the energy price
shocks, and increased again in the early 1980s when the severity of
the debt crisis became apparent. These credit lines have, however,
typically come with various forms of conditionality attached,[12] which
have involved requirements relating to external sector liberalization
(reductions in tariffs and quotas, and/or devaluation) and changes
in internal policies. Conditionality has frequently been criticized by
developing countries as imposing unilateral liberalization in the form
of lowered tariffs and fewer import restrictions, often accompanied by
exchange rate adjustments. In return, these countries receive loans,
but no credit is given for liberalization in subsequent international
negotiations.[13] Instead, they have to adjust to a liberalized domestic
market without gaining the additional benefits of improved access to
export markets for goods being promoted under these programmes.
These programmes require changes in domestic policies such as tax
increases, expenditure cuts and interest rate increases. Failure to
comply with these conditions leads to cancellation of the credit
arrangements. The degree of conditionality has in some cases
resulted in countries refusing IMF credits.[14]

ICAs

Another key element of the global trading system central to
the interests of developing countries are ICAs. Most developing
countries are exporters of commodities rather than manufactures,
and volatility in commodity export terms of trade and their
continued erosion, in part due to competition from synthetics,
is a central developing country concern. Most of the post-war
attempts at commodity agreements have failed (with the exception
of OPEC), partly because of the inability of groups of producing
countries to agree on the allocation of production quotas. The
1980 agreement on a Common Fund for commodities still awaits
ratification by the US Congress. How to proceed and what to

request of the developed world in this area are also issues for developing countries.

Other Arrangements

Other parts of the global trading system are less central to developing countries, but for completeness should be noted. Trade in temperate zone agricultural products is an important area of conflict[15] since developed country policies in this area can have serious repercussions in developing countries whether they be importers or competing exporters. This trade is in disarray, largely because domestic policies in developed countries remain free from any internationally-negotiated disciplines. A small number of developing countries (most notably Argentina) would significantly benefit from improvements in international discipline over domestic programmes in this area.

Trade in services is another important area (see Chapter 7 of this volume and Stalson, 1985). This area is currently relatively free of formal trade barriers, but domestic regulatory policies substantially restrict cross-border transactions. This area has been the subject of parallel negotiations in the Uruguay Round reflecting, in part, an effort to prevent future protectionist measures being used in services. This inclusion was resisted by ten 'hardline' developing countries[16] on the grounds that existing derogations from the GATT (such as textiles) should be dealt with first, before any new issues (such as services) were added to the negotiating agenda.[17]

In summary, developing countries face a global trading system in which they have obtained the institutional benefit of S & D status, but outside the GSP this has not yielded them significant benefits in the form of improved access. The small number that are major exporters of manufactures face market access problems which seem to have grown in importance in recent years. Difficulties occur mainly with voluntary restraint agreements, but the growing use of contingent protection is also a problem. A much larger number of developing countries are exporters of commodities, and have obtained little or nothing of value to them from ICAs, most of which have now broken down. Those with debt problems do not have an institutional mechanism they can use to link debt service assurances to improved access in order to generate the required export earnings. In addition these countries have

increasingly encountered pressures for domestic liberalization as
part of the conditionality associated with IMF and World Bank
support packages.

EVALUATING THE OPTIONS FOR DEVELOPING COUNTRIES

In approaching this wide-ranging system the issue for developing
countries is how best to use it and, if necessary restructure it to
their own advantage. Like developed countries, developing countries
want to have improved and more secure market access abroad for
their exports, and improved and less volatile terms of trade. They
also have to decide whether and how far they can liberalize domestically. They must assess whether linking domestic liberalization to
improved access via reciprocal bargaining is an advisable strategy
for them, and how far reciprocal bargaining under existing GATT
rules will take them. It is also necessary to evaluate what changes
in the system may be needed to broaden their negotiating opportunities.

Throughout this process, they have to live with the fact that
increasingly they are a large heterogeneous group of countries with
divergent interests. There are differences in size, with large countries
such as China, India and Brazil contrasting with small countries in
the Caribbean and the Pacific Islands and elsewhere. There are
both higher and lower income countries; and differences between
major manufacturing exporters and commodity-based exporters;
heavy debtor and largely non-debtor countries; differences in the
orientation of policies between an 'outward' orientation and 'inward'
orientation.

Although these differences have always been there, they seem
to have become more prominent in recent years. In the past, such
differences did not prevent developing countries from supporting a
common strategy in trade negotiations with developed countries.
Through the 1960s and 1970s, they tended to adopt a joint posture
of using UNCTAD to push for S & D status based on their strong
belief in the desirability of industrialization and their need for supporting domestic policies, including protection. The main objectives
underlying their joint strategy were that their own trade policies
should remain free from any internationally negotiated discipline

for both goods and factor flows, and that preferential access for their exports should be granted to them unilaterally by developed countries. Other objectives included more stability, and ultimately improvement, in their commodity-based terms of trade; increased aid flows; and the maintenance of controls over inward investment on sovereignty grounds.

The Options

The onset of new GATT negotiations, combined with a sense that the global trading system has undergone major change, seems to have caused several developing countries to begin to re-evaluate their approach. A small number are active in current GATT negotiating committees;[18] and developing countries undoubtedly played a major role in Punta del Este during the launch of the Uruguay round. There seems to be a growing awareness therefore that there are options for developing countries other than the approaches of the past, and that these should be evaluated.

As a group; developing countries can continue with their previous approach: namely requesting more concrete benefits from S & D status, including more preferential market access than they already have under GSP.

Alternatively, they can weaken their demands for enhancement of special and differential status and move toward reciprocal bargaining within the existing framework of the GATT, attempting to bargain access to their own markets for improved access to developed country markets. In moving toward reciprocal bargaining, they could attempt to negotiate as a single bloc with a single negotiator (which would almost certainly be infeasible given their differences of interest), negotiate through subgroups on specific issues (which also has difficulties, such as what concessions might be made to achieve progress on any given issue), or negotiate individually (which has the problem that each country's leverage is limited).

Another option would be that developing countries could instead concentrate their energies on seeking major institutional change, arguing that for meaningful reciprocal bargaining to occur between developed and developing countries, ways must be found of allowing for wider bargaining than is currently possible. The argument would be that the present system does not allow for issues such as commodities, debt and trade linkages, financial aspects of trade liberalization and IMF conditionality to be brought into any reciprocal bargaining. This is an argument for something close to the 'global negotiations' in the UN which were terminated in 1980 when the Reagan administration came to power.[19]

Individually, countries have an even wider menu of possibilities. They can largely ignore multilateral trade negotiations, reasoning that they are small and without influence in negotiations. As trade issues arise, they can act pragmatically, accepting the system as given, trying to protect and widen market niches for their exports where they have access. Also, for many developing countries domestic policy impediments to improved trade performance are probably more important than improved market access.[20]

Alternatively, individual developing countries can try to improve their access through international negotiations. If they are large enough and believe that it is realistic for them to have some influence on the outcome, they can actively participate in ongoing negotiations in GATT. They can also attempt bilateral negotiations with their major developed country trading partners, as Mexico did in its 1984 negotiation of bilateral subsidies and safeguard agreements with the US prior to joining GATT. They may also join or form coalitions on issues of importance to them either with other developing countries, such as the group on services prior to Punta del Este, or with various combinations of developed and developing countries as in the Cairns agricultural group.

Another option for them is to seek expanded trade on a wide range of products with neighbouring developing countries,[21] through customs and payments unions, even though most attempts to do this have proved to be failures. Finally, they can individually make or endorse calls for institutional change to deal with what they see as neglected issues of prime concern to both themselves and other developing countries.

These strategies are not mutually exclusive, and it may make sense for countries to use several of them at the same time. Countries can endorse bloc-wide calls for improved access being granted to them unilaterally, while at the same time pragmatically pursuing their own interests through other negotiating channels. Consistency in position across different approaches may be more of a concern for large countries than for small countries which have little influence over the overall system design.

The Bloc-Wide Approach

In the 1960s and 1970s, developing countries largely adopted a common bloc-wide approach to global trade matters,[22] to the relative exclusion of subgroup or individual country strategies. Their attempt to achieve enhancement of benefits under S & D status was based on the assertion that the problems of developing countries, while special, were none the less common to them all. This bloc-wide strategy appeared at the time to make good sense. With limited economic leverage available to them, achieving S & D was thought by developing countries largely to involve the bloc-wide strategy of exploiting the geo-political rather than the strictly economic interests of developed countries. The leverage was the developed countries' desire to have developing countries included in a global system of multilateral institutions designed by the Western powers, even if it meant that their participation had to be on special terms.

Developing countries used a variety of arguments to support their position. Some of these appeared in the influential Haberler report to GATT on trends in international trade (GATT, 1958) and others in the subsequent Prebisch (1964) UNCTAD report.

The central thesis underlying the developing countries' argument was that their trade problems are inherently different from those of developed countries. This claim was based on a number of premises.

1. Balance-of-payments deficits, along with foreign exchange shortages, it was argued, were endemic to the low-income status of developing countries. As long as they persisted, it would be difficult for any significant liberalization in developing countries to occur.
2. Developing country export prospects were poor because their exports were relatively income inelastic. A significant improvement in their balance-of-payments situation was thus unlikely, even if growth occurred in the developed world.
3. Growth requires industrialization which, in turn, requires domestic import-substitution policies (protection). On these grounds, trade liberalization achieved through reciprocally-bargained reductions in protection would be undesirable.

Developing countries thus argued that they should be free from any internationally-negotiated discipline over their own trade policies, and it was felt that they would not be in a position to liberalize for many years to come. Multilaterally-negotiated liberalization was therefore impossible, since with this view of the world there is nothing for developing countries to negotiate away, and preferential access to developed country markets was needed to offset their poor export prospects.

Developing countries also made the argument that their being granted S & D status was consistent with the self-interest of developed countries. They argued as follows:

1. The absence of discipline over their trade policies, combined with unilateral concessions by the developed world, would foster growth in developing countries, eventually leading to larger developed country exports.[23]
2. Developed country geo-political interests are helped by granting developing countries preferential market access in that growth tends to encourage more liberal political regimes.
3. Global justice dictates that trade concessions be made by the developed world as part of a broader redistributive trade and aid package to the developing world.

In seeking to advance their claims for S & D status, a bloc-wide approach among developing countries emerged in the 1960s, which manifested itself in UNCTAD. Solidarity within the group of developing countries was stressed, reflecting the belief that their common interests could only be advanced through collective action. Thus, while the developing countries sought to have their trade problems labelled as special, at the same time they also argued that these problems were common to all developing countries, and therefore that they should all be accorded S & D status.

The approach employed to achieve these objectives was to focus on the developed countries' desire to build global multilateral institutions to regulate world trade with the widest possible membership.[24] In the 1960s, developing country participation in GATT and the IMF was believed by both developed and developing countries to be in the interest of the Western powers, since it limited Soviet influence in the developing world. This belief allowed developing countries to strike a bargain: to participate in the multilateral institutional structure designed by the developed countries, but only on their own special terms. Newly independent developing countries joining the system in the 1960s also did not take on any disciplines over their own trade-restricting policies. A special status for them under GATT began to emerge, which has been called 'non-contracting-contracting party' status.[25] In 1965 this was formally recognized in Part IV of GATT which laid down the principles of S & D status.

S & D in the mid-1960s led in the early 1970s to the GSP.[26] Under the various GSP schemes introduced by the major developed countries, developing countries were granted preferential market access on a range of imports. Generally such imports had to be non-competitive with developed countries' products, and a variety of other restrictions applied, such as market share criteria.

GSP is usually cited as the one major concrete benefit for developing countries stemming directly from S & D. However, the benefits to developing countries from GSP are also widely believed to be small. In addition most of the benefits accrue to a small number of countries. Recent research by Karsenty and Laird (1986) using detailed UNCTAD data, suggests that in 1983, imports by GSP donor countries from GSP receiver countries were only 2 per cent higher than they would otherwise have been. In addition, they estimate that over 50 per cent of the benefits of GSP accrued to four beneficiaries: Hong Kong, Korea, Taiwan, and Brazil.[27] Furthermore, even full extension of GSP by including currently excluded products (such as textiles and food) and the removal of limits on the amount of imports subject to preferential treatment would only increase these gains by a factor of three.[28]

In retrospect, the wisdom of using a strategy of a bloc-wide approach to seek enhancements to S & D can be challenged, but there are arguments both ways. On the pro side, if developing countries do truly need freedom from international discipline over their own policies in order to pursue their developmental objectives, there is nothing they have to offer in reciprocal bargaining. Given the premise of an inability to liberalize, seeking S & D status and especially unilateral trade preferences from developed countries follows naturally. Developing countries acting collectively exploit the maximum leverage available to them to achieve their objectives, this leverage being the developed countries' desire for as wide a membership as possible in multilateral institutions.

Furthermore, if one believes that developed countries will inevitably use protection to resist domestic adjustments, a strategy of seeking enhanced S & D status may well offer the best hope for developing countries as a group to achieve some respite from developed country protective actions, many of which are aimed at other developed countries but none the less affect developing countries. This, in retrospect, has probably proved a forlorn hope, but given the limited economic leverage developing countries perceived themselves to have in earlier global negotiations there seemed to be few options available.

There are several arguments against the bloc-wide S & D strategy. First, developing countries tend to be small and trade theory suggests that they suffer more than large countries from their own trade restrictions.[29] One can also question the basic premise that the trade problems developing countries have are special. Many neo-classical economists would argue that there is nothing in low income status *per se* which implies that balance-of-payments problems are inevitable, or that trade-restricting developmental policies are necessarily desirable. And pessimism over developing countries' export prospects has not proved to be correct for those rapidly growing NICs with significant exports of manufactures.

Furthermore, one can argue that the escape from international discipline under GATT which developing countries have sought through S & D has proved to be something of a mirage. Freedom from GATT discipline on the grounds that chronic balance-of-payments deficits make liberalization difficult has its mirror image in increased discipline from the IMF, World Bank and the financial community, through conditionality linked to requests for credits. And the liberalization that has occurred has resulted from tie-ins to credits, and has not been bargained in exchange for improved access to developed country markets.

Finally, even if no major improvement in access to developed country markets results, participating in a process of reciprocally-bargained international discipline can still provide important benefits to developing countries. One of the prominent themes in the debates on the role of GATT in the late 1940s was its use as a masthead for those groups within countries that wanted to achieve a more liberal trading order.[30] Domestic protectionist pressures, it was argued, could be more easily resisted if pro-liberalization groups within countries could point to international treaties which rule out the type of protection being sought. S & D status implies an approach quite the opposite of one providing support for pro-liberalization groups within developing countries.

The arguments in favour of S & D status carried the day in the 1960s, with the creation of UNCTAD in 1964, the introduction of

Part IV of GATT in 1965, the GATT waiver for the GSP in 1971, and the introduction of country GSP schemes in the mid-1970s. As noted above, however, the concrete benefits that have accrued to developing countries as a result of S & D status seem to have been small, and have been concentrated on a small number of higher-income manufacturing developing country exporters. GSP benefits are not negotiated reciprocally but are a unilateral concession by developed countries, from which developing countries can be, have been, and are being graduated.[31] And while some other small benefits from S & D can be claimed, such as the conditional application of some of the GATT codes negotiated in the Tokyo Round, these concessions have been of marginal significance.[32] Indeed, as Fuentes argues (in Chapter 11, volume 2 of this study), the absence of an injury test for US countervail under the subsidies code has been harmful for non-signatory developing countries.

The bloc-wide strategy that developing countries followed in the 1960s and 1970s is therefore now under re-evaluation. The least developed and lower income countries see themselves as not benefiting from GSP, and some query the value of their continued adherence to a bloc-wide strategy. Richer countries that have been GSP beneficiaries see growing discriminatory trade barriers against their manufactured exports as a reason to consider an approach involving more reciprocity. And growing heterogeneity among the interests of individual developing countries makes it difficult to maintain the cohesiveness of a coalition involving all countries.

Alternatives to a Bloc-Wide Approach

The cohesiveness of the grand coalition of all developing countries is weakening, which has encouraged several countries to look at other approaches to dealing with their trade problems. This process has its own element of dynamic instability since, once the coalition of all developing countries becomes weakened, the benefits to individual countries from adhering so strongly to a bloc-wide approach are diminished. In the long run, therefore, the issue may be not only whether developing countries should rely on bloc-wide strategies as in the past, but whether bloc-wide strategies will remain feasible.

A number of developments both in the developing world and more widely in the trading system have served to weaken the common coalitional approach. One is that the belief in the developing world in the desirability of trade-restricting developmental strategies is no longer as uniform or as strong as it was in the 1950s and 1960s. Over the years neo-classical economists have repeatedly stressed the costs of anti-comparative advantage import-substituting trade policies, the gains from trade and the virtues of unilateral trade liberalization.[33] This line of thinking has had its effect, especially since high growth and import substitution have not gone hand in hand. Strong growth performance has come in the outward-oriented Pacific-rim economies of Korea, Taiwan, Hong Kong, and Singapore.[34]

In addition, a small number of developing countries, led by Korea, have been able to liberalize their payments regime and achieve rapid growth. This experience, as well as that of others, has led to a questioning of the credibility of claims that the trade policies of developing countries are as special as S & D advocates have claimed.

A further development has been rapid growth in manufactured exports for a few key developing countries, predominantly those same economies which have achieved high income growth (Korea, Taiwan, Hong Kong, Singapore and Brazil).[35] As this export growth has occurred, these economies have all encountered increasing difficulty in accessing developed country markets.[36] Young (1987) points out that 95 per cent of Korean exports are now in manufactures; and around 50 per cent of exports to the USA are restricted in one way or another by voluntary restraints, CVDs and other forms of restrictive measures. The problems which confront such countries trying to sustain export growth in the face of these barriers are not adequately dealt with by an approach that simply stresses enhancement of S & D status. Korea has thus become a strong advocate of a reciprocal bargaining approach.

Another development is that, relative to the mid-1960s when UNCTAD was formed and Part IV of GATT was negotiated, the developed country desire for strong global multilateral institutions appears to have weakened.[37] In part this is because the USA is no longer so hegemonic, but it also reflects a noticeable erosion of developed country commitment to global institution-building which was initiated with such fervour in the late 1940s.

The large debt of developing countries has also emerged as a problem for the trading system,[38] and as a source of leverage for developing countries with market access problems. Linking firmer assurances on debt service to improved market access[39] for exports has, for instance, been an approach which Brazil has suggested on a number of occasions.

As a result of these changes, there is now increased discussion of coalitional activity, both among sub-groups of developing countries, and between developed and developing countries. However, co-alitions are difficult to form and equally difficult to maintain. Even if agreement on common objectives can be obtained, agreement on how far countries are individually willing to go to achieve the objectives is difficult.

Thus far in the current trade round coalitions involving developing countries seem to have been largely 'agenda moving' rather than 'negotiating' coalitions. There are two major examples. The ten 'hardline' developing countries, led by India and Brazil, which argued strongly against including services on the agenda for the next MTN, were successful in eventually obtaining a twin-track approach in the negotiations which keeps services as a separate negotiating group. They achieved this even though Argentina and Uruguay eventually split away from the group to lend their support to a higher profile for agriculture in the Round. On agriculture, a group of 14 developed and developing countries (the Cairns Group) successfully pushed for its inclusion in the MTN as a high-profile issue.

At the ministerial meeting that initiated the Uruguay Round in Punta del Este, the USA and other developed countries found themselves discussing substantive trade issues with a number of Latin American and African countries, a phenomenon not seen in previous rounds of negotiations. Thus, despite the difficulties of coalition formation, participation in smaller group activity outside the grand coalition of all developing countries is now accepted as offering direct benefits to individual developing countries.

What might developing countries achieve through a different approach, and what might such approaches entail? There seem to be two broad classifications of approach: one which maintains a bloc-wide approach but seeks something different from enhanced S & D, and the other which uses subgroups to achieve more narrowly defined ends.

If developing countries maintain a bloc-wide approach they could either attempt to bargain reciprocally in GATT as a group, or use their group leverage to seek changes in the institutional framework within which negotiations take place.

Bargaining reciprocally in GATT poses three problems. The first is how much leverage developing countries as a group might have in such negotiations. This is a contentious issue since, while developing countries as a group account for only a small amount of world trade, their growth rate is higher than that of the developed world; leverage in negotiations over long-term trading rules should reflect expected size as much as current trade levels. Moreover, North–South trade is still largely an exchange of commodities and raw materials for manufactures.[40] A cohesive coalition able to use, for instance, threats of interrupted supplies of commodities has enormous potential leverage, even if this remains an unlikely event at present. Hence the commodity composition of trade and other factors, as well as relative country size, have to be taken into account in assessing leverage.

The second problem for developing countries would be how to maintain a cohesive coalition while bargaining as a group. Their individual interests are so different that prior negotiations among developing countries would seem to be called for to come to an agreement on what could be negotiated with the developed world. This would involve evaluating what concessions could be given in return, and at what point individual countries could withdraw and advance their own objectives on a go-it-alone basis. Even if such a process were successful, a negotiator for the developing world would have to be agreed upon who could quickly respond to the ebb and flow of negotiation. The pressures such a process would create within a group of all developing countries could well prove impossible to contain, fracturing the negotiating group.

Another issue is whether developing countries would see much benefit from negotiating reciprocally as a group in GATT, given both the structure of GATT and the agenda for the current MTN. The major issues of concern to developing countries – VERs for manufacturing exporters, debt and trade linkages for most and commodity issues for the majority – are not formally part of the MTN, and neither is there much prospect of active negotiations on these items in GATT. So many of the issues on the agenda for the current MTN – for instance intellectual property, services and trade-related investment – are of such limited immediate interest to developing countries that one can reasonably question why developing countries would choose to enter such a process.

Developing countries might instead try to use a bloc-wide approach to try to force institutional changes which more fully accommodate their interests. Included could be a recognition of financial liberalization by a developing country as a negotiable concession (see Clarete and Whalley, Chapter 4 in this volume); more fully incorporating commodities into global reciprocal bargaining; and linking debt repayment to more secure access to developed country export markets. None of these, however, is free of problems.

What exactly would firmer guarantees of debt servicing mean, and in what sense is that negotiable for market access? Presumably, market access could be withdrawn if debt servicing faltered, but the debt itself reflects previous transactions and is a sunk cost from the point of view of the lending countries. Access would effectively be bargained for cash, which is way outside the coverage of GATT.

Commodities also pose many problems. Developing countries do not want improved access as much as they seek improved and more stable terms of trade.[41] The GATT does not seem to be the framework in which to bargain access to developing country markets on the one hand, or for improvements of the type developing countries seek on the other. And what would be the concrete negotiating instrument on commodities, and the size of the developed country subscription to the Common Fund?

While there is little doubt that issues of major concern to developing countries are not covered by the current global institutional structure, radical change in this structure seems an equally difficult goal for developing countries to achieve. Many developing countries have thus found themselves beginning to think about either subgroup coalitional activities or, more typically, a go-it-alone approach to dealing with their trade problems. This is revealed by the experiences of the eleven participating countries in this project.

Notes

1.   An earlier version of this chapter was prepared for a meeting of the Ford Foundation project on Trade Policy and the Developing World held in Ottawa, 17–20 August, 1987. We are grateful to Ken Lewis, Trade Negotiations Office, Ottawa, for helpful discussions.
2.   The second of these volumes contains studies by participants from the 11 countries represented in the project. A volume of preliminary studies (*Dealing with the North*) was published as a research monograph by the CSIER, in 1987 and contains the papers from the first project conference held in Oaxaca, Mexico, in July 1986.
3.   See also the discussion of US policy options in trade with developing countries in Preeg (1985).
4.   The countries involved in this project are Argentina, Brazil, China, Costa Rica, India, the Philippines, Korea, Kenya, Tanzania, Nigeria and Mexico.

5.   For a much more detailed discussion see Hudec (1987) who presents
      a comprehensive legal history of the evolution of developing coun-
      tries' special treatment within the GATT. See also Dam (1970).
6.   Japan is an exception, with only modest growth in the trade-to-GNP
      ratio.
7.   See World Bank (1987), Table 8.3, p. 142.
8.   For further detailed discussion, see UNCTAD (1986b), p. 5.
9.   Often using GATT Article XVIII–B (balance of payments) as
      a justification.
10.   See IMF (1986).
11.   See Meltzer (1986).
12.   For more detail, see Guitian (1981).
13.   This idea of giving 'credit' to the developing countries that
      have undergone unilateral liberalization as part of IMF and World
      Bank programmes is being given serious consideration, provided the
      countries agree to bind the measures.
14.   Nigeria and Brazil are recent examples of this.
15.   See Trela, Whalley and Wigle (1987).
16.   Brazil, India, Egypt, Yugoslavia, Peru, Nicaragua, Cuba, Nigeria,
      Tanzania and Argentina (which subsequently dropped out).
17.   The Brazilian position on this issue, typical of the hardline group,
      is described in Abreu and Fritsch, Chapter 6 of this volume.
18.   For example, representatives from the following countries chair
      negotiating groups: Malaysia and Côte d'Ivoire (Tropical Products),
      Korea (MTN Agreements and Arrangements), Brazil (Safeguards),
      Hong Kong (Subsidies and Countervailing Measures), and Uruguay
      (Dispute Settlement).
19.   These global negotiations were to be held during a Special Session
      of the General Assembly in 1980 and were perceived as an attempt
      to achieve some progress towards the NIEO. Items to be discussed
      included raw materials, energy, trade, development, money and
      finance. Preparations broke down during 1980 when groups from
      North and South could not agree on procedures such as whether
      negotiations would take place in specialized agencies (North's
      preference) or in a forum such as the UN (South's preference).
20.   See, for example, Lipumba (Chapter 4 in volume 2).
21.   For further discussion of the potential of SST, see UNCTAD
      (1986a).
22.   This is best represented by the G77 in UNCTAD which has
      been largely responsible for voicing the position of the developing
      countries. For example, see Nyerere (1979). For further discussion
      of the G77, see Sauvant (1981).
23.   Similar arguments of self-interest have been used on other issues;
      for instance, there is the argument that commodity agreements give
      stability to buyers as well as sellers, and thus should be more strongly
      supported by developed countries.
24.   See the discussion of both this point and the entire history of the
      evolution of developing countries' legal relationship with GATT in
      Hudec (1987).

25. Wolf (1986).
26. For detailed discussion of the GSP, see Murray (1977).
27. Also, studies of GSP in the EEC show that imports from non-beneficiaries have grown at a faster rate than those from GSP countries (World Bank, 1987, p. 167).
28. See also the discussion in Brown (1988) and Baldwin and Murray (1977).
29. For example, Clarete and Whalley (1985) estimate that eliminating tariffs, quotas and export taxes in the Philippines in 1978 would have increased GNP by 5.2 per cent.
30. See the discussion in Hudec (1987).
31. The USA announced this year that Taiwan's GSP benefits will be reduced to US$2 billion, a cut-back of 37.5 per cent compared with to 1985. Korea's benefits will be cut by 24 per cent of its 1985 benefits (Far Eastern Economic Review, January 15, 1987, p. 50). According to Young (1987), Korea would gladly graduate from GSP and pursue lower MFN tariff rates if it meant respite from the 301 actions threatened by the USA and the threatened market denial in exchange for greater US access to the Korean market, especially in areas of agriculture, insurance and intellectual property.
32. This sentiment now seems to be widely shared. For example, the World Bank (1987) says: 'It has been suggested that by accepting S & D treatment the developing countries have struck a Faustian bargain. In exchange for preferences, which have brought them limited and risky gains, they have given up a voice in reciprocal trade negotiations and left themselves open to attack by protectionists in the industrial countries' (p. 167). See also Dam (1970), p. 649, and Wolf (1984).
33. See, for example, Balassa and Associates (1971), Krueger (1978), Balassa (1980), and Frank (1981).
34. See World Bank (1987), p. 85 and Figure 5.3, p. 86.
35. See GATT (1986), Tables A17, A37.
36. For further details on protectionism facing developing countries, see UNCTAD (1986b).
37. For further discussion, see Krasner (1985).
38. A further set of problems is the protectionist policies in creditor countries which hamper exports from the indebted countries, thus impeding their ability to service their debt.
39. For discussion of how trade policy changes in the developed markets could help alleviate the debt crisis, see Laird and Yeats (1987).
40. See Ikiara, Chapter 2 in volume 2.
41. This position is cited in Behrman (1978).

References

Balassa, B. (1980) 'The Process of Industrial Development and Alternative Development Strategies', World Bank Working Paper 438 (Washington, DC: World Bank).

Balassa, B. and Associates (1971) *The Structure of Protection in Developing Countries* (Baltimore, Maryland: Johns Hopkins Press).

Baldwin, R.F. and T. Murray (1977) 'MFN Tariff Reductions and Developing Country Trade Benefits Under the GSP', *Economic Journal*, 87, pp. 30–46.

Behrman, J. (1978) *Development, The International Economic Order and Commodity Agreements* (Reading, Mass.: Addison-Wesley).

Brown, D.K. (1988) 'Trade Preferences for the Developing Countries: A Survey of Results', *Journal of Development Studies*, 24 (3), pp. 335–63.

Clarete, R. and Whalley, J.(1985) 'Interactions between the Trade Policies and Domestic Distortions: The Philippine Case', CSIER Working Paper 8522C (London, Canada: CSIER, University of Western Ontario).

Dam, K.W. (1970) *The GATT: Law and International Economic Organisation* (University of Chicago Press).

Frank, I. (1981) 'Trade Policy Issues for the Developing Countries in the 1980s', World Bank Staff Working Paper 478 (Washington, DC: World Bank).

GATT (1958) *Trends in International Trade* (Haberler Report) (Geneva: GATT).

GATT (1986) *Text of the General Agreement on Tariffs and Trade* (Geneva: GATT).

Guitian, M. (1981) *Fund Conditionality: Evolution of Principles and Practices* (Washington, DC: IMF).

Hudec, R.E. (1987) *Developing Countries in the GATT Legal System* (London: Macmillan, for TPRC).

IMF (1986) *Exchange Arrangements and Exchange Restrictions Annual Report 1986* (Washington, DC: IMF).

Karsenty, G. and Laird S. (1986) 'The Generalized System of Preferences: A Quantitative Assessment of the Direct Trade Effects and of Policy Options', UNCTAD Discussion Paper 18 (Geneva: UNCTAD).

Krasner, S. (1985) *Structural Conflict: The Third World Against Global Liberalization* (Berkeley, Calif: University of California Press).

Krueger, A.O. (1978) *Liberalization Attempts and Consequences*, NBER (Cambridge, Mass: Ballinger).

Laird, S. and Yeats, A.J. (1987) 'On the Potential Contribution of Trade Policy Initiatives for Alleviating the International Debt Crisis', *Journal of Economics and Business*, 39 (3), pp. 209–24.

Meltzer, R.I. (1986) 'The US Renewal of the GSP', *Journal of World Trade Law* 20 (5), pp. 507–25.

Murray, T. (1977) *Trade Preferences for Developing Countries* (London: Macmillan).

Nyerere, J. (1979) 'Third World Negotiating Strategy', *Third World Quarterly* 1 and 2 (April).

Prebisch, R. (1962) 'The Economic Development of Latin America and its Principal Problems', *Economic Bulletin for Latin America*, 7, pp. 1–22 (first published as an independent booklet by UN ECLA, 1950).

Prebisch, R. (ed.) (1964) *Towards a New Trade Policy for Development: Proceedings of the United Nations Conference on Trade and Development*, (Geneva: UNCTAD), 23 March–16 June, vol. 2.

Preeg, E.H. (ed.) (1985) *Hard Bargaining Ahead: U.S. Trade Policy and Developing Countries* (Washington, DC: Overseas Development Council).

Sauvant, K. (1981) *The Group of 77: Evolution, Structure, Organization* (New York: Oceana Publications).

Stalson, H. (1985) *U.S. Service Exports and Foreign Barriers: An Agenda for Negotiations*, National Planning Association Report 219 (Washington, DC: National Planning Association).

Trela, I., Whalley J. and Wigle R. (1987) 'International Trade in Grains: Domestic Policies and Trade Impacts', *Scandinavian Journal of Economics* 89 (3), pp. 271–283.

UNCTAD (1986a) 'On the Potential for Expanding South-South Trade through the Extension of Mutual Preferences among Developing Countries', Discussion Paper 16 (Geneva: UNCTAD).

UNCTAD (1986b) *Protectionism and Structural Adjustment*, TD/B/1081 (Part I) (Geneva: UNCTAD), 23 January.

Whalley, J. (ed.) (1987) *Dealing with the North: Developing Countries and the Global Trading System* (London, Canada: CSIER, University of Western Ontario).

Wolf, M. (1984) 'Two-Edged Sword: Demands of Developing Countries and the Trading System', in J. Bhagwati and J.G. Ruggie (eds) *Power, Passions, and Purpose: Prospects for North–South Negotiations* (Cambridge, Mass: MIT Press).

Wolf, M. (1986) 'Developing Countries in the Global Trading System', CSIER Global Perspectives Working Paper 1986-02-G (London, Canada: University of Western Ontario).

World Bank (1987) *World Bank World Development Report 1987* (Washington, DC: Oxford University Press).

Young, S. (1987) 'South Korea', in Whalley (1987).

2 A Game-Theoretic View of International Trade Negotiations: Implications for the Developing Countries[1]

John McMillan

INTRODUCTION

The chapters in this book propose changing the global trading system, to make it work more in the developing countries' interests. What would be the consequences for the developing countries of redesigning the global trading system? Before fixing something, one should understand how it works. This chapter uses game theory to try to throw some light on how the global trading system works.

After developing a game-theoretic interpretation of some of the institutions of world trade, it will be argued that developing countries could gain from adopting an activist role in trade negotiations.

Arbitrariness is an essential feature of any negotiation, whether among nations or among individuals. If a negotiation is potentially fruitful in that there is some overlap of interests among the participants, then usually there will be not one but many possible agreements which will leave all better off than the status quo. In tariff negotiations, for example, there are many different combinations of mutual tariff reductions which would leave each country gaining from the change. This multiplicity of mutually beneficial moves means that there are returns from being actively involved in the process, trying to push the agreement in a favourable direction, since there are many different changes that one's negotiation partner would be willing to agree to.

Since there are many potential agreements that make all participants better off, the fact that the negotiations do not break down is more important to the negotiators than a precise weighing of the gains and losses from the agreement. It follows that there is an advantage to what one might call 'phoney precision' in negotiation. This is illustrated by the rule that has evolved to govern tariff negotiations within GATT. Under the norm of reciprocity, countries in effect barter tariff reductions in such a way as to result in a perceived balance of concessions. The value of a tariff reduction is measured by the percentage tariff cut multiplied by the volume of imports affected. From an economic point of view this measure is meaningless; but, in view of the multiplicity of mutually beneficial agreements, this meaninglessness does not matter. Reciprocity so defined can be simply and unambiguously measured; and it therefore serves as a focal point upon which an agreement can coalesce.

This view of the outcome of the negotiation process as being essentially arbitrary generates qualified optimism about the prospects for success in negotiations over matters more complex than tariff reduction. Consider, for example, a question of concern to both developed and developing nations: how to reduce the subsidies that nations give to their exporting or import-competing industries. The OECD has recently proposed ways of measuring the size of subsidies. Such measures can be criticized for the inevitably arbitrary assumptions upon which they are based. But, once again, phoney precision is useful in negotiations. In order to produce a focal point, it is helpful if there is an accepted way of keeping score in the process of mutual concession-giving. Because there are many potential mutually acceptable agreements, it does not matter that the way of quantifying concessions is itself arbitrary. An agreement on a common definition of the size of subsidies would move the parties a long way toward an agreement to reduce them.

THE TARIFF-SETTING GAME

Game theory analyses situations in which each agent's well-being depends not only on his or her own actions, but also on the actions of others; and all of the agents take these interdependencies into account when deciding their actions. Thus, just as an oligopolist's profit depends on rivals' price decisions, a trading nation's welfare depends on other countries' tariff decisions.

In 1953 Harry Johnson developed an analysis of interdependent tariff-setting that is essentially game-theoretic (although, like the Molière character who did not know he was speaking prose, Johnson was apparently unaware that he was dealing with game theory). Each country is modelled as choosing a tariff rate. To the extent that the country is large enough to be able to influence world prices, one country's tariff affects the other countries' welfare. As is standard in trade theory, each country is assumed to seek to maximize its social utility, which is a function of total domestic consumption of each commodity.

At an equilibrium of this game, each country chooses its best tariff given its rational expectation of the other countries' tariff choices. Johnson shows that this equilibrium tariff is equal to the inverse of the elasticity of demand for the country's exports (Johnson, 1953). It can also be shown that if all countries simultaneously lowered their tariffs below their equilibrium levels, all would gain (McMillan, 1986, pp. 29–31). Thus there is a sense in which the equilibrium, established by the individually rational actions of each country, is collectively irrational. No country can, by its own actions, make itself better off than at the equilibrium: but all countries would gain if some degree of cooperation could somehow be achieved so that coordinated tariff reductions occurred.

Does this model capture the essential features of trade-policy interactions? Two empirical observations suggest that it does not. First, what drives the model is countries setting tariffs so as to improve their terms of trade. Many countries, and in particular most developing countries, are too small to be able to affect world prices. A small country faces an infinitely elastic export demand; thus Johnson's result predicts that small countries will eliminate all barriers to imports. The most casual empiricism contradicts this prediction. Second, in an empirical implementation of Johnson's model, Hamilton and Whalley (1983) estimate equilibrium tariffs for the USA and the EEC to be in excess of 50 per cent: much higher than existing tariffs, but about the level of the tariffs that ruled after the tariff wars of the 1930s. This suggests that since the Second World War the developed countries have succeeded in reducing tariffs far below what is implied by Johnson's model. Evidently Johnson's analysis omits some mechanism that allows coordinated improvements to be made.

The next section will suggest a resolution of the first objection to the Johnson model: that the countries' aims are not adequately represented by the utility function which is conventionally assumed in the theory of international trade. The next section after that will suggest a resolution of the second objection: that a static model ignores the potential for cooperation inherent in the ongoing nature of international relationships.

PLAYERS, PAY-OFFS AND STRATEGIES

In the abstract, a game has three components: the players; a pay-off function for each player; and a set of strategies for each player. Before modelling a real-world situation as a game, we must address the questions of who the players are, what their aims are and what actions are available to them.

For the trade-negotiations game, the obvious answer to the first question is that the players are the nations. This is not, however, the only way of modelling trade negotiations. To answer certain questions requires that the nation's internal decision- making process be considered; for this purpose, the players might be, for example, labour and capital or Congress and the Executive Branch. For still other questions, it might be adequate to represent as players blocs of several nations. Nevertheless, the discussion to follow will presume that the players are nations.

What is the strategy set in the trade-negotiations game? This is essentially a rephrasing of the question 'What is the agenda for negotiation?' The answer is not obvious; the strategy set is larger than the traditional GATT agenda, in which strategies are choices of tariff rates. The strategy set might also encompass the various non-tariff barriers to trade and, potentially relevant to developing countries, it might range further beyond the current purview of GATT to include balance-of-payments, international-debt and global-security factors. Whether these other instruments should actually be used by the developing countries depends upon the predicted responses of the other countries.

Finally, what are the countries' aims? The idea underlying the rules of GATT as well as the positions taken by the negotiating countries seems to be that exports are a good thing and imports are a bad thing. The typical economist's view, in contrast, is that the purpose of the economic system is to provide individuals with consumption goods; imports achieve this, and exports are merely a means to this end, needed to pay for the imports. Quantitative evidence on this divergence of views comes from the computations by Brown and Whalley (1980) of the welfare consequences of the various tariff-cutting formulae proposed during the Tokyo Round negotiations. Using standard welfare measures, Brown and Whalley found that each of the USA, the EEC and Japan would have gained more from other countries' proposals being adopted than from their own. This could be explained as a series of mistakes. But more understanding of the process is to be gained if we presume that the countries' negotiators know what they are doing, but that their objectives are not captured by economists' welfare measures.

In order to build a positive or descriptive model, we must investigate the domestic politics of the trading nations. The Stolper-Samuelson theorem implies that changes in trade policy inevitably are redistributional: Some citizens gain, others lose. Thus interest groups lobby for different trade policies. The negotiators' aims can be taken to reflect the workings of this political process. The players in the trade-negotiations game, the nations, can therefore be taken as having utility functions that summarize the outcome of the domestic lobbying. In turn, the political lobbying is itself a game.[2] To analyse the trade-negotiations game it may not be necessary to model explicitly the domestic political game, or to understand in detail how the domestic political process works. It may be enough to know the country's preference ordering that emerges; this can be regarded as a reduced form of the domestic game. In other words, it may be enough for some purposes to regard the country as a black box, provided the objectives the modeler attributes to it are consistent with what actually occurs within the black box. The results of past trade negotiations provide some data on the negotiators' revealed preferences. For instance, econometric studies of the post-Kennedy Round tariff reductions in the USA have indicated that smaller-than-average tariff reductions occurred in industries with higher-than-average labour adjustment costs. Evidently the negotiators sought to protect declining industries and industries with a high proportion of unskilled or elderly workers.[3]

ENFORCING COOPERATION

Two basic distinctions in game theory are between zero-sum and non-zero-sum games, and between cooperative and non-cooperative games. The trade-negotiations game is non-zero-sum; that is, the sum of the players' pay-offs varies depending on their actions. Because the game is non-zero-sum, the nations have a common interest in reducing trade barriers; but they have conflicting interests over how the gains from cooperation are to be distributed among them. A cooperative game is defined by the ability of the players to make binding agreements; otherwise, it is non-cooperative.

In a cooperative game the outcome must be Pareto efficient. The argument is simple: from any non-Pareto-efficient point, there is by definition some movement that makes some agents better off and none worse off; since binding agreements can be made, such a movement can be presumed to occur.

The outcome of a non-cooperative game is a Nash equilibrium: each agent does the best he or she can given his or her rational expectation of the other agents' actions. In contrast to cooperative games, a non-cooperative non-zero-sum game, if played only once, typically has an outcome that is not Pareto efficient (Dubey, 1980). This is because no agent has an incentive to take into account the effects of his or her own actions on the other agents' well-being. There is some alternative set of actions that would make all the agents better off; but it is in no agent's interest unilaterally to act differently. The resulting contradiction between what is individually rational and what is collectively rational is exemplified by the prisoner's dilemma, and also by Cournot's oligopolists, who fail to maximize total industry profit. Furthermore, as we have seen, the equilibrium in Johnson's tariff-setting game has this property.

This unfortunate feature may disappear if the game is played repeatedly rather than just once. Provided the agents are sufficiently patient, an efficient outcome can be maintained as a dynamic Nash equilibrium if the agents use strategies which threaten retaliation should anyone deviate from his or her part of the efficient action (Friedman, 1986). Thus cooperative behaviour is enforced by the talion: the law of retaliation in which the punishment resembles the offence committed. In this way, for example, a cartel can maintain itself by having each member threaten to start a price war should any member engage in price cutting.

Three caveats must be added. First, the possibility of efficient equilibria requires that the agents do not discount the future too heavily. At any play of the game, an agent faces an immediate temptation to deviate from his or her part of the Pareto-efficient action. Agent A might be deterred by the other agents using 'trigger' strategies: threatening to retaliate in future periods should A defect. Thus the potential deviator faces a trade-off between a short-term gain and a long-term loss; the trigger strategies work as a deterrent only if A does not discount the future too much. We shall throughout assume that this is the case. Second, efficient outcomes are not the only equilibria. Playing the static Nash equilibrium repeatedly is an equilibrium of the dynamic game, as is every outcome that is better in the Pareto sense than the static Nash equilibrium. Also, there are typically many Pareto-efficient outcomes. Thus there are many equilibria and game theory does not predict which equilibrium will be reached. Third, the workability of trigger strategies requires that deviations from the prescribed actions be observable. Uncertainty limits the range of outcomes Pareto-superior to the static Nash equilibrium that can be dynamic equilibria (Porter, 1983).

What is the relevance of these theorems to the international trade game? Because there is no international authority with the coercive power to enforce the terms of contracts, games among nations are necessarily non-cooperative games. From the point of view of the developed nations, at least, GATT has been remarkably successful in reducing tariffs. Given that the international trade game is a non-cooperative game, how has GATT succeeded in generating multilateral tariff reductions? The answer is provided by Dam (1970, p. 79):

> The essence of the GATT system lies not in the abstract legal relationships created by a tariff concession but rather in the enforcement mechanism. Under Article XXIII the principal sanction for the increase of a duty in violation of a binding is the suspension by interested contracting parties of concessions made to the offending contracting party. There is no punitive sanction for nonperformance of the promise implicit in a tariff concession. The consequence of nonperformance is thus merely the re-establishment, at the option of an interested party and subject to the approval of the contracting parties, of the pre-existing situation (although the retaliatory suspension may be on items not originally negotiated with the offending contracting party).

GATT's enforcement mechanism, as described by Dam, resembles the retaliatory strategies in repeated games exposited above; thus the repeated game seems appropriate as a model of the GATT enforcement mechanism.

Incidentally, retaliatory trade restrictions are not a recent innovation. Adam Smith remarked upon their use:

> The case in which it may sometimes be a matter of deliberation how far it is proper to continue the free importation of certain foreign goods is, when some foreign nation restrains by high duties or prohibitions the importation of some of our manufactures into

their country. Revenge in this case naturally dictates retaliation, and that we should impose the like duties and prohibitions upon the importation of some or all of their manufactures into ours. Nations, accordingly, seldom fail to retaliate in this manner. (Smith, 1952, p. 199).

It must be stressed that efficient outcomes are not the only equilibria of repeated games. The repeated playing of the equilibrium of the single-play game, with its suboptimal outcome, remains an equilibrium of the dynamic game; as does every outcome between this and any efficient outcomes. Thus there is a surfeit of equilibria. Game theory does not predict an efficient outcome in a repeated game; it only shows that such an outcome is possible. This is sometimes forgotten. For instance, in a historical study of trade wars, Conybeare (1986) suggests that 'The most interesting analytic question is why several hundred years of iterated conflict could produce no lasting cooperation' (p. 156); Conybeare proposes several explanations. But there is no paradox here: non-cooperation is one of the equilibria. Game theory offers no guarantee that, when there are multiple equilibria, a Pareto-efficient equilibrium emerges. The players can be trapped in a low-level equilibrium.

THE NEGOTIATION PROCESS

The prisoner's dilemma has become a cliché of game theory. It will be argued here that to model an international confrontation as a prisoner's dilemma is to trivialize it.[4] The prisoner's dilemma is a very special game, in that it has only one outcome in which both agents are better off than in the static equilibrium. Thus, if the players can somehow ensure that an efficient equilibrium is reached, there is no further source of conflict. Real-world games are much more subtle: they have many efficient outcomes, with the potential for conflicts over how the gains from cooperation are to be shared. To end an analysis of an international situation with the observation that repetition of the game can induce cooperative behaviour is to leave unaddressed what is arguably the most important question: the division of the gains from cooperation.

The theory of cooperative games was designed to address questions about which Pareto-efficient outcome will be reached. A set of supposedly reasonable but essentially arbitrary axioms is proposed, and by applying them a particular efficient outcome is picked out. But this is entirely axiomatic reasoning: no behaviour by rational economic agents is being modelled. Most cooperative-game solution concepts, such as the Nash bargaining solution and the Shapley value, seem to bear little resemblance to the way international negotiations actually proceed. More recently there has been developed a non-cooperative theory of bargaining, in which the costs of delaying agreement, combined with the assumption that players not only act rationally but also form their expectations about others' actions rationally, yield a unique outcome (Rubinstein, 1987). Although this strategic approach is of great importance for economic theory, the existing analyses seem to be too stylized to be applicable to the international-negotiations game.

We must look, then, to less formally developed ideas in order to understand the negotiating process. Schelling (1960) proposes that focal points can be used to resolve multiple-equilibrium problems in games. A bargaining equilibrium is reached when the bargainers' expectations converge: when they share mutually consistent perceptions about what outcomes the others will agree to. At an equilibrium, 'each expects the other not to expect to be expected to retreat' (Schelling, 1960, p. 70). That there are many equilibria means that there are many outcomes that can be generated by mutually consistent expectations (or, more precisely, there are many subgame-perfect Nash equilibria). A focal point arises if there is some feature of the bargaining situation that serves to focus each agent's attention on a particular equilibrium point, and therefore to coordinate the agents' expectations.

The concept of focal point is not precisely defined. For this reason it must be used with care, lest it degenerate into a question-begging concept: a particular equilibrium occurs because it occurs. This trap can be avoided by listing at the outset the possible determinants of focal points. There are several; a particular outcome might be highlighted by historical precedent; or by some natural mathematical symmetry; or through the intervention of an impartial mediator (Kreps, 1984, Mandel, 1985, Roth, 1985, Myerson, 1986).

Laboratory experiments on a simplified bargaining situation conducted by Roth and his co-authors (Roth, 1987) yield some lessons about focal points. The subjects bargained for tokens, which were essentially lottery tickets. Each token was worth four times more to one bargainer than to his rival. When this asymmetry was not public knowledge, most agreements divided the tokens evenly;

this is a natural focal point. When the asymmetry was partially or completely known, two focal points typically emerged: each player got either an equal number of the (unequally valued) tokens, or an equal expected value of monetary reward. In repeated plays, the experimenter could manipulate a bargainer's expectations about what his or her opponent would agree to, suggesting that focal points can be established by precedent. Although equal division may be motivated by the bargainers' notions of fairness, there is evidence against this interpretation. When there were two focal points, each bargainer argued for the one that most favoured him or her; also, the frequency of disagreement increased with the distance between focal points, suggesting some kind of strategic behaviour.

One of the main features of the GATT negotiating procedure is the principle of reciprocity: the custom of rewarding another country's concessions by concessions of equal value. Although the preamble of the General Agreement mentions the desirability of 'reciprocal and mutually advantageous arrangements directed to the substantial reduction of tariffs and other barriers to trade' (GATT, 1986a, p. 1), reciprocity is not defined in the General Agreement. Custom has, however, given it a definition: countries in effect trade tariff reductions in such a way as to result in a perceived balance of concessions. The size of a tariff reduction is traditionally measured by the percentage tariff cut multiplied by the value of imports affected.[5] Thus, out of the many possible directions of mutual tariff reduction, a few possible directions are selected for consideration. The reciprocity custom serves to focus the negotiators' attention on a small subset of the possible tariff-reduction combinations: it establishes a Schelling-type focal point.

Reciprocity therefore has the useful effect of reducing the extent of arbitrariness in the negotiating process. As Dam (1970, pp. 88–90) notes, however, the norm of reciprocity is itself arbitrary; Dam describes it as an 'absurd' and 'naive' way of measuring the value of a tariff reduction. The economic effect of a tariff reduction is only loosely related to the volume of trade that it affects; also important are the demand and supply elasticities. Dam suggests that, instead of the volume-of-imports criterion, there should be a criterion based on some estimate, (albeit necessarily inexact) of the change in imports that will result from the tariff change.

If we view the reciprocity norm in focal-point terms, however, its arbitrariness is not a drawback. From a status quo point that is not Pareto efficient there are many mutually advantageous potential agreements. Because of the multiplicity of possible outcomes that would leave all players better off than the status quo, the negotiating process is by its very nature arbitrary. Reciprocity serves to establish a focal point because it is a simple rule cemented by long-standing custom. Its exactness is its virtue. A more economically meaningful but less exact rule, perhaps requiring quantitative estimates of demand and supply elasticities, would leave more scope for disagreement among the bargainers and therefore result in a higher probability of breakdown.

This interpretation of reciprocity is consistent with a lesson that can be extrapolated from the bargaining experiments reported by Roth (1987), summarized above. In these experiments there was a marked tendency for the bargainers to settle for a 50–50 split, despite the fact that units of measurement by which the 50–50 split was defined were arbitrary: the 50–50 split was nominal rather than real. Given the multiplicity of ways of improving upon the status quo, what seems to be needed for a bargaining settlement to be reached is a commonly-agreed way of keeping score in the process of mutual concession-giving; and it does not seem to matter that the units in which the score is kept have no real meaning, or that different but arguably equally valid units of measurement could be devised. In the Roth experiments, the bargainers failed to reach agreement in typically one-sixth to one-quarter of the cases; this is surprisingly frequent given the contrived simplicity of the experimental bargaining situation. We can conclude that, because of the multiplicity of ways of making all parties to a negotiation better off, the exact, true division of the gains from agreement is less important to the negotiators than the fact that the negotiations do not break down. Hence the appearance of equal division may be enough to generate agreement.

In the Tokyo Round negotiations, 'the way reciprocity gets put into practice is through a calculation of balance in the concessions that are being exchanged. This calculation of balance is quantitative, and it produces numerical measures that allow negotiators to evaluate the equivalence of the concessions offered by each side' (Winham, 1986, p. 266). According to one of the participants the final meeting on tariffs ended up being a series of 'long battles fought with hand calculators' (Winham, 1986, p. 266). Moreover, such quid-pro-quo bargaining was not restricted to tariffs. Reciprocity was also applied in the negotiations about NTB codes in the Tokyo Round, with negotiators demanding 'payment' for any actions they took (Winham, 1986, Chapters 6 and 7). For instance, in exchange for an alteration in its method of assessing taxes on distilled spirits, the USA extracted tariff reductions from the EEC and Canada. The US negotiators carefully calculated in dollar terms what they were giving and receiving over this tax issue; although, once again, the measures of the gains and losses made no economic sense.

RECIPROCITY AND THE DEVELOPING COUNTRIES

GATT's relationship with the developing countries has long been based on the principle of non-reciprocal and preferential treatment. This rests, at least on the face of it, on the idea that poor countries' development can be aided by preferential access to developed countries' markets. Recently critics of GATT's treatment of the developing countries have pointed out that practice has not lived up to this ideal. The principle of preferential access has failed to guarantee that the developed countries are open to developing-country exports. This has led to some questioning of the preferential-access and non-reciprocity provisions. Would the developing countries be better off if they were not accorded special status?

GATT rules do not prevent the developing countries from engaging in reciprocal bargaining; but they prevent developed countries from insisting upon it (GATT, 1986b, p. 192). Our analysis of bargaining suggests that, by not requiring that reciprocity be extended to the developing nations, the GATT rules may hinder the developing countries from using a potentially effective bargaining strategy. Developed countries, negotiating among themselves, can offer access to their own markets in exchange for access for their exports. Such offers are credible because the possibility of retaliation provides sanctions against non-performance. For the developing countries, in contrast, the insistence upon preferential status means that they are excluded from the process of finding mutually advantageous reductions in trade restrictions. Non-participants are unlikely to receive much from any agreement that is reached. This common-sense point is confirmed by non-cooperative game theory: if one player makes all the offers, that player gets the better of the bargain (Ausable and Deneckere, 1987).

While a theoretical analysis such as this can identify potential gains from extending reciprocity to the developing countries, it cannot establish its feasibility. It is often argued that reciprocity would not be effective because the developing countries lack the necessary bargaining power. Whether reciprocity for the developing countries would be workable is an open empirical question.

The term 'bargaining power', though often glibly used, is notoriously difficult to define in a precise, measurable and non-tautological way. However, the discussion of reciprocity and retaliation suggests a simple definition that is adequate for our purposes: one's bargaining power is greater the more one has to offer that the other party wants (via reciprocal bargaining) and, conversely, the more the other party would be harmed if one withheld what one has (in retaliation for violation of the agreement).

The aspect of a country's bargaining power in either GATT-based or bilateral trade negotiations that first comes to mind is its ability to offer or withhold access to its domestic market. Does this give significant bargaining power to developing countries, or is it so small as to be useless in negotiations? There is evidence to suggest that market access can in some instances be a viable bargaining tool for developing countries. Some, such as India and Brazil, have domestic markets that are large by any standards. Taiwan's share of world exports now exceeds Switzerland's and Sweden's and is almost one-fifth of the USA's share; while Hong Kong and Korea are not far behind Taiwan (GATT, 1987). Developing countries have a large share of the production and trade in some particular commodities; for instance, Malaysia is a dominant actor in the world markets for palm oil, rubber, copra and tin (Newbery, 1981). In a number of instances, developing countries' threats have achieved their desired ends. The People's Republic of China once threatened to cease grain purchases from the USA if new textile import restrictions were imposed. Malaysia induced Sweden to remove import restrictions on rubber boots by threatening to stop its imports of Swedish trucks. Chile secured access for some of its agricultural exports in Japan by threatening to cease its importation of Japanese cars.[6]

Quantitative evidence on the returns to activist negotiation comes from a study of the consequences of the Kennedy Round by Finger (1979). The nine developing countries that actively participated in the Kennedy Round negotiations induced the USA to lower trade barriers on 33 per cent of its imports from them.[7] This is less than the major developed countries or the other developed countries achieved (70 per cent and 49 per cent, respectively), but markedly more than the inactive developing countries (5 per cent). This perhaps underestimates the returns from active negotiation, for participation in the Kennedy Round by the 'active' developing countries did not necessarily consist of meaningful bargaining. An additional point is that what is under consideration is a set of procedures for trade policy that can be expected to be in place for several years. Thus the current size of developing countries' markets is less relevant than the future size; at current growth rates, the markets of countries like Korea and Brazil can be expected to be increasingly important. The developing countries played a more active and effective role in the negotiations in the Tokyo Round in the 1970s than in the Kennedy Round in the 1960s (Winham, 1986, pp. 272–3), which suggests that their influence is increasing over time.

Furthermore, the developing countries' bargaining options might be broader than just the offering of access to their own markets; trade flows measure only a part of the developing countries' potential bargaining power. The agenda might be expanded to encompass payment regimes, international debt, or global security (Hamilton and Whalley, 1988). Dixit (1987) argues that small countries often have an impact in international relations that is disproportionate to their size. For instance, the Philippines gains strategic leverage in trade negotiations with the USA from the USA's desire to keep its military bases in the Philippines. One interpretation of the history of the GSP is that its very existence is evidence of the bargaining power which the developing countries can extract from security matters. In this account, the GSP was a concession wrung from the Western powers in the 1950s in exchange for the developing countries' participation in the non-Communist bloc rather than the Communist bloc.

Regardless of the effectiveness for a developing country of extended reciprocity in its international interactions, there would be a welfare-improving effect on the political-economy game played within each developing country (sketched in the section on Players, Pay-offs and Strategies above). Admitting the principle of reciprocity strengthens the hand of the free-trade lobby in domestic bargaining, for a reduction in trade restrictions can be sold as the concession needed to ensure market access for the country's exporters. Acceding to the discipline of retaliation has a similar effect: the threat of retaliation from other countries provides an incentive for exporters to engage in lobbying against protection (Abbott, 1985). By making itself subject to GATT-based reciprocity, the government of a developing country would reduce the power of domestic interest groups by reducing its own scope for action. This voluntary relinquishing of power over trade policy would be analogous to the US Congress passing control over trade policy to the Executive Branch, in the Reciprocal Trade Agreements Act of 1934, on the grounds that the Executive Branch would be less responsive to interest groups than Congress itself.

In the focal-point interpretation, GATT's success in reducing tariffs on developed-country trade stems from the simplicity of the reciprocity custom that has evolved: the straightforward focal point is equal volumes of trade. If reciprocity is to be extended to issues of concern to the developing nations, such as agricultural trade and NTBs, equally simple focal points will have to be devised. Similarly, if the agenda is to be expanded to include international-debt and global-security considerations, workable focal points will have to be found. These focal points must be determined by something that is easily observable to all parties, and based on facts about which there is no scope for disagreement. Whether such focal points can be found remains an open question. If they cannot, it may be difficult or impossible for agreements to be reached. Consider for example the vexed question of how to get agreement on reducing the extent to which nations subsidize their industries; agriculture is the prime example. The OECD has recently developed what it calls Producer Subsidy Equivalents and Consumer Subsidy Equivalents, which attempt to measure the trade impacts of subsidies. There are, of course, severe problems of measurement here; some arbitrariness is unavoidable. But, analogous with the arbitrariness inherent in measuring the value of a tariff reduction, it does not much matter how the arbitrariness be resolved. Since there are many mutually advantageous potential agreements, there are many different ways of measuring the economic impact of a subsidy as a way of keeping score in the process of mutual concession-giving. If the focal-point model of the bargaining process is correct, then agreeing on a common definition of the size of subsidies would move the parties a long way toward an agreement on reducing them.

CONCLUSION

It has been suggested that the multiplicity of equilibria caused by the ongoing nature of the trade-negotiations game creates two distinct roles for GATT. One role is to ensure that the nations are not trapped in a low-level equilibrium, as apparently they were in the 1930s. Cooperation is achieved through the retaliation possibilities inherent in, the dynamics of the game. The other role is to provide a mechanism for selecting a particular outcome from the set of efficient outcomes and for resolving conflicts over how the gains from cooperation are to be divided. In this, the principle of reciprocity focuses the bargainers' attention on a small set of possible directions of change.

With some oversimplification, one can characterize relations among developed countries as being mediated by their self-interest, via reciprocity and retaliation. In contrast, relations between developing and developed countries are dependent, under the GSP, on the developed countries' goodwill. The developed countries have been remarkably successful in achieving tariff reductions. Evidently, and not surprisingly, self-interest is a powerful force in international relations. Can this force be turned to the developing countries' advantage? Perhaps it can, by using the mechanisms of reciprocity and retaliation which have worked for the developed countries. This might make the developing countries' access to developed countries' markets more secure, for it would be dependent on the developed countries' self-interest rather than, as now, on their goodwill.

Notes

1. I thank Ashok Desai, Michael Finger, Glenn Harrison, Lawrence Krause, John Whalley, Martin Wolf, and the participants in the Ford Foundation project for comments.
2. For analyses of some aspects of this game, see Hansen and Jaskold-Gabszewicz (1972), Brock and Magee (1978) and Bhagwati (1982).
3. The cited results are due to Cheh (1974) and Bale (1977). For further empirical analysis of the redistributional implications and the domestic political economy of tariff-setting, see Bayard and Orr (1980), Finger, Hall and Nelson (1982), Marvell and Ray (1983), and Ray (1981) on the USA; Caves (1976) and Helleiner (1977) on Canada; and Reidel (1977) on Germany.
4. Open to such criticism are the articles in Oye (1986), analyses of the politics of international security and economic conflicts that take as their basis the prisoner's dilemma game.
5. On the use in the Tokyo Round and the Kennedy Round of this definition of reciprocity, see Evans (1971, pp. 314–15) and Winham (1986, pp. 201, 266). This is what Bhagwati and Irwin (1987) term 'first-difference' reciprocity.

6.   The first two of these cases are cited by Hudec (1987). The third comes from a World Bank official.
7.   The nine active' developing countries were Argentina, Brazil, Chile, Dominican Republic, India, Jamaica, South Korea, Peru and Trinidad and Tobago.

References

Abbott, K.W. (1985) 'The Trading Nation's Dilemma: The Functions of the Law of International Trade', *Harvard International Law Journal* 26, (Spring), pp. 501–32.

Ausable, L.M., and Deneckere, R.J. (1987) 'A Direct Mechanism Characterization of Sequential Bargaining with One-Sided Incomplete Information', Discussion Paper No. 728, Northwestern University, April, forthcoming in *Journal of Economic Theory*.

Bale, M.D. (1977) 'United States Concessions in the Kennedy Round and Short-Run Labour Adjustment Costs: Further Evidence', *Journal of International Economics*, 7 (May), pp. 145–8.

Bayard, T. and Orr, J. (1980) 'Trade and Employment Effects of Tariff Reductions Agreed to in the MTN', Economic Discussion Paper No. 1, Bureau of International Labor Affairs (Washington, DC: US Department of Labor), April.

Bhagwati, J.N. (ed.) (1982) *Import Competition and Response* (University of Chicago Press).

Bhagwati, J.N., and Irwin, D.A. (1987) 'The Return of the Reciprocitarians – US Trade Policy Today', *The World Economy*, 10 (June), pp. 109–300.

Brock, W.A., and Magee, S.P. (1978) 'The Economics of Special Interest Politics: The Case of the Tariff', *American Economic Review: Papers and Proceedings*, 68, pp. 246–50.

Brown, F. and Whalley, J. (1980) 'General Equilibrium Evaluations of Tariff-Cutting Proposals in the Tokyo Round and Comparisons with More Extensive Liberalization of World Trade', *Economic Journal* 90 (December), pp. 838–66.

Caves, R.E. (1976) 'Economic Models of Political Choice: Canada's Tariff Structure', *Canadian Journal of Economics* 9 (May), pp. 278–300.

Cheh, J.H. (1974) 'United States Concessions in the Kennedy Round and Short-Run Labor Adjustment Costs', *Journal of International Economics*, 4 (November), pp. 323–40.

Conybeare, J. (1986) 'Trade Wars: A Comparative Study of Anglo–Hanse, Franco–Italian, and Hawley–Smoot Conflicts', in Oye (1986).

Dam, K.W. (1970) *The GATT: Law and International Economic Organization* (University of Chicago Press).

Dixit, A. (1987) 'Issues of Strategic Trade Policy for Small Countries', *Scandinavian Journal of Economics*, 89, pp. 349-68.

Dubey, P. (1980) 'Nash Equilibria of Market Games: Finiteness and Efficiency', *Journal of Economic Theory*, 22, pp. 363–76.

Evans, J.W. (1971) *The Kennedy Round in American Trade Policy* (Cambridge, Mass.: Harvard University Press).

Finger, J.M. (1979) 'Trade Liberalization: A Public Choice Perspective', in R.C. Amacher, G. Haberler and T.D. Willett (eds) *Challenges to a Liberal International Order* (Washington, DC: American Enterprise Institute).

Finger, J.M., Hall, H.K. and Nelson, D.D. (1982) 'The Political Economy of Administered Protection', *American Economic Review*, 72 (June), pp. 452–66.

Friedman, J.W. (1986) *Game Theory with Applications in Economics*, (Oxford University Press).

GATT (1986a) *Text of the General Agreement on Tariffs and Trade* (Geneva: GATT).

GATT (1986b) *The Texts of the Tokyo Round Agreements* (Geneva: GATT).

GATT (1987) 'International Trade in 1986 and Current Prospects', Press Release, 23 March.

Hamilton, B. and Whalley, J. (1983) 'Optimal Tariff Calculations in Alternative Trade Models and some Possible Implications for Current World Trading Arrangements', *Journal of International Economics*, 15 pp. 323–48.

Hamilton, C. and Whalley, J. (1988) 'Strategic Options for Developing Countries in the Global Trading System', mimeo (London, Canada: University of Western Ontario).

Hansen, T. and Jaskold-Gabszewicz, J. (1972) 'Collusion of Factor Owners and the Distribution of Factor Output', *Journal of Economic Theory*, 4, pp. 1–18.

Helleiner, G.K. (1977) 'The Political Economy of Canada's Tariff Structure: An Alternative Model', *Canadian Journal of Economics*, 10 (May), pp. 318–25.

Hudec, R.E. (1987) *Developing Countries in the GATT Legal System* (London: Macmillan for TPRC).

Johnson, H.G. (1953) 'Optimum Tariffs and Retaliation', *Review of Economic Studies*, 21, pp. 142–53.

Kreps, D.M. (1984) 'Corporate Culture and Economic Theory', mimeo, Stanford University, May.

Mandel, M.J. (1985) 'Focal Points and Wage Bargaining', mimeo, Harvard University, June.

Marvell, H.P. and Ray, E.J. (1983) 'The Kennedy Round: Evidence on the Regulation of International Trade in the United States', *American Economic Review*, 73 (March), pp. 190–7.

McMillan, J. (1986) *Game Theory in International Economics* (New York: Harwood).

Myerson, R.B. (1986) 'Negotiation in Games: A Theoretical Overview', in W.P. Heller, R.M. Starr and D.A. Starrett (eds) *Uncertainty, Information and Communication: Essays in Honor of Kenneth J. Arrow*, vol. III (New York: Cambridge University Press).

Newbery, D.M.G. (1981) 'Commodity Price Stabilization in Imperfectly Competitive Markets', Discussion Paper No. 32 (Washington, DC: Development Research Center, World Bank).

Oye, K.A. (ed.) (1986) *Cooperation Under Anarchy* (Princeton University Press).

Porter, R.H. (1983) 'Optimal Cartel Trigger Price Strategies', *Journal of Economic Theory* 29, pp. 313–38.

Ray, E.J. (1981) 'The Determinants of Tariff and Nontariff Restrictions in the United States', *Journal of Political Economy*, 89 (February), 105–21.

Reidel, J. (1977) 'Tariff Concessions in the Kennedy Round and the Structure of Protection in West Germany: An Economic Assessment', *Journal of International Economics*, 7 (May), pp. 133–43.

Roth, A.E. (1985) 'Toward a Focal-Point Theory of Bargaining', in A.E. Roth (ed.), *Game-Theoretic Models of Bargaining* (Cambridge University Press).

Roth, A.E. (1987) 'Bargaining Phenomena and Bargaining Theory', in A.E. Roth (ed.), *Laboratory Experimentation in Economics: Six Points of View* (Cambridge University Press).

Rubinstein, A. (1987) 'A Sequential Strategic Theory of Bargaining' in T. Bewley (ed.), *Advances in Economic Theory: Fifth World Congress*, (Cambridge University Press).

Schelling, T.C. (1960) *The Strategy of Conflict* (Cambridge, Mass: Harvard University Press).

Smith, A. (1952) *An Enquiry into the Nature and Causes of the Wealth of Nations* Chicago: Encyclopedia Britannica).

Winham, G.R. (1986) *International Trade and the Tokyo Round Negotiation* (Princeton University Press).

3 The Havana Charter Experience: Lessons for Developing Countries

Janette Mark and Ann Weston

INTRODUCTION

How differently things would have turned out had the ITO been established is one of those 'what would have happened if' questions that can never be answered. The fact that the GATT was only one part of a larger conception was later to play its part in the developing countries' view that the GATT was an inadequate instrument and unresponsive to their needs.[1]

Developing countries have long been discontented with the international trading system and, as the major remnant of the attempt to reorder trade relations at the end of the Second World War, GATT has been a constant target of their dissatisfaction. They argue that GATT, as it is now structured, fails to protect their interests and ignores many issues important to them.

To some extent these concerns are being addressed in the Uruguay Round of MTN which aims to improve the functioning of the GATT system and strengthen GATT's institutional basis.[2] In addition some contentious North–South issues (such as textiles, clothing and agriculture) will be raised. But many major trade policy problems for developing countries, such as the depressed market for commodities, fluctuating exchange rates and the increasing debt-servicing burden, will not be on the GATT agenda.

A key issue for developing countries therefore is whether to seek reforms within GATT, or pursue a more radical approach. In particular, over the years there has been an increasing sense of nostalgia in some quarters about the Havana Charter and the ITO, and a suggestion that the broader framework of the ITO would have led to more order and less tension in international trade relations than exists today.

Thus this chapter is not simply a history lesson; a major

goal is to bridge the gap between past and present, and to determine whether the, ITO provides a good (and realistic) model for reforming the trade system and reducing tensions between North and South. In the next section we examine the background to the Havana Charter, what the Charter involved and why the ITO never got off the drawing board. This is followed by a review of developing countries' major concerns when the Charter was negotiated and with GATT today, and brief comments on whether they would have been handled differently under the ITO. In the fourth we consider how developing country discontent with the GATT led to the establishment of UNCTAD and other proposals for changing the institutional basis of the international trading system. Our conclusions are summarized in the final section.

THE HISTORICAL CONTEST

Few questioned the need for some kind of trade organization. The great differences of opinion were about the powers the international body should have, the practices that were to be allowed, the extent to which existing trade barriers were to come into play for countries whose economic position had been seriously damaged by the war.[3]

There was a flurry of activity among the major trading nations during and immediately after the Second World War that focused attention on establishing a liberal trading system based on such principles as MFN treatment, non-discrimination and reciprocal negotiations. The goal was to increase world commerce by reducing tariffs and outlawing recourse to trade restrictions and, in turn, to spur economic development and restore some sense of order to international trade relations.

The experience of the 1930s had shown that a country's national policies could adversely affect the economic health of other countries; in particular, the policies of larger economic powers could be devastating for small, open countries. This was especially true of trade policy; the escalation of bilateral trade frictions and rising protectionism characteristic of the Depression had to be avoided.

There was also an underlying belief – among the Western nations at least – in free enterprise and the power of the marketplace; provide the private sector with a secure, stable and predictable environment – both at home and abroad – and growth and development would follow. Of course there would always be special cases that required the assistance of government but these were expected to be in the minority. In any event, such intervention, so far as it affected other countries, was now considered an international issue.

The discussions surrounding the formation of a new trade organization proved to be an arduous task, partly because of the breadth of issues involved but also because of the increasingly large number of countries in the discussion (at the Havana Conference in particular), and the balancing act needed to reconcile conflicting national and international policies. Thus, despite agreement that economic cooperation was a prerequisite for peace and prosperity, a common view on the extent and nature of cooperation in the trade field was not easily found.

In a Nutshell

In December 1945, the USA presented its *Proposals for the Expansion of World Trade and Employment* to ECOSOC as the basis for the discussion about the future of trading relationships. Since this document had been drafted in close cooperation with the UK, and to a lesser extent Canada, it reflected the prevailing concerns outlined above. The clear intention was to create a liberal trading system that would foster growth and stability, both economic and political.

Upon receiving the US proposals, ECOSOC appointed a preparatory committee with representation by 17 countries, including six now developing, to prepare a draft agreement for an international trade organization.[4] After three meetings of the committee during which major points of both principle and technical details were contested, a substantially revised draft surfaced. On 21 November, 1947, representatives of over 50 countries – including 32 developing – gathered in Havana for the International Conference on Trade and Employment to discuss and negotiate a further 800 amendments to the draft charter for a world trade organization. Four months later, on 24 March 1948, the conference was concluded and *The*

Charter of the International Trade Organization was signed by 53 countries.[5]

GATT

The road from the unveiling of the American proposals to the conclusion of the Havana Conference in 1948 was a long one and, in the interim, some countries decided to take a slight detour. On the suggestion of the USA, 23 countries – including 11 developing – convened a meeting in April 1947 to negotiate multilateral tariff reductions.[6] After a few months of negotiations, these countries placed the results under a General Agreement on Tariffs and Trade – GATT. For the most part, GATT rules were drawn from the commercial policy chapter of the draft Charter and thus reflected the original American proposals. It was assumed that when the proposed ITO was put in place, the results of the GATT negotiation would be incorporated into it. However, when countries met in Annecy for a second time under the auspices of GATT in 1949, the future of the Charter was uncertain and GATT members, by then totalling 33, took measures to make their arrangement somewhat more permanent, although there was no mention of providing it with any institutional support.

Why was the Charter not Ratified?

By 1948, post-war trade negotiations had produced both a comprehensive trade charter backed by a strong institution and a provisional agreement with a narrow mandate and slight institutional structure. In the end, it was GATT that survived. The Havana Charter was in effect stillborn.

Both the 'success' and 'failure' of the Charter for a world trade organization rested in the fact that it was a negotiated document. It differed sufficiently from the original American proposals to indicate that a real compromise was achieved over the course of three years. The ultimate concessions came from the American delegation which was willing to give way on major points to the developing countries so as to achieve an agreement with universal membership. In the end, however, intense American domestic opposition to the Charter effectively killed the initiative, with no recourse to further negotiation. Knowing that it had little chance of success, the Administration decided on 6 December, 1950 not to resubmit the Charter to Congress for ratification.

It was the institutional structure, perhaps as much as the nature of the rules it was intended to administer, that eventually led to the US failure to ratify the Havana Charter. There was strong opposition in Congress to surrendering some of its authority over trade policy to an international organization in which the US would have little control, even with the support of its developed country allies. However, those that feared the power given to the proposed ITO over national policies were joined in their effort to kill the Charter by two main camps. On the one hand were the perfectionists, or free traders. From this group's vantage point the Charter was too one-sided; it contained so many loopholes and strayed far enough from the basic principles of free trade that the end result was considered worse than having no agreement at all. Furthermore, some elements appeared to contradict free enterprise values; they noted references to full employment, commodity provisions that allowed government regulation and references to restrictive business practice condoning interference with private investors.

At the opposite end were the protectionists. This group voiced the familiar argument that the American economy would be ruined by a flood of imports if the Charter was ratified. They also concurred that the ITO would tie the hands of government and interfere too much in domestic affairs. In other words, despite all the loopholes (some of which were included at the insistence of the US), this group argued that the Charter did not go far enough to protect their interests and American sovereignty.

It is perhaps simplistic to put so much weight on American opposition to the Charter; certainly, there were second thoughts in other capitals as well once the ink had dried and domestic debate proceeded. However, it remains that the USA was the most important actor and any organization – be it political, economic or technical – to which it did not belong had little chance of survival let alone effectiveness. Consequently, even many of those countries that did ratify the Charter included a provision that their ratification was subject to US membership.

DEVELOPING COUNTRY CONCERNS: THEN AND NOW

The majority of countries that are now considered to be 'developing' were still many years away from independence when discussions about a new trade organization began after 1945. None the less, approximately 30 'underdeveloped countries' – as they were then known – participated in the Havana Conference and signed the Charter.[7] In this section we look at the way developing countries' immediate concerns with economic development and commodities were handled. We also consider whether the enactment of the ITO would have helped to resolve some of the other trade issues which preoccupy developing countries today; specifically, the discriminatory restraints on their manufactured exports, the inadequate rules for agricultural trade, the 'new' areas of services and investment and the trade-debt link. The broader issue of institutional reform is dealt with in the next major section.

Economic Development

The original US proposals made little reference to the particular needs of the developing countries; the US assumed that if every country adhered to some basic rules and freed international trade and capital flows, economic growth and development would follow. Although the Americans approved of helping needy countries, they felt that this responsibility was more appropriate for other agencies and organizations which provided development aid and technical assistance (such as ECOSOC and IBRD).

This 'hands-off' approach met with immediate opposition from India and some Latin American countries. Their representatives argued that developing countries could not compete on an equal footing with the industrialized countries; the Charter's rules had to allow for the industrialization policies many developing countries were introducing. While the US proposals recognized that tariffs or direct subsidies might be needed to support industrialization in special cases, the fact that they specifically ruled out the use of import quotas or tariff preferences over and above those that already existed became the topic of heated debate.[8] Developing countries favoured the use of tariff preferences as a tool for increasing trade with their regional neighbours but they were particularly concerned about the right to use quotas to promote their industrialization. Given the philosophical differences, a major disagreement between the US and the developing countries – joined by Australia – became the focus of considerable animosity.

To defuse this conflict, which was quickly souring the work of the Preparatory Committee, a separate committee on industrial development was created with representatives from Australia and some developing countries, amongst others. The committee was responsible for drafting a new objective for the Charter, namely: 'To foster and assist industrial and general economic development, particularly of those countries which are still in the early stages of industrial development, and to encourage the international flow of capital for productive investment.'[9]

After extensive negotiation, the committee presented an entirely new chapter to the draft Charter that incorporated the concerns raised by the developing countries, especially in the use of special measures for industrialization. Chapter III, 'Economic Development and Reconstruction', stressed the importance to international trade of the 'economic development of all countries, particularly those in which resources are as yet relatively undeveloped, as well as the reconstruction of . . . economies . . . devastated by war' (Article 8).

Chapter III itself covered three broad areas that were of special importance to the developing countries: industrialization, foreign investment and trade. On industrialization the proposed ITO was to play an essentially advisory role, assisting members to draw up industrialization plans, while leaving their financing and implementation to other agencies.

The provisions relating to international investment prompted lengthy debate. Interestingly, this issue was introduced at the insistence of the American delegation, which wanted to incorporate rights for foreign investors that would protect them from potentially harmful host-country policies (such as expropriation). However, by the time the final draft was written, this intent had been completely turned around; the developing countries succeeded in incorporating rights for the capital-importing country, including the right to expropriate a foreign investor's plant as long as 'just compensation' was paid. As mentioned above, this was one of the issues which eventually contributed to the downfall of the Charter.

By far the most important focus of Chapter III was on trade. Again after considerable debate, the Charter recognized the occasional need, in the course of economic development, to protect domestic infant industries using measures otherwise in contravention of the Charter (such as quotas or tariff preferences). At the same time, numerous conditions were attached to safeguard against their abuse. In particular, countries were required to consult with affected countries and get the approval of the ITO before the measures could be introduced; strict time limits were also stipulated and penalties could be levied if they were not met.

There were also several conditions on the use of tariff preferences: prior approval had to be sought and would only be given for agreements between neighbouring countries or members of the same economic region, for products on which preferences were found to be essential to the creation or development of an industry or agricultural sector, and for up to ten years in the first instance. Compensation for third countries could be required, possibly by the reduction of duties, or the guaranteeing of fixed tariff margins on their exports. Rule-breaking, that is not getting two-thirds of ITO members' support for an initiative, could lead to the loss of rights under the Charter.

That a new chapter on economic development was included in the Havana Charter to meet the concerns raised by the participating developing countries reflects the active role played by these countries in the post-war institution-building process, and indicates that they carried enough influence – both numerically and politically – to have an impact; and the economically dominant countries clearly wanted to include these countries in the planning process. However, increasing the number of participating countries introduced more conflict into the negotiating process and, in the end, weakened what consensus had existed.

Neither was the result entirely satisfying for developing countries. While the inclusion of Chapter III did meet some of their concerns, many countries felt that the attached conditions were too restrictive and that they impinged upon their sovereignty; one country, Argentina, refused to sign the Charter on these grounds. At the other extreme, free traders in developed countries, and especially in the USA, complained that the new provisions introduced too many loopholes and moved the Charter too far from its original principles.

Initially, GATT made only passing reference to development concerns primarily because it was drawn up before the debate over the provisions for economic development was resolved in the Havana Conference preparatory committee. Besides its preamble, which lists one of the objectives of trade as 'raising standards of living, ensuring full employment and . . . developing the full use of the resources of the world', trade measures were allowed to deal with some problems commonly experienced by developing countries, although they were originally introduced largely for the benefit of the European countries. These included restrictions to safeguard balance of payments (Article XII) and discriminatory restrictions on imports for balance-of-payments purposes (Article XIV).

It was not until 1955, following substantial revisions to GATT, that safeguard action and balance-of-payments measures were allowed specifically for development purposes (Article XVIII). Subsequent changes, in particular the addition of Part IV in 1965 and, at the end of the Tokyo Round, the Enabling Clause, formally endorsed the special trade needs of countries in the course of economic development that went far beyond what was envisaged in the Havana Charter.[10] Thus developing countries are unlikely to favour returning to the Charter's limited notion of S & D treatment.[11]

Commodities

Another important issue that drew the participating developing countries into the post-war trade debate was the treatment of commodity production and trade. At the time, many were more economically dependent on commodity exports than they are today and had been seriously affected by the collapse of commodity prices in the Depression (in response to which several countries jointly had introduced restrictions on various exports such as rubber, sugar, tea and tin).

The Havana Charter included a Chapter (VI) devoted to ICAs which, for the most part, was based on the original American proposals. It endorsed the need for ICAs, but with fairly narrow objectives and under strict conditions. Commodity agreements were to help producers adjust to changing markets and, at the same time, protect the interests of consumers. ICAs would only be allowed for up to five years in the first instance if there were a 'burdensome' surplus affecting small producers and likely to lead to substantial unemployment, and if consumers were ensured adequate supplies at fair prices.

Some producing countries, especially those from Latin America, were critical of the American proposals; at the Havana conference they opposed consumer representation and demanded that ICAs include minimum prices. However, firm rejection by the USA and other developed countries meant that 1930s-style producer-only cartels would not be allowed under the Charter.

None the less, the commodity chapter was still criticized by the American business community which opposed any government-controlled cartels. As one key American delegate noted, the chapter was found to be lacking because it sought out the middle ground and stuck to it: 'It neither prohibits commodity agreements nor promotes them.'[12]

When the Charter was dropped and Chapter VI was not subsumed into GATT, the responsibility for ICA initiatives was left with the UN ICCICA, set up under ECOSOC in 1947. In 1954 the UN Commission on International Commodity Trade was established to look after the broader issues of commodity production and trade; in the mid-1960s both were replaced by UNCTAD and its permanent Committee on Commodities.

GATT initially said little about commodities, other than allowing ICAs (Article XX-H) that would otherwise contravene GATT rules because of restrictions on exports and/or imports, or discrimination, as long as they conformed to the principles of Chapter VI of the Havana Charter. In 1965 the addition of Part IV recognized the need for measures to 'attain stable, equitable and remunerative prices' for primary products (as well as improved market access), and the Trade and Development Committee set up a group on international commodity problems. But for the most part commodity issues were dealt with outside the mainstream of the international trading system. It was not until a more active approach was taken by UNCTAD that GATT slowly gave more attention to this important Third World issue.

Agricultural Trade

GATT's poor record in liberalizing agricultural trade has also been cited by developing countries as a major shortcoming, but not because it fell far short of what had been intended in the Charter. Two major exemptions for agriculture were spelled out in the Charter's Commercial Chapter (IV). Import quotas on agriculture and fishery products were allowed to supplement surplus disposal programmes and domestic production and marketing controls, provided that the quotas did not reduce the share of imports in a domestic market or discriminate between imports. Export subsidies were also allowed on all primary commodities, under certain conditions. In neither case was prior approval of other members required, though advance notice of quotas was necessary. For the most part, these provisions were drafted in such a way that the US farm programme would be consistent with the Havana Charter and thus the latter would gain Senate support.

Not surprisingly, similar US pressures led to special treatment of agricultural and other primary commodities in the GATT. Initially the main exemption was for quotas to support government measures (for example, production controls or measures to remove temporary surpluses), subject to the same provisos as in the Charter. In addition, the 'Grandfather Clause' granted immunity to many agricultural (and other) programmes that existed at the time of accession to GATT. It seems likely that these would have been maintained if the Charter had been enforced.

Since 1947, GATT exemptions for agriculture have grown. For example, in 1955 the USA sought a waiver for import fees and/or quotas on various products, even though they were not all subject to production controls, with no time limit. An exemption of primary commodities from the prohibition on export subsidies (broadly in keeping with the previously agreed Article 27 of the Charter) was also added in 1955 (Article XVI-B), again at the insistence of the USA. This particular provision provoked serious objections from Canada and other small commodity exporting countries who argued that they could not afford to subsidize their exports, and who saw the tighter ban on subsidies for manufactured exports as proof that the GATT was operating in favour of established industrial exporters. Indeed, the lengthy negotiations required to secure some exemptions in the Charter for countries in the course of industrialization, while agriculture was largely excluded from the rules of both the Charter and the GATT, left developing countries, in particular, feeling the brunt of bias.

Discriminatory Restraints

More recently, developing countries have been concerned by the unfavourable treatment of their exports of manufactured goods, especially textiles and clothing. As has been discussed, the provisions for economic development and commodities preoccupied the underdeveloped countries at Havana. At the time, they were more concerned with promoting domestic industrialization than with the treatment of their manufactured exports. However, from the mid-1950s, as some developing countries (and Japan) began to industrialize and build up export capabilities outside their traditional areas, restricted access to developed country markets for their manufactured exports became a major issue. Such discriminatory restrictions remain the most blatant contravention of developing country rights under GATT.

The history of special protection for textiles and clothing is a long one; barriers to developed country markets have existed since the 1930s when a few countries imposed import controls on Japanese apparel. As already noted, it was this kind of protectionism that the Havana Charter – and subsequently GATT - was supposed to prevent.

Yet it is unlikely that the ITO, any more than GATT, would have been able to resist pressure for special restrictions on the textile and clothing trade or prevent the proliferation of voluntary export restraints in other areas. In the first place, the commercial policy provisions of the Charter (such as safeguard clauses and controls on quantity restrictions) were simply transferred to GATT, as were the basic principles of non-discrimination and MFN treatment. Second, there is little to suggest that the stronger institutional presence of the ITO could have held back protectionist demands for controls on low-cost exports from developing countries. As was evident in the case of agriculture, countries with significant economic power are often able to secure derogations, whatever the principles and penalties. In contrast, the rights and interests of smaller countries are often ignored. For these and other reasons, most developing countries have felt like outsiders within the GATT system, viewing it as a 'rich man's club'.

'New' Areas

A major issue raised in the preparations for the Uruguay Round was whether to extend GATT to 'new' areas such as trade in services and trade-related investment issues, as suggested by some developed countries. A number of developing countries argued that GATT should complete its existing agenda, particularly with regard to strengthening its controls over safeguards and grey-area measures, before embarking on new business.

Like GATT, the prime objective of the Charter was to increase the exchange of goods, with no reference to services. However, in the context of RBPs, and as a result of pressure from many developing countries, the Charter acknowledged that services such as transportation, telecommunications, insurance and bank commercial services were substantial elements in international trade and that RBPs in such services could seriously affect trade in goods (Chapter V, Article 53). A procedure was therefore established for the settlement of disagreements over RBPs in services, bilaterally and then multilaterally by the ITO, but only if no other relevant intergovernmental organization existed.

As was the case for many issues that had been covered by the Charter, multilateral discussion of services proceeded in other fora (for instance, OECD, IATA, UNCTAD and ITU). GATT has some jurisdiction over services: there is a special mention of motion picture films and certain GATT articles and codes apply to various services that are complementary to trade in goods (such as banking, shipping and export insurance). But services that substitute for trade in goods, or are traded without a relationship to goods, are only covered to the extent that Article XXIX commits Contracting Parties to observe Chapter V of the Havana Charter: that is, relating to RBPs on certain services. If the American-led initiative to establish a multilateral framework of principles and rules for trade in services is successful during the course of the Uruguay Round, it will most certainly go far beyond the original scope of the Havana Charter.

As already discussed, the Havana Charter's provisions on the treatment of private investment were included in the economic development chapter. At that time, the USA argued that protection for foreign investors was needed to encourage the flow of capital for productive investment. Because of its specific concern about the treatment of investment in the developing countries, the USA wanted a commitment to provide 'adequate security', while 'avoiding discrimination', and only making 'reasonable requirements' of foreign investors; although these terms were not defined, the commitment did not appear to go as far as requiring national treatment as in the case of goods. The sanction for breaking these undertakings was to be the loss of trade concessions in the market of any complaining capital-exporting country, with ultimate appeal for adjudication to the International Court of Justice.

In response to the US proposals, the developing countries sought exemptions such as permission, on balance-of-payments grounds, to block the transfer of funds paid for nationalization of a foreign enterprise. This particular provision was dropped, but developing countries were allowed flexibility in deciding how much and on what terms foreign investment would enter their countries; safeguards were also permitted to prevent foreign investors 'interfering' in their internal affairs. While recognizing the need for additional bilateral agreements, the ITO was authorized to begin the formulation of a more detailed investment code.

In the current trade negotiations, the focus will be almost exclusively on the trade-related aspects of investment. Developing countries have raised concerns that broader issues such as the right of establishment and national treatment for foreign investors will be raised in the context of the services negotiations. If so, they have argued (with one eye on the Havana Charter) that restrictive business practices should also be discussed.

The Havana Charter recognized that foreign exchange controls could frustrate efforts to liberalize trade, and that import restrictions could upset attempts to stabilize exchange rates. Thus ITO signatories would be required either to join the IMF or have a special exchange agreement. The Charter prescribed in some detail cooperation between the ITO and the IMF (Article 24). For example, in deciding whether import restrictions (under Article 21) were warranted, the ITO would ask the IMF to determine whether a country's balance of payments was serious (for example, very low or rapidly declining reserves)[13]. Similarly, consideration of discriminatory import restrictions by countries with exchange controls would take into account whether the IMF found such action to be consistent with its Articles. In return, the ITO would report to the IMF when it considered that a country's exchange restrictions were affecting its obligations under the Havana Charter.

Since these provisions were included in the Charter's Commercial Policy chapter, they were carried over into GATT (Article XV) virtually verbatim. The links with the IMF have remained close but essentially one-way and limited to discussion of import restrictions introduced on balance-of-payments grounds. With the growing need for improved international macroeconomic coordination, GATT's failure to develop this linkage between trade and financial issues beyond what was originally envisaged in the Havana Charter has been the subject of criticism.[14]

FILLING THE INSTITUTIONAL VOID

As has been shown, the Havana Charter offered a much broader framework for dealing with international trade relations than presently exists. It also provided for a much more powerful organization to oversee those relations. When the Havana Charter failed to win the ratification of Congress, GATT was left to fill the immediate void in the trade policy area, a function it in fact had been filling since 1947. Subsequently, many of the other items that died with the Charter were picked up by other institutions; of these UNCTAD was the most important and ambitious. For the most part, however, these other institutions haave not been able to accomplish what had been envisaged in the Havana Charter; and neither have they successfully integrated the developing countries into the international trading system.

The GATT and UNCTAD

The near-accidental beginnings of GATT – and the expectation that it would be overtaken by the ITO – meant that it had no institutional existence.[15] It was merely an agreement. A secretariat was set up but its primary purpose was to organize and service tariff negotiations between GATT signatories. Although it has gradually expanded, it remains small compared to many other international bodies (350 staff compared to the IMF's 1 700, for example). This has necessarily limited its capacity to play a more proactive role in international trade policy-making, whether it be in terms of monitoring changes in any national policies (trade or otherwise) that affect trade[16] and ensuring adherence to GATT rules, providing technical advice or building links with other organizations in trade-related fields. Traditionally there has also been a lack of high-level political representation at most GATT meetings; unlike the OECD, where trade ministers meet annually, GATT ministerial meetings are exceptional.

For their part, developing countries have not been satisfied with GATT's rules or its weak institutional structure. This discontent, combined with a desire to promote broader international cooperation in the field of trade and development, led to the first UN Conference on Trade and Development in 1964, and the establishment of UNCTAD as a new permanent institution.

UNCTAD reflected, for the most part, developing countries' frustration with the GATT; its bias in favor of developed country trade interests (in terms of the balance of rights and obligations expected of GATT members, the issue areas covered and the preoccupation with trade barriers among Western developed countries), its failure to recognize the special role of trade in economic development and its weak institutional basis. In UNCTAD the developing countries saw the possibility of resurrecting the ITO, an agency with the broad range of functions originally proposed in the Havana Charter, but with somewhat different rules.[17] Developed countries, while supporting UNCTAD's initiation for political reasons, opposed any suggestion that it replace the GATT as the central body with responsibility for the management of the international trading system. In fact, they saw UNCTAD 'as a compromise arrangement between a non-existent ITO on the one hand and an already established ITO on the other'.[18]

The creation of this new organization appeared initially to serve the developing countries well. It encouraged GATT to review again its relationship to their trade concerns and, amongst other changes, led to the creation of Part IV and the Committee on Trade and Development. At the same time the UNCTAD Secretariat became a very vocal exponent of their interests. It espoused the need for a NIEO which, in the area of trade, included structural adjustment and tariff preferences in the North to allow for expansion of developing countries' exports, the creation of a Common Fund for Commodities, and special measures for the least developed countries.

It is now widely recognized, however, that UNCTAD has had its limitations. A major problem has been the unwillingness of most developed countries to reach agreements within UNCTAD that are legally binding (as in GATT), opting instead for recommendatory resolutions. Another is that the bloc approach, which originally helped to strengthen the presentation of developing country concerns, has become highly confrontational, making UNCTAD less productive than it might otherwise be. At the same time, inadequate acknowledgement of the growing diversity within the developing country group has undermined the credibility of some of their demands. Finally, the Secretariat's espousal of developing country interests has weakened its capacity to act as a mediator in international trade negotiations.[19] There has also been a problem of overlap with GATT in certain trade policy areas, in which UNCTAD has developed a major role, raising the institutional issue of policy coordination, if not integration.

Proposals for Change

Although GATT and other organizations filled part of the void left by the demise of the Havana Charter, it is generally acknowledged (albeit with different degrees of conviction) that current arrangements are not adequate to deal with the complexities of the global economy; developing countries in particular are still unhappy with the way in which the 'system' is structured. Certainly, there are elements of UNCTAD's approach to international trade which, if merged with some of GATT's, could create an organization more effective and yet sensitive to the relationship between trade and development.

In particular, it may be in developing countries' long-term interest if UNCTAD's integrative approach (essentially that of the ITO) were married with GATT's legally binding, and yet increasingly flexible, approach to bargaining (for example, with the possibility of forming coalitions that cut across traditional country groupings being formed for different issues, and negotiations between smaller groups) provided there is some way to integrate the concerns of those excluded from GATT negotiations, especially the smaller developing countries. The OECD may also provide a useful model in some respects, notably as a forum for ongoing intergovernmental discussion of a broad range of interrelated economic issues such as trade, domestic adjustment, and fiscal and monetary policies.

Over the years there has been no shortage of proposals for reform of the trading system. While these have primarily involved discussion of new rules, the issue of institutional structure has also been paramount. Some, such as the GATT working group in 1955, and the American Society for International Law in 1976, proposed completely new organizations: the OTC to oversee GATT, and the WTO respectively. In 1981, Camps and Gwin also published an elaborate outline for a new PTO to replace both GATT and UNCTAD: in effect a new ITO. Others, like the Leutwiler group reporting in 1985 to the Director-General of GATT, focused instead on new structures within GATT as a way of making it more effective. Essentially these proposals have concentrated on ways to increase country involvement (through changes in the institutional structure and the voting system), new functions and new links with other organizations, all of which would be welcome changes to current arrangements.

While such major changes may be necessary to establish a more effective organization, there must be some doubt about their political acceptability in the current environment. Despite a general recognition that national economies have become increasingly interdependent over the last 40 years, and that trade liberalization is even more critical now to stimulate economic growth, economic nationalism and scepticism about surrendering sovereignty to international institutions remain strong in many parts of the world. Certainly none of the major reform proposals has proved any more politically acceptable to the USA than the ITO was in 1948. And now, as then, no reform initiative is likely to be taken up without widespread support.

CONCLUSIONS

In this chapter we have tried to speculate whether the developing countries would have found the international trading arena more congenial today if the Havana Charter had been ratified. Many developing countries were involved in the Havana negotiations – indeed the process marked the beginning of the North-South dialogue – and held high hopes for the ITO. The question is whether many of their current concerns would have been more easily resolved, or even not arisen, if the ITO had been in place since 1949.

As we have seen, there are many respects in which GATT has evolved from Chapter IV of the Havana Charter, on which it was based, to take into account some of the special needs of developing countries. While GATT rules may still not satisfy some developing countries, a return to the Havana Charter would cost them even these gains. At the same time, some of GATT's present weaknesses (for instance, on agriculture, new areas and bilateral sanctions) stem largely from provisions written into the Charter. On the other hand, the ITO's broader issue coverage, its larger institutional presence and the associated scope for greater monitoring and coordination of trade policies, may have helped fill the void which exists today.

There is a danger, however, in ascribing too much importance to an institution. With its complex institutional structure, as well as its broad coverage, the ITO may well not have been able to prevent the deterioration in international trade relations. Most likely, it too would have been strained by the same outside economic and political pressures that have led countries to break the spirit of GATT (especially with regard to the use of discriminatory restraints against developing country exports) and to oppose increasing accountability to external agencies over domestic policies, even when these affect trade.

Notes

1. Camps and Gwin (1981), p. 117.
2. See GATT (1986).
3. Diebold (1952), p. 4.
4. Australia, Belgium-Luxembourg, Brazil, Canada, Chile, China, Cuba, Czechoslovakia, France, India, Lebanon, the Netherlands, New Zealand, Norway, Union of South Africa, UK and USA.
5. Participants at the Havana Conference included those on the Preparatory Committee and Afghanistan, Austria, Bolivia, Burma, Ceylon, Colombia, Costa Rica, Denmark, Dominican Republic, Ecuador, Egypt, El Salvador, Greece, Guatemala, Haiti, Indonesia, Iran, Iraq, Ireland, Italy, Liberia, Mexico, Nicaragua, Pakistan, Panama, Peru, the Philippines, Portugal, Southern Rhodesia, Sweden, Switzerland, Syria, Transjordan, Uruguay, Venezuela.
6. Australia, Belgium, Brazil, Burma, Canada, Ceylon, Chile, China, Colombia, Czechoslovakia, France, India, Lebanon, Luxembourg, the Netherlands, Norway, New Zealand, Pakistan, Southern Rhodesia, Syria, Union of South Africa, UK and USA.
7. Just as it is difficult today to determine whether some countries are more developed than developing, particularly with respect to the issue of appropriate trade rights and obligations, the same problem arose when the rules for an international trade organization were being discussed 40 years ago. Perhaps the most obvious borderline cases at the time were Australia and New Zealand.
8. The issue of preferences was an especially contentious one between the USA and the UK, with the USA insisting that the Imperial Preference system be abolished.
9. Charter, Chapter I, Article 1 (Canada, 1949).
10. See Hudec (1987) for a full discussion.
11. The extent to which S & D treatment has actually benefited developing countries is a matter of some debate with some critics arguing that they might have been able to secure greater and bound access to developed country markets if they had offered reciprocal cuts. See Hudec (1987).
12. Wilcox (1949), p. 124.

64   *The Havana Charter Experience*

13.   According to one interpretation at the time (Wilcox, 1949), this
       provision should have reduced US concern with possible abuse
       of Article 21, given its weighted vote in the IMF. However, the
       IMF's role was to be one of technical assistance, rather than of
       decision-making.
14.   See Hufbauer and Schott (1985).
15.   Sylvia Ostry, Canada's ambassador for the MTN, has called this
       institutional weakness one of GATTs 'birth defects' (Per Jacobson
       lecture, September 1987).
16.   This would complement the IMF's increasing surveillance of its
       members' macroeconomic policies.
17.   Camps and Gwin (1981), p. 144.
18.   UNCTAD (1985), p. 10.
19.   Weiss (1986), p. 134. The recent creation of a separate Third
       World Secretariat to research and articulate developing country
       interests in international trade (and financial) issues may signal
       that developing countries themselves are willing to see UNCTAD
       become more independent.

References

American Society of International Law (1976) *Panel on International Trade
Policy and Institutions: Re-making the System of World Trade*, Studies in
International Law Policy, no.12.
Bidwell, P.W. and Diebold, W., Jr (1949) 'The United States and the
International Trade Organization.' *International Conciliation*, 2 (December), pp. 187–239.
Bronz, G. (1956) 'An International Trade Organization: The Second
Attempt', *Harvard Law Review*, 69.
Brown, W.A., Jr (1950) *The United States and the Restoration of World
Trade: An Analysis and Appraisal of the ITO Charter and the General
Agreement on Tariffs and Trade*, (Washington, DC: The Brookings
Institution).
Camps, M. and Gwin, C. (1981) *Collective Management: the Reform
of Global Economic Organizations* (New York: McGraw-Hill).
Canada (1949) *Final Act of the United Nations Conference on Trade
and Employment. Held at Havana from November 21, 1947 to March
24, 1948, and Related Documents*, Treaty Series, 1948, No.32 (Ottawa:
King's Printer).
Cortney, P. (1949) *The Economic Munich: The ITO Charter, Inflation
and Liberty: The 1929 Lesson* (New York Philosophical Library).
Curzon, G. and Curzon, V. (1976) 'The Management of Trade Relations
in the GATT', in A. Shonfield (ed.), *International Economic Relations of
the Western World 1959-1971 (vol. 1)* (Toronto: Oxford University Press,
for the Royal Institute of International Affairs).
Dam, K.W. (1970) *The GATT: Law and International Economic Organization* (University of Chicago Press).
Diebold, W., Jr (1952) *The End of the I.T.O.*, Essays in International

Finance, No.16 (Princeton: International Finance Section, Department of Economic and Social Institutions, Princeton University), October.

Gardner, N.R. (1980) *Sterling–Dollar Diplomacy in Current Perspective: The Origins and the Prospects of Our International Economic Order* (New York: Columbia University Press).

GATT (1985) *Trade Policies for a Better Future: Proposals for Action* (Geneva: GATT), March.

GATT (1986) 'Ministerial Declaration on the Uruguay Round', 20 September.

Hudec, R.E. (1987) *Developing Countries in the GATT Legal System* (London: Macmillan for TPRC).

Hufbauer, G. and Schott, J. (1985) *Trading for Growth: The Next Round of Trade Negotiations* (Washington, DC: IIE).

McGovern, E. (1986) *International Trade Regulation: GATT, the United States and the European Community* (Exeter: Globefield Press).

Patterson, G. (1986) 'The GATT and Negotiating International Trade Rules', in A.K. Henderson (ed.) *Negotiating World Order: The Artisanship and Architecture of Global Diplomacy* (Boston: Scholarly Resources).

Spero, J.E. (1981) *The Politics of International Economic Relations*, 2nd edn, (New York: St. Martin's Press).

UNCTAD (1985) *The History of UNCTAD 1964–1984* (New York: UN).

Weiss, T.G. (1986) *Multilateral Development Diplomacy in UNCTAD: The Lessons of Group Negotiations, 1964–84* (London: Macmillan).

Wilcox, C. (1949) *A Charter for World Trade* (New York: Macmillan).

Wilgress, E.D. (1949) *A New Attempt at Internationalism: The International Trade Conferences and the Charter: A Study of Ends and Means*, University of Geneva, Thesis No. 62.

4 Trade-Restricting Effects of Exchange Rate Regimes: Implications for Developed–Developing Country Trade Negotiations

Ramon L. Clarete and John Whalley

INTRODUCTION

Reciprocal bargaining among developed countries under GATT focuses on both an explicit and implicit bargain. Explicit bargains involve mutual reductions in real-side barriers (tariffs). The implicit bargain is that negotiating parties will maintain full convertibility of domestic currencies so that reductions in real-side trade barriers will have an effect on trade.

In contrast, most developing countries have inconvertible currencies, and fix or manage their exchange rates in ways which result in excess domestic demand for foreign exchange. As a result, rationing devices such as auctions or priority allocation schemes have to be used to allocate foreign exchange among users. Because the implicit bargain does not hold, explicit reciprocal bargaining between developed and developing countries on real-side trade restrictions cannot proceed.

In this chapter, we argue that foreign exchange arrangements in developing countries not only have the effect of restraining real-side trade flows but are one of the major impediments to a fuller integration of developing countries into the trading system. Our argument is that these rationing devices are an integral, and typically the central, part of the system of trade-restricting commercial policies used in most developing countries. Because they are not recognized as a negotiable barrier in GATT, reciprocal bargaining between developed and developing countries covering only real-side trade restrictions, as takes place in GATT, is of little interest to either party. Negotiated reductions in real-side barriers in developing countries largely result in tightened rationing of foreign exchange with real trade flows little changed. Developed countries become frustrated by liberalization that produces little increase in trade flows. Developing countries are frustrated by their inability to bargain away their own financial liberalization for improved access to developed country markets.

We suggest that liberalization of domestic foreign exchange arrangements by developing countries should be treated as a concession in trade negotiations akin to tariff reductions. Either tariff increases to offset the elimination of implicit barriers under any move to full convertibility should be allowed, or the implicit barriers associated with foreign exchange schemes should be bargainable. The current GATT framework does not allow changes in foreign exchange arrangements to be treated in this way since it largely covers trade-restricting measures found in developed countries. Any attempt to integrate developing countries more fully into the present multilateral system of internationally-negotiated disciplines is unlikely to succeed unless it allows for a wider range of trade restrictions to be bargained in some way.

This line of argument raises many thorny issues. Realistically, can negotiated international disciplines be used to limit the use of trade-restricting foreign exchange arrangements? How can full convertibility be achieved, and subsequently enforced? What forms of transparency, bindings, and so forth should, or even could, form part of an international negotiation process covering those impediments? How could negotiations proceed without a commodity basis for an exchange of concessions, and without principal suppliers with whom to negotiate? And what does the trade-restricting nature of these arrangements and any move towards enlarged reciprocal bargaining imply for the current separation of spheres of responsibility between GATT, the IMF, and the World Bank?

Our bottom line is that despite many implementation difficulties, current global institutional arrangements are ill-suited to the task of achieving negotiated multilateral disciplines covering the use of key trade-restricting practices in both developed and developing countries. GATT is a framework covering only traditional real-side trade restrictions such as tariffs and quotas, not non-traditional instruments, including rationed foreign exchange. And while the IMF exerts some discipline over foreign exchange arrangements, this is not a result of multilateral negotiations in which trade concessions are exchanged. Instead, conditionality with lines of credit linked to domestic policy reforms, devaluation, and/or conventional trade liberalization measures, such as reductions in quotas and tariffs, has been the rule.

While perhaps easier to describe at this stage in generalities rather than in concrete detail, we none the less suggest that an integrated negotiating format spanning traditional trade restrictions and non-traditional trade-restricting measures would allow for a wider exchange of concessions between developed and developing countries than currently. This involves developed countries acknowledging financial liberalization as a concession which can be negotiated, as well as developing a process which allows for rationing devices to be converted into negotiable instruments. Allowing tariff increases in developing countries in return for a move toward full convertibility is one approach, with tariffs then bargained downward in multilateral negotiations. Another is to move toward transparency through auctioned quotas and negotiated bindings on the premium value associated with quotas to be enforced through exchange rate changes and/or domestic monetary policy. Eventual reductions in premium values would, with luck, occur through multilateral negotiations, much as has occurred with tariffs. A redefinition of the role of the IMF would be a natural component of such a change, and in the penultimate section we describe the form of change we have in mind.

FOREIGN EXCHANGE DISTORTIONS AS TRADE RESTRICTIONS

Foreign exchange restrictions are both complex and comprehensive.[1] All 11 countries represented in this project use them. All have licensing schemes for the allocation of foreign exchange for authorized imports and surrender requirements for exporters. All require exports to be paid for in convertible currencies. Five of the eleven have multiple exchange rates for import and/or export transactions.

It is unclear whether generally in the developing world the use of these restrictions is becoming more or less widespread, since even when used their severity tends to change over time due to periodic devaluations and/or domestic policy reforms. In Eastern and Southern Africa, for example, the use of the major import restrictions (including payments restrictions) seems to be growing. In 1967 there were no payments restrictions in any of seven Eastern and Southern African countries. By 1982, in all of these countries payments restrictions co-existed with real-side import barriers, and over the period the number of countries that resorted to payments-based trade impediments steadily grew (see Gulhati, Bose and Atukorala, 1985). Despite the pervasive use of these restrictions, however, theoretical and empirical literature on their effects remains limited, with most trade policy work still devoted to tariffs and quotas.[2]

The way in which these arrangements restrict trade is as follows.[3] If a fixed (or controlled) exchange rate policy is adopted, but without the accommodative domestic monetary policy needed for an equilibrium outcome in which full convertibility is achieved, excess demand for foreign exchange results. Foreign exchange earnings of exporters are required to be surrendered to the central bank, and the resulting foreign exchange is rationed using a priority (or other) allocation scheme among importers.

Under such a regime, monetary policy is no longer neutral, and can have substantial real-side effects on trade flows through the rationing of foreign exchange. Classical literature on exchange rate regimes usually stresses the irrelevance of the exchange rate regime and the neutrality of money for international transactions. The argument is that under flexible exchange rates, rates will be endogenously determined in an international economy once domestic monetary policies are selected. Subsequent changes in monetary policies will affect only exchange rates; real trade flows will remain unchanged. Where exchange rates are fixed, the fixed exchange rates imply the form domestic monetary policies must take to support an international equilibrium in which currencies are freely exchangeable at the fixed rates.

The case which applies to most developing countries is that in which monetary policy is not accommodative in this way, and there is an excess supply of domestic currency at the fixed exchange rate. Without sufficient foreign capital inflows to cover the resulting trade deficit, excess demand for foreign exchange results. Hence some form of rationing is required, along with compulsory surrender of foreign exchange by exporters. If exporters were able to sell their foreign exchange on a free market they would receive a higher exchange rate, but they are compelled to comply with the surrender requirement and, in effect, face a tax on their export earnings.

One simple process for allocating foreign exchange which illustrates the effects on trade is auctions. If we assume that rights to purchase foreign exchange at the fixed exchange rate are auctioned, a premium value will result (that is, the domestic currency price of the right to purchase foreign exchange from the central bank at the official rate). Because they have to pay a premium to acquire foreign exchange, importers in effect pay a combined (premium-inclusive) exchange rate which is higher than the official rate. The need to pay this premium restricts trade in ways akin to a tariff, since exporters only receive the official rate.

Fixed exchange rates with non-accommodative domestic monetary policies and rationing thus drive a wedge between domestic prices and the world prices at which the country trades.[4] As a result, policy reforms which relax foreign exchange rationing will tend to expand trade.

The trade-restricting effects of foreign exchange rationing can be eliminated either by a devaluation[5] or by restrictive monetary policy. By allowing the exchange rate to find its equilibrium value, or by letting the domestic money supply accommodate to the fixed exchange rate, the premium value is driven down to zero, bringing the economy back to a free trade equilibrium. The difference is that under a devaluation the price level rises, while under restrictive monetary policies it falls. Since rationing of foreign exchange is identical in its effects to a tariff, policy reforms which aim to phase out rationing can be viewed as a trade concession by importing countries in the same manner as tariff reductions or the lifting of import restrictions.

More complex foreign exchange allocation schemes than auctioned quotas can be used, and this can change the impact on trade flows. Foreign exchange is usually allocated rather than auctioned, and frequently by commodity, with basic foods and raw materials receiving the highest priority, capital goods and equipment the next, and consumer goods the lowest. Government trading enterprises also often receive the largest share of foreign exchange allocations, along with established importers. In such cases the net effect is an implicit protective structure akin to a multi-rate tariff, with more than one implicit premium value on rationed foreign exchange, reflecting the allocation scheme adopted.

Where foreign exchange is administratively allocated between essential and non-essential imports, black markets for foreign exchange typically develop, induced by the exchange allocation process. Such markets reflect incentives for exporters to avoid surrendering foreign exchange to the central bank at the fixed exchange rate, and incentives to acquire foreign exchange outside the priority allocation scheme to finance either smuggling or importing on open general licensing. In such cases illegal importers gain by reselling imports at the higher domestic prices which occur because of the trade restrictions on imports. The differences between black market and official exchange rates reflect both the degree of trade distortion implied by the exchange rate regime and the enforcement and penalty system used to prosecute black marketeers.[6]

Foreign exchange systems are therefore central to an understanding of trade policies in developing countries since trade-restricting regimes in these countries involve a combined set of commercial policies which cover both the financial and real sides of trade and payments flows. These two sets of restrictions combine to yield one single set of distortions which restrict trade in severe ways. Importantly, financial impediments typically provide the binding restriction on trade flows. Thus, in an economy where tariffs operate and where there is also foreign exchange rationing, the binding restriction on foreign trade is not the tariff but the availability of foreign exchange. Under auctioned foreign exchange quotas, reductions in tariffs simply have the effect of increasing the premium value on domestic foreign exchange markets, but do not significantly liberalize trade. To liberalize trade in most developing countries, it is necessary not only to reduce real-side trade policies but also the financial component of trade restrictions operating through the exchange rate regime and foreign exchange rationing.

NEGOTIATING EXCHANGE RATE LIBERALIZATION

Any attempt to integrate developing countries more fully into the trading system has, in our judgement, to recognize the central role that the trade-restricting effects of exchange rate policies play in developing countries. There is currently no framework through which developed countries can negotiate improved international disciplines over these key trade restrictions in developing countries, and neither can developing countries negotiate trade concessions from developed countries in return for financial liberalization. This institutional problem is at the heart of the current difficulties facing the global trading system, as far as the participation of developing countries is concerned.

The negotiating framework of GATT does not cover such restrictions, and is thus unsatisfactory from the point of view of all

negotiating parties. From a developed country point of view, negotiated reductions in real-side trade policies by developing countries
will typically be ineffective in significantly improving their market
access. This is because without removal of restrictions on payments
arrangements, real-side liberalization will produce offsetting changes
in (either implicit or explicit) foreign exchange premia which leave
real trade flows largely unaffected. From a developing country point
of view, financial liberalization is not treated as a concession within
the existing global negotiating framework, and cannot be bargained
for improvements in market access abroad. This is why we suggest
that changes in both these arrangements and the institutional
structure through which reciprocal bargaining on trade measures
occurs are needed to integrate developing countries into the trading
system.

The way forward seems to be for all parties to acknowledge
the integrated nature of trade-restricting policies in developing
countries, including financial as well as real-side trade policies. The
trade-restricting effects of all domestic policies must be considered
in negotiations. Developed countries need to recognize liberalization
of financial policies in developing countries as a concession to be
negotiated, and an area over which international disciplines can
be negotiated in comparable ways to tariffs. Developing countries
need to be prepared to accept more discipline over their own
domestic policies, bargaining away financial impediments to trade
for improved access to their trading partners' markets.

One approach to broadening the scope of GATT negotiations is
to provide incentives for developing countries to move toward full
convertibility of their domestic currencies. It is simplistic to expect
developing countries unilaterally to adopt freely floating exchange
rates because of the large domestic adjustments that this may imply.
Also, with volatile terms of trade facing individual countries, fixing
the exchange rate is seen as a policy which provides some degree of
insulation for domestic producers. The situation in which developing
countries find themselves parallels that of many European countries
in the 1940s and 1950s when recovering from their wartime experiences under inconvertibility and exchange controls. The redesigned
trading system of the late 1940s was in part a response to the
European situation, involving a fixed exchange rate system with
the IMF operating as an institution recycling resources from surplus
to deficit countries, and GATT serving as a real-side trade barrier
bargaining framework which only slowly became operational as full

convertibility was restored. This came to be replaced in the 1970s by a system of flexible exchange rates among developed countries. Some scheme to cushion adjustment costs as developing countries also move toward full convertibility, and incentives for them to do so both seem needed.

How could one proceed? One route is to think in terms of international negotiations which build on the GATT approach of transparency, bindings and eventual negotiations used to achieve reductions in trade barriers among developed countries over the last 40 years. Transparency would require that the full trade-restricting effects of domestic exchange rate arrangements be made more visible. Bindings, followed by negotiations, would then be the subsequent steps. If the implicit barrier is negotiated down to zero, at that point full convertibility will have been achieved.

Auctioning of foreign exchange quotas by developing countries would seem to be the first step in achieving transparency. A commitment to the use of auctioned quotas might thus be a first concession to be sought by the developed world. This would also have the benefit for governments in developing countries of converting existing foreign exchange allocation mechanisms into arrangements which generate revenue for them. Where priority allocation systems for foreign exchange are already in use, auctioning of quotas could be done on a commodity-specific basis, in effect converting existing allocation arrangements into more visible commodity-specific tariff-like instruments.

One difficulty, however, with commodity-specific foreign exchange auctions is that recontracting can take place among importers across commodities. Importers of essential commodities allocated foreign exchange by the government could resell part of their foreign exchange holdings to importers of non-essential goods. One option may be to auction packages of foreign exchange and import licences for specific commodities. Under this approach a government could first decide how to allocate the country's foreign exchange earnings among various categories of imports. The government would then conduct commodity-specific auctions of the packages of foreign exchange and import licenses.

The combined trade-restricting wedge implied by tariffs, quotas and foreign exchange rationing could then become the subject of bindings or negotiations, or each part of the combined wedge could be bound. This wedge would be calculated from the successful auction bids, and hence negotiations would focus not simply on tariffs or quotas as at present. Bindings could be undertaken on the combined wedge. Violations of bindings would result in a withdrawal of equivalent concessions as currently under GATT; to keep combined protective wedges within bound ranges, domestic monetary policy and/or devaluations would be the policy instruments which would probably have to be used.

To illustrate this idea, consider a particular import, M. The domestic price of M is given by: $P = e\pi(1 + \lambda)(1 + t)$ where e is the official (overvalued) exchange rate, λ is the foreign exchange premium, π is the border price of M in foreign currency, and t is the tariff rate. In this case the combined wedge is equal to $[t + \pi(1 + t)]$, which for simplicity we define as θ. The value of π is calculated from auctioning foreign exchange allocated to import M. The country agrees to bind θ in exchange for concessions from its negotiating partner.

There are, however, several problems with this approach. One is that the market for foreign exchange quotas generating premium values may be highly volatile, perhaps oscillating around a given level during any period of time. λ may rise temporarily to violate the binding but then fall. Does this constitute a violation of the reciprocal agreement giving the country's trading partners the right to withdraw concessions from it? Presumably not, if the movement of λ is self-reversing; or if some moving average of λ is still within bounds. Where one draws the line on a violation is thus problematical. Another problem may be export booms which drive λ down to zero. Should the country be allowed to raise its tariffs as long as they are within previously-agreed bindings on the combined wedge? There are also administrative problems. Who monitors the use of domestic policies adopted to meet bindings on premium values in contracting countries with only partially convertible currencies? Is it up to partner countries? Does the GATT secretariat do this? Should the IMF be asked to help monitor domestic policies to ensure compliance with GATT commitments?

One positive note seems to be that there is solid evidence suggesting that foreign exchange auctions are feasible (IMF, 1987a). According to a recent IMF study (Quirk *et al.*, 1987), 15 developing countries have successfully floated their exchange rates using an interbank market arrangement or by auctioning foreign exchange quotas. Under the auction system, exporters have been required to surrender their earnings to the central bank at the prevailing exchange rate. The amount to be auctioned for merchandise imports is determined after the government has set aside foreign exchange for official purposes, such as external debt service or accumulation of international reserves. The government sets the minimum bid price, and individual bids are accepted for as long as they exceed the previous highest bid. When the supply is exhausted, the last bid determines the market-clearing price. Problems have arisen with this approach due to 'the retention and sequestering of exchange for official purposes', as well as the uncertainty and risk of exchange loss which exporters suffer since they have to surrender their earnings based on the last auction rate.

Notwithstanding the administrative problems, this approach seems to give developing countries more time to adjust as they move towards full convertibility of their currencies. As long as the combined wedge of trade restrictions is within bounds, they have the freedom to decide how best to allocate their foreign exchange earnings among imports, and between imports and official uses. They can vary tariff rates, devalue their domestic currency or, if needed, lower aggregate demand during times of poor export performance, without losing any trade concessions they may have negotiated.

Another way to proceed is to encourage developing countries to adopt a freely floating exchange rate prior to reciprocal negotiations on barriers. This involves developed countries allowing developing countries with inconvertible currencies to convert λ into a tariff in return for adopting a freely floating exchange rate. Thus, using the same notation introduced earlier, θ becomes the new tariff rate for import M, and the country adopts a unified, fully flexible exchange rate policy. Reciprocal bargaining then proceeds on the basis of the increased tariff.

This may seem a strange bargain since tariffs are first increased in developing countries before negotiations on market access by developed countries begin. The bargain in this case is for developing countries permanently to change their exchange rate regime, which would be a major concession for many developing countries, in return for the agreed conversion of the implicit barrier into an explicit tariff. Converting λ into a tariff involves choosing the current official fixed exchange rate as the initial rate in a flexible exchange rate policy, while at the same time making trade policies transparent, one of GATT's basic principles. In succeeding GATT negotiations, the focus of bargaining would be on tariffs, which would have been previously bound at θ. Another way to look at the concession made by developing countries under this approach is that they commit themselves permanently to bind λ to zero, which then opens the door to these countries to become more active participants in subsequent GATT negotiations.

The advantage of this approach is that the implicit contract in GATT is then observed by all members: all currencies are convertible and only real-side trade impediments are relevant in the negotiations. Second, this approach does not demand the same amount of administrative resources as the first.

There are, however, problems. Capital flight is a major short-run problem with this approach. If expectations develop that the government may not keep to a flexible exchange rate policy, large capital movements out of the country may result. If this happens it will realize what speculators had anticipated, making the problem worse. It may be necessary, therefore, for controls on capital movements to remain, even as domestic currencies are becoming convertible, considerably complicating the nature of the agreement of barriers being substituted for financial impediments.

These are our two approaches to financial liberalization in developing countries designed to bring them more fully into the sphere of reciprocal bargaining. There are undoubtedly other approaches, and each will have its problems. The basic objective of achieving full convertibility and transparency so as to allow for bindings and negotiations does, however, seem to us to be the way forward.

THE GATT, THE IMF, AND DISCIPLINE OVER REAL-SIDE AND FINANCIAL TRADE RESTRICTIONS

The interactions between real-side and financial impediments to trade flows outlined in the second section are central to the choices which developing countries face in deciding how best to pursue their own participation in the present trading system as reflected in the rules and arrangements embodied in GATT and the IMF. As the global trading system has evolved in the post-war years, these two separate and quite distinct institutions have each taken on their own separate spheres of responsibility. This has, in part, led to the difficulties of treating financial liberalization by developing countries as negotiable instruments in reciprocal bargaining. Thus the proposal of broadening the scope of such negotiations to include financial liberalization also has important implications for these two important global institutions.

The GATT and BOP Problems of Developing Countries

GATT serves several functions. One is to provide a set of rules governing the behaviour of countries in formulating their own trade policies. A second is to serve as a forum for multilateral trade negotiations, wherein its contracting parties exchange mutually beneficial trade concessions. GATT also provides a mechanism for resolving trade disputes among its members, as well as a process allowing for withdrawal of concessions to help in enforcement of agreements. Its two central features are the MFN principle (which prohibits discrimination among suppliers from other countries at the member's border) and national treatment (which prohibits discrimination in favour of domestic producers over foreign suppliers beyond the national border). So GATT also represents a commitment to lowered trade barriers, which has mainly been accomplished through a sequence of multilateral negotiations on tariff reductions, although other trade impediments, such as government procurement, subsidies and AD duties, have also been discussed. These have typically been dealt with through codes agreed to by groups of signatory countries, although the outcomes have generally been less satisfactory than with tariffs.

As far as the topic of this chapter is concerned, however, nowhere in either the original GATT articles or in subsequent GATT negotiations have the trade-restricting effects of exchange and financial arrangements been explicitly recognized. Liberalization of such arrangements is not treated as a trade concession comparable to a tariff reduction. Reductions in tariffs are always regarded as trade-liberalizing even if financial and exchange rate impediments apply. The focus of GATT negotiations has thus been largely on reducing or regulating real-side trade-restricting measures commonly found in developed countries. The unfortunate part of this is that it is in developing countries that the most severely trade-restricting regimes occur, and these simultaneously offer the largest source of mutual gain from trade liberalization.

Since financial arrangements typically dominate real-side trade restrictions in restraining trade in developing countries, the net effect is that these countries appear to feel limited in the ways in which they can participate vis-à-vis each other in GATT negotiations. Developed countries seem to assume that developing countries have little to make by way of meaningful concessions, and hence little to contribute to a mutual exchange. They also seem well aware that liberalization of tariffs and quotas by developing countries may do little to yield improved access to these markets. The system thus excludes the concessions which developing countries could offer based on financial and exchange rate arrangements.

Any changes to the present structure of GATT to accommodate reciprocal bargaining over financial liberalization by developing countries has to begin from the present GATT articles. Article XV recognizes that GATT's jurisdiction is over real-side trade impediments and that exchange and financial arrangements are under the IMF. The idea is that once BOP equilibrium is achieved and sustained with IMF support, trade can then be increased by lowering real-side trade impediments through multilateral trade negotiations under GATT. This reflects the prevailing view in the late 1940s that under the then fixed exchange rate system, the attainment of BOP equilibrium was to be achieved by the IMF recycling trade surpluses to deficit countries in order to defend the fixed parities. According to this view of the fixed exchange rate system, BOP difficulties are seen as being largely short-term once full convertibility has been achieved. Article XV therefore represents an impediment to reciprocal bargaining of the type we suggest, since it assumes away the importance of financial impediments to trade. It acknowledges separate roles for GATT and the IMF, and implicitly sees BOP deficits as being temporary phenomena rather than long-term and policy-induced, and being accompanied by trade-restricting financial arrangements.

GATT arrangements are also in part to blame for the widespread non-observance of the implicit contract on convertibility as far as developing countries are concerned since it treats developing countries quite liberally with respect to BOP problems, which weakens any pressures on them to align their domestic policies so as to achieve and sustain convertibility.

Import restrictions are permitted for BOP reasons under Articles XII and XVIII-B of GATT. Article XII applies to all contracting parties facing a threat of a serious decline in monetary reserves. The threat of a payments crisis must be 'imminent', or the monetary reserves of the country invoking Article XII must be 'very low' for GATT to approve the use of trade restrictions. The country is expected to take up corrective measures in order to solve its BOP problems. Once approved, the BOP restrictions, as well as the policies meant to solve the payments problems of the country, are to be reviewed annually by GATT.

In practice, however, only a few (and typically developed) countries have invoked Article XII and imposed BOP trade restrictions. The reason is that the majority of such restrictions have been imposed by developing countries, who cite Article XVIII-B which is written specifically for them. Its requirements for imposing import restrictions are more liberal and the surveillance of trade restrictions and related domestic policies are weaker compared to those under Article XII.[7] For example, the consultations with GATT are conducted every year under Article XII as opposed to once every two years with Article XVIII-B.[8] In such consultations, the conditions which led to the imposition of restrictions as well as the alternative policy decisions taken to solve the payments problems are reviewed by GATT.[9]

Most of the consultations that have taken place since 1974 involving the GATT Committee on Balance of Payments Restrictions proceeded based on Article XVIII-B requirements (see Anjaria, 1987; Eglin, 1987). Of 24 countries which imposed import restrictions for BOP purposes between 1974 and 1986, 19 invoked Article XVIII-B, three invoked Article XII and, for two countries, the Article used to justify the restrictions is not stated. No developing country cited Article XII.

As Eglin (1987) points out there are several factors in this system which undermine the surveillance of import restrictions used for BOP purposes, which in turn have resulted in only weak discipline over developing countries using such restrictions. The Balance of Payments Committee has no means of ensuring that countries using BOP restrictions are doing so in conformity with both its findings and general GATT principles. Notification by contracting parties tends to be incomplete. Indeed the process has become so ineffective that those countries adversely affected by trade restrictions used by trading partners usually do not report such cases to the Committee.[10] Countries can also employ trade restrictions for BOP purposes prior to consultation with GATT. Consultations under Article XVIII-B and Article XII thus typically do little to dissuade developing countries from imposing trade restrictions.

This all makes it relatively easy for developing countries to impose trade barriers for BOP purposes under Article XVIII-B. This in part reflects the view underlying GATT, namely that payments problems for such countries are structural and endemic in nature. BOP problems 'will tend to be generated by . . . the [in]adequacy of the reserves in relation to their programme of economic development'.

Accordingly developing countries 'may need over a period of time to control the general level of their imports' to safeguard their external positions.[11]

GATT fails to acknowledge that payments problems of developing countries may be induced by domestic exchange rate and monetary policies, and that the resulting financial arrangements may themselves restrict trade. Allowing developing countries to control imports only reduces the pressure on such countries to restore discipline and consistency in their economic policies. Hence, payments problems may be unnecessarily prolonged, may tend to worsen, and their trade-restricting effects eventually come to dominate all other trade impediments. Changes are needed in GATT in order for wider reciprocal bargaining to occur.

Some proposals have been made for GATT reforms to strengthen discipline over international trade transactions such as the tightening of Article XVIII-B to minimize the use by developing countries of BOP restrictions, although these will not facilitate the form of reciprocal bargaining we propose. Eglin (1987) proposes eliminating Article XVIII-B and treating both developed and developing countries equally under Article XII as far as BOP restrictions are concerned. Recognizing that agreement by the contracting parties over this is unlikely, he also suggests the following specific proposals for reform of the current surveillance procedures in GATT on BOP restrictions: (i) requiring time limits for the use of Articles XII and XVIII-B, after which continued use of BOP restrictions by any country would result in its trading partners seeking compensation for damages sustained; (ii) introducing accelerated consultations after a grace period to exert additional pressure on the country to withdraw its BOP import restrictions; (iii) removing simplified BOP consultations which have proved to be ineffective in persuading countries to drop BOP import restrictions; and (iv) instituting regular annual consultations in GATT for all countries.

A related proposal is for some form of concessions to be exchanged on Article XVIII-B and Article XIX between developing and developed countries. The idea is that developing countries may either give up Article XVIII-B and accept Article XII BOP provisions like other countries, or accept more discipline on the use of balance-of-payments restrictions in exchange for developed countries making concessions in Article XIX on the use of safeguards. Article XIX allows emergency action on imports of particular products, and has been used by developed countries to protect industries facing import surges. The imposition of time limits on the use of such measures (degressivity) is the most frequent developing country request.

The above concrete proposals are put forward for achieving firmer discipline over the use of BOP restrictions. However, even if they occur, they do nothing to address the need for reciprocal bargaining to include financial liberalization, and our belief is that ultimately new GATT articles would be required. An integral part of this would also be a redefinition of the role of the IMF, which would involve changes to Article XV.

Developing Countries and the IMF

The IMF is also the key to international economic arrangements which have evolved during the post-war years. Established during the Bretton Woods conference in 1944, the mandate of this multilateral agency is to help promote and maintain employment and living standards in all its member countries by fostering orderly exchange and financial arrangements among its member countries. Like GATT, it also aims to expand world trade, especially by promoting currency convertibility and resolving BOP problems. It provides financial support for BOP purposes, and if need be oversees domestic policies of its members which are relevant to BOP difficulties. This dual role of policy surveillance and financing is manifest in the practice of conditionality. Conditionality stems from the mandate to establish safeguards over the use of the agency's resources as stated in Article V(3a) of the IMF Agreement. In 1979, the agency's executive board issued guidelines on access to Fund resources and the use of stand-by arrangements, leading to the existing sets of terms and conditions which have evolved through years of conditional lending to members. Stand-by arrangements range from a period of one year up to three years, while compliance of members with the terms set in any Fund programme is evaluated on the basis of a number of performance criteria which normally are confined to macroeconomic variables.

The IMF's financial resources come from member countries which are required to deposit a quota of resources determined by income and the extent to which their respective currencies are used in international trade. A quarter of the quota is to be deposited in terms of gold or convertible currency, with the rest in the currency of the depositor country. Loans up to the country's quota can normally be extended in five equal tranches, with the first tranche, called the reserve tranche, extendable to the depositor without any conditions. The other four tranches, called the credit tranches, have conditions attached to them in varying levels of severity.

Broadly, IMF loans may be classified into those with low and high conditionality. Low conditionality simply requires that the borrower who is experiencing a BOP deficit be taking measures to correct it. The country is given 'the overwhelming benefit of the doubt' that it is undertaking reasonable efforts to reduce its payments difficulties (Williamson, 1982). The IMF low conditionality credit facilities include the first credit tranche, the Compensatory Financing Facility, the Oil Facility in the 1970s, the Buffer Stock Financing Facility and the Trust Fund. High conditionality loans, on the other hand, require the borrower to implement a specific set of corrective measures recommended by the IMF to restore balance in payments. Resources are usually provided under stand-by arrangements lasting up to three years. These provide the borrower with access to Fund resources in a series of instalments subject to the borrower's compliance with the terms of the arrangement. This, in turn, is evaluated on the basis of a specific set of performance criteria. The upper credit tranches, the Extended Facility, the Supplementary Financing Facility, and recently the SAF, are high conditionality credit facilities.

These current lending practices of the IMF make it an important lender to many developing countries. Industrialized countries ordinarily regard the agency not as a source of credit, since they can always borrow from private commercial banks, but rather as an institution which channels aid to developing countries in the form of concessional credit. Developing countries, on the other hand, particularly the poorer ones, are generally deemed not to be creditworthy by the private banking sector, and thus see the IMF as their lender of first resort. Also, many developing countries suffer from structural BOP disequilibria, which many of the IMF high conditionality facilities are tailored for. Relatively successful developing countries tend to suffer from temporary lapses of creditworthiness which they see as able to be restored if they enter into stand-by or extended arrangements with the IMF which, in turn, has to approve their domestic policies.

The latest credit arrangement is the SAF (IMF, 1986), approved by the IMF in March 1986. This facility is to assist poor developing countries with endemic BOP problems in carrying out economic policy reforms. In June 1987, it was proposed to triple the SAF resources currently amounting to SDR 3 billion (IMF, 1987b).

The escalating conditionality manifest in the agency's credit facilities reflects the IMF view of the causes of the BOP problems of its members. BOP deficits, according to Williamson (1982), are classified by the IMF into three types: temporary deficits which are self-reversing, deficits caused by excess demands and those caused by overvaluation of the local currency. While the first two types may be regarded as temporary disequilibria, the last is viewed as a 'fundamental disequilibrium' in external payments. Low conditionality facilities are applied to temporary BOP deficits, while high conditionality loans are used to address fundamental payments problems. The oil shocks of the 1970s provided the basis for a fourth type of deficit: those induced by non-seasonal terms-of-trade changes in response to which the economy finds it costly to adjust. The Extended Facility and the SAF are meant to respond to such types of deficits.

The breadth of conditionality, however, has set off active debates both over the merits of conditionality itself, and as to whether conditionality has had positive effects in inducing policy changes which have improved the payments position for debtor industries.[12] According to a recent report of the Group of 24 (IMF, 1987c) on the IMF's role in promoting adjustment with growth, the agency 'generally has insisted on heavy reliance on demand management policies for correcting maladjustments in external payments'. Typically stand-by arrangements require 'excessive' reduction of domestic aggregate demand, cuts in real wages, lower government spending, sharp currency devaluations and import liberalization. These objectives are spelled out in performance criteria which, the report says, have proliferated, tightening conditionality as a result.

Thus the Group of 24 concludes that the current practice of conditionality 'has not generally been satisfactory' (IMF, 1987c). Programmes were costly for the developing countries and worsened income distribution. Economic growth was sacrificed for a 'quick reversal of balance of payments deficits' through demand compression, and devaluations only worsened domestic inflation. The Group calls for a more flexible implementation of Fund programmes, stressing that growth and distribution concerns should not be unduly neglected in the effort to achieve BOP viability for all members.[13]

Another view is that conditionality has provided a vehicle through which some degree of liberalization has resulted, but as a concession for credits to developing countries to help with payments difficulties rather than through reciprocal bargaining. The net result has been that international discipline over trade and domestic polices which developing countries thought they had avoided under GATT through their successful claims for S&D status in the 1960s have been replaced by unilateral discipline undertaken by developing countries because of conditionality attached to IMF loans. The IMF has thus taken on a role which, in effect, fills a vacuum left by the lack of coverage by GATT of financial impediments to trade. As was argued above, GATT does not cover the trade-restricting effects of financial policies, and it has been unable to provide any framework for international negotiations covering these measures.

Also, under conditionality developing countries are committed to honouring their obligations under lending programmes of the IMF for the duration of the programme. After this period of time, they are again free to choose what economic policies they wish to follow. Hence the discipline over trade and domestic policies which IMF conditionality extracts from developing countries as 'payment' for credit concessions is temporary. In contrast, trade arrangements under GATT remain in force indefinitely, or until a new agreement is made by the contracting parties. Developing countries may thus find it worthwhile to see if the discipline they agree to under IMF conditionality programmes can in some relatively modest way be negotiated by them for improved market access under GATT, such as offering to undertake IMF conditions permanently in return for concessions on access.

In the short run, the IMF has clearly played a major role in providing credit and policy surveillance through its current programmes. In the long run, if our approach of expanding the scope of GATT negotiations to cover financial liberalization were to be followed, the agency would have to cooperate more fully with GATT to help monitor compliance by member countries of negotiated bindings over financial distortions. Surveillance of undertakings made in such negotiations could usefully build on existing IMF activities in this area. GATT–IMF cooperation is currently limited under GATT consultation related to BOP restrictions as provided in Article XV. Such cooperation could be broadened to monitor the compliance of developing countries with other GATT obligations. The IMF has the advantage over GATT in such surveillance since it requires ongoing scrutiny of the financial and stabilization policies of individual developing countries.

GATT and the IMF clearly play complementary roles, although within the current institutional structure the full dimensions of this complementarity are not reflected in their current operations. A process of imposing unilateral discipline on developing countries through credit negotiations does not allow for negotiation of mutually-agreed disciplines on the use of all trade-restricting policies, including domestic financial policies. By restricting its attention to real-side trade measures and not encompassing financial restrictions on trade and their real-side effects, GATT provides no mechanism for negotiating effective discipline on the key trade-restricting policies in developing countries. Hence our view is that the separation of responsibility between GATT and the IMF is part of the difficulty of how to integrate developing countries more fully into the trading system. Our proposal is to broaden reciprocal bargaining under GATT to include financial impediments to trade. This would expand the scope of GATT and, if in the longer term developing countries were to move to full convertibility as part of this process, the role of the IMF would appear to be much reduced, perhaps emphasizing surveillance.

CONCLUSION

In this chapter we focused on financial impediments to trade flows in developing countries associated with their fixed exchange rate regime and rationing of foreign exchange. We suggested that bargaining on real-side trade measures among developed countries makes sense because they maintain convertibility. Such bargaining between developed and developing countries makes little sense while the latter maintain inconvertibility. Developed countries become frustrated since real-side liberalization produces little increase in trade in developing countries, because financial restrictions are the binding impediments. Developing countries become frustrated since financial liberalization by them is not treated as a concession. We concluded that GATT needs changing to widen the range of potential reciprocal bargains. We also discussed concrete proposals as to how a return to convertibility can take place in these countries.

Our view is that wide-ranging changes in the global trading system are needed to encompass both financial and real-side trade restrictions to help move substantive developed–developing country trade negotiations forwards. We argue that unless financial restrictions in developing country trade policies are dealt with centrally, there can be little substantive liberalization of trade between developed and developing countries. A negotiating framework is needed which allows for a mutual exchange of concessions covering both financial and real-side impediments to trade.

Notes

1.   See 1985-86 IMF *Handbook of Foreign Exchange Restrictions.*
2.   Exchange controls have received some attention in the macro literature, but less attention in micro trade literature, although their trade-restricting effects are generally well known (see Bhagwati and Srinivasan, 1984).
3.   See Clarete and Whalley (1986) for a formal analysis of foreign exchange rationing schemes and a calculation of their economic impacts based on an applied general equilibrium model of the Philippines.
4.   While these distortions operate in much the same manner as tariffs, an important difference is that when external shocks hit the economy the tariff equivalent implied by these restrictions will change.
5.   Usually a devaluation is viewed as increasing exports and reducing imports, and consequently improving the trade deficit. This occurs, however, where the trade deficit is accommodated by an inflow of foreign capital, and where there is no need to ration foreign exchange. Here we argue that a devaluation expands imports in the presence of rationing (the regime which currently applies to most developing countries).
6.   Thus, even if foreign exchange liberalization can be agreed to be a trade concession, it is misleading to use black market prices of foreign exchange as an indication of the restrictiveness of foreign exchange regimes. This is because countries do not use the same enforcement procedures for the surrender of export earnings, and neither do they treat parallel foreign exchange markets uniformly. See Nguyen and Whalley (1985) for an analysis of the co-existence of equilibria on black and white (official) markets.
7.   For example, Article XII requires that the threat of a serious decline of the country's foreign exchange reserves be 'imminent' before import restrictions can be applied. However, this word is deleted in Article XVIII-B.
8.   Officially, this is 'in view of the practical difficulties which [developing] countries may have in preparing the necessary documentation and in sending the experts to attend these consultations'. See GATT (1955), p. 184.
9.   Consultations of this nature are classified as either 'full' or 'simplified'. Full consultations are required when a country imposes new restrictions or intensifies existing ones. The IMF representative is also invited to attend such consultations to discuss the IMF assessment of the country's economic situation. Simplified consultations

are required periodically to monitor the progress of the country in solving the payments problems as well as its application of the authorized trade restrictions. See Eglin (1987) and Anjaria (1987) for a discussion of how such consultations work.

10. This limited use of reverse notification is especially common in cases involving small developing countries. With negligible trade with the rest of the world, such countries escape GATT discipline since their trading partners are hardly affected by their actions and usually do not report any violations of GATT agreements by them.

11. See GATT (1955), p. 183.

12. See especially Williamson (1983), but also the debates within the IMF in Connors (1979), Crockett (1981), Kelley (1982), and Khan and Knight (1983). Balassa and McCarthy (1984) provide a compendium of adjustment experience in a number of developing countries relevant to this debate.

13. It is unclear, though, how flexible implementation of such programmes can be redesigned without losing whatever little discipline the agency has succeeded in promoting among many developing countries. Also, stressing financing so as to promote growth and distribution in the face of widespread distortions in developing countries might be counterproductive, and in the long run would do such countries more harm than good. As Guitian (1987) argues: 'Unless the growth associated with such financing reflects its efficient use, it will not be sustained. Indeed, growth in the future may have been mortgaged with financing undertaken in excess of the economy's absorptive and productive capacities.'

References

Anjaria, S. (1987) 'Balance of Payments and Related Issues in the Uruguay Round of Trade Negotiations'. *The World Bank Economic Review*, 1 (4).

Balassa, B. and McCarthy, F.D. (1984) 'Adjustment Policies in Developing Countries, 1979-1983: An Update', World Bank Staff Working Papers, No. 675 (Washington, DC: World Bank).

Bhagwati, J. and Srinivasan, T.N. (1984) *Lectures in International Trade* (Cambridge, Mass: MIT Press).

Clarete, R. and Whalley, J. (1986) 'Equilibrium in the Presence of Foreign Exchange Premia', CSIER Working Paper 8613C (London, Canada: University of Western Ontario).

Connors, T.A. (1979) 'The Apparent Effects of Recent IMF Stabilization Programs', IMF Discussion Paper, No. 135 (Washington, DC: IMF), April.

Crockett, A.D. (1981) 'Stabilization Policies in Developing Countries: Some Policy Considerations', *IMF Staff Papers* (Washington, DC: IMF), pp. 54-79.

Eglin, R. (1987), 'Surveillance of Balance-of-Payments Measures in the GATT', *The World Economy*, 10 (1), pp. 1–26.

GATT (1955), *Basic Instruments and Selected Documents, Third Supplement* (Geneva: GATT).

Guitian, M. (1987) 'The Fund's Role in Adjustment', *Finance and Development*, 24 (2), pp. 3–6.

Gulhati, R., Bose, S. and Atukorala, V. (1985) 'Exchange Rate Polices in Eastern and Southern Africa, 1965-1983', World Bank Staff Working Paper, No. 720 (Washington, DC: World Bank).

IMF (1986) 'The IMF's Structural Adjustment Facility', *Finance and Development*, 23 (2) p. 39.

IMF (1987a) 'Camdessus Welcomes Summit Support for SAP', IMF Survey (Washington, DC: IMF), 29 June.

IMF (1987b) 'Developing Countries Prove Successful in Introducing Floating Exchange Rates', IMF Survey (Washington, DC: IMF), 1 June.

IMF (1987c) 'Group of 24 Report', IMF Survey Supplement (Washington, DC: IMF), 10 August.

Kelley, M.R. (1982) 'Fiscal Adjustment and Fund Supported Programs, 1971–80', IMF Staff Papers (Washington, DC: IMF) pp. 561–602.

Khan, M.S. and Knight, M.D. (1983) 'Determinants of Current Account Balances of Non-Oil Developing Countries in the 1970s: An Empirical Analysis', IMF Staff Papers (Washington, DC: IMF), pp. 819-42.

Nguyen, T.N. and Whalley, J. (1985) 'Coexistence of Equilibria on Black and White Markets', CSIER Working Paper 8523C (London, Canada: University of Western Ontario).

Quirk, P., Christensen, B., Huh, K. and Sasaki, T. (1987) 'Floating Exchange Rates in Developing Countries: Recent Experience with Auction and Interbank Markets', Occasional Paper No.53 (Washington, DC: IMF).

Williamson, J. (1982), *The Lending Policies of the International Monetary Fund* (Washington, DC:IIE).

Williamson, J. (ed.) (1983) *IMF Conditionality* (Washington, DC: IIE).

Part II

Developing Country
Objectives in the System

5 Primary Commodities in the International Trading System[1]

T. Ademola Oyejide

INTRODUCTION

Primary commodities provide a significant component of world merchandise trade. Although primary commodity trade is dominated by the industrialized countries, the LDCs are substantially more dependent on it in terms of their national income, export earnings and employment.

As a result of this dependence, several characteristics of primary commodity trade pose significant problems for the LDCs. Countries which are heavily dependent on primary commodity exports tend to suffer from declines in their terms of trade; instability of prices and export earnings of primary commodities constitute additional sources of problems. Furthermore, tariffs, NTBs and tariff escalation in the developed countries substantially constrain market access both for raw and processed forms of primary commodities, while non-competitive marketing arrangements and market structures deny the LDCs the full benefits derivable from their primary commodity exports particularly in processed forms.

This chapter argues that these issues represent the main concerns of the LDCs with respect to the treatment of primary commodities in the international trading system. It argues also that the numerous multilateral initiatives which have been mounted to tackle these problems have left them largely unresolved. Because of GATT's narrow focus, its institutional weakness and the dominant interests of the developed countries' coalition which its negotiating format and operating procedures reflect, the concerns of the LDCs relating to primary commodity trade have never been part of the organization's central focus. Yet, as the main organization responsible for managing the global trading system, GATT needs to deal with the concerns of the developed and developing world in a more balanced manner.

This chapter suggests that a reform process should be set in motion not necessarily to create new organizational forms for dealing with trade and related matters but to modify GATT's structure, mandate and procedures so that issues considered important by the LDCs

91

can receive as much attention as those which affect the interests of the industrialized countries. This reform process may be difficult and protracted, but it is argued that the enhanced participation of the LDCs and the apparent willingness of the developed world to liberalize primary commodity trade make this a feasible option.

SIZE AND STRUCTURE OF PRIMARY COMMODITY TRADE

The term primary commodities covers a whole range of products that can be classified into several broad groups, depending on one's objective. Based on the UN's SITC, primary commodities include agricultural and mineral products defined largely as SITC sections 0, 1 and 4, including division 68 and item 522.56. This definition offers two broad groups; one covers agricultural primary commodities, and the other includes minerals, ores and metals.

Agricultural primary commodities have several subdivisions. Broadly, they can be divided into food and raw materials, excluding synthetics. Food products are made up of food, beverages, tobacco, oilseeds and oleaginous fruits, animal and vegetable oils and fats. Agricultural raw materials include cotton and cotton yarn, jute and jute products, hard fibres and products, rubber and timber. Food products can be further divided into at least two broad categories. In one class are temperate zone food products while a second group covers tropical food products. The latter group is dominated by tropical beverages, such as coffee, cocoa and tea; while the former group includes food grains, dairy products, meat and poultry among others. It may also be necessary to distinguish between agricultural raw materials which face significant competition from synthetics (for example, natural rubber) and those that do not, or not to a large extent. International discussions of primary commodities have utilized aspects of these distinctions between different components of primary products.

Trade in primary commodities is a significant part of world merchandise trade. Table 5.1 provides relevant data. The value of total primary commodity exports rose from US\$ 85.7 billion in 1970 to US\$ 319.7 billion in 1983. In comparison, the value of all merchandise exports went up from US\$ 316.4 billion to US\$ 1 820.1 billion over the same period. These figures indicate that while the value of primary commodity exports increased over 1970–83, the value of total merchandise exports grew even faster. Hence, the share of primary

commodity exports out of total merchandise trade declined sharply
from 27.1 per cent in 1970 to 17.6 per cent in 1983. Agricultural
commodities (Food products) contributed 72.3 per cent of primary
commodity export earnings in 1970, while minerals, ores and metals
accounted for 27.7 per cent in the same year.

Table 5.1   Structure of world trade (US$ billion)

	1970	*1980*	*1983*
All primary commodities	85.7	373.2	319.7
Food products	62.0	278.9	247.9
Minerals, ores and metals	23.7	94.3	71.8
All merchandise trade	316.4	2 014.4	1 820.1

Source: UNCTAD, *Yearbook of International Commodity Statistics*, 1985.

Regional distribution of total primary commodity exports and
imports is shown in Table 5.2. Looking first at export value, the
share of developed market economies increased from 58.4 per cent
in 1970 to 64 per cent in 1983. Over the same period, the share of
the LDCs fell from 32.6 per cent to 29.3 per cent. Africa's share
fell steadily from 8.8 per cent in 1970 to 4.9 per cent in 1983;
Asia managed to increase its share steadily over the same period,
from 9.8 per cent to 10.8 per cent; while the performance of Latin
America and the Caribbean was mixed: its share declined from 13.6
per cent in 1970 to 12.3 per cent in 1980 and then increased to 13.2
per cent in 1983. The dominance of developed market economies in
primary commodity trade is more sharply reflected in regional shares
of imports; but import distribution also reveals a trend that is roughly
the opposite of that shown by exports. Thus, although the share of
primary commodity imports accounted for by the developed market
economies remained quite substantial, the trend was downward; from
75.6 per cent in 1970 to 65.8 per cent in 1983. Correspondingly, the
share of the LDCs which was only 14.3 per cent in 1970 rose to 22.5
per cent by 1983.

It is clear from the above that trade in primary commodities is
dominated by the industrialized countries. In fact, this dominance
extends also to the 18 IPC commodities selected by UNCTAD as
those in which LDCs have primary export interests. As Table 5.3
shows, only four (Brazil, Malaysia, Cuba and Indonesia) of the ten
principal exporters of the 18 IPC commodities are LDCs. In addition,

the developed country exporters accounted for 64.0 per cent and 55.7 per cent in 1972 and 1983 respectively of the total exports of the top ten exporters; they also provided 26.0 per cent and 27.6 per cent of world exports of the 18 IPC commodities over the same period.

In spite of the dominant position of developed countries in primary commodity trade, LDCs are much more dependent on primary commodities for their export earnings than are the industrialized countries. Table 5.4 offers data on an aspect of this comparison. The

Table 5.2   Share of regions in world primary commodity trade

	1966	1970	1975	1980	1983
Exports (%)					
World	100.0	100.0	100.0	100.0	100.0
Developed market economy countries	56.5	58.4	61.9	65.2	64.0
Developing countries	33.6	32.6	29.0	28.3	29.3
Africa	9.0	8.8	6.6	5.2	4.9
Latin America/Caribbean	13.6	13.6	12.7	12.3	13.2
Asia	10.8	9.8	9.2	10.3	10.8
Socialist countries of Eastern Europe	8.2	7.8	7.3	5.3	5.3
Socialist countries of Asia	1.8	1.3	1.7	1.3	1.4
Imports (%)					
World	100.0	100.0	100.0	100.0	100.0
Developed market economy countries	74.2	75.6	68.8	68.5	65.8
Developing countries	15.0	14.3	19.0	20.3	22.5
Africa	3.0	2.5	4.2	4.1	4.8
Latin America/Caribbean	4.6	4.5	5.0	5.4	5.1
Asia	7.2	7.0	9.0	10.6	12.4
Socialist countries of Eastern Europe	9.3	8.8	10.8	9.4	9.8
Socialist countries of Asia	1.6	1.3	1.4	1.8	1.9

Source: UNCTAD, *Yearbook of International Commodity Statistics*, 1985

Table 5.3   Value of exports of 18 IPC commodities from the ten principal exporters (US$ billion)

	1972	1980	1983
Developed	8.9	30.1	25.6
USA	3.1	13.2	11.2
Australia	1.4	4.2	3.8
France	0.9	3.6	3.0
Canada	1.4	3.3	2.6
USSR	1.5	2.9	2.5
Germany (Fed. Rep)	0.65	2.9	2.5
LDC	5.0	23.6	20.4
Brazil	2.4	7.5	6.5
Malaysia	1.3	6.8	6.2
Cuba	0.6	4.6	4.8
Indonesia	0.7	4.7	2.9
World	34.2	113.1	92.6

Source: UNCTAD, *Yearbook of International Commodity Statistics*, 1985

share of primary commodities in total merchandise exports of both the developed market economy countries and the socialist countries of Eastern Europe is generally below the world average over the 1966–1983 period. The world average itself declined steadily from 32 per cent in 1966 to 18 per cent in 1983. In the same way, the share of primary commodities in the total merchandise exports of the developed market economy countries fell from 26 per cent to 18 per cent; while that of socialist Eastern Europe declined from 25 per cent to 10 per cent over the same period. The LDCs' share also fell, of course, and on the aggregate, quite dramatically: from 55 per cent in 1966 to 21 per cent in 1983. But when oil-exporters are excluded, the LDCs' share remained as high as 36 per cent in 1983.

COMMODITY TERMS OF TRADE AND INSTABILITY ISSUES

Primary commodities have several features that condition their trade prospects which, in turn, influence the attitude of policy makers to them in both the industrialized world and the LDCs. Many of the problems associated with primary commodity trade can be traced to one or several of these features. Foremost among

Table 5.4   Share (%) of primary commodities in all merchandise exports by region

	1966	1970	1980	1983
World	31.6	27.1	18.5	17.6
Developed market economy countries	25.9	22.2	19.1	17.5
Developing countries	54.7	48.7	18.6	20.5
Developing countries*	72.8	67.1	41.0	35.6
Africa*	69.0	58.6	20.5	26.1
Latin America/Caribbean	65.6	65.2	39.7	38.8
Latin America/Caribbean*	83.7	80.7	56.0	56.1
Asia*	57.3	47.5	26.0	20.8
Socialist countries of Eastern Europe	25.2	21.5	12.6	9.7

* Excluding major oil-exporters.

Source: UNCTAD, *Yearbook of International Commodity Statistics*, 1985.

these are issues related to changes in commodity terms of trade and the degree of instability in both price and export earnings.

Commodity or net barter terms of trade describe the relationship between prices of exports and prices of imports. A country's net barter terms of trade deteriorate when its export prices decline relative to its import prices. The general view held by LDCs is that, in broad terms, there has been a deterioration in the terms of trade of primary commodity exporters. This view has received analytical support from the well-known Prebisch–Singer thesis (Prebisch, 1949; Singer, 1950). But the theoretical basis and the statistical evidence for the thesis have often been challenged. In spite of the continuing controversy about and endless debate on the issue, the tendency toward a long-term secular decline in primary commodity prices, either in real terms or relative to the prices of manufactured products, remains an enduring concern of the LDCs, particularly those that are heavily dependent on foreign exchange earnings from a few primary commodities. It is believed that a downward trend in the real prices of commodities, other than petroleum, is perceptible from the mid-1950s, and may have worsened since the early 1970s. Table 5.5 provides some evidence to show that the annual growth rate of commodity prices has been negative for the 1950–82 period, and for most of the subperiods in between. Evidence for a more recent period, 1982–6, conveys the same impression (see Table 5.6): by and large, the trend of

Table 5.5   Annual growth rates (%) of commodity prices (constant US$)

	1950–9	*1950–79*	*1950–82*	*1960–9*	*1970–9*
33 commodities	-2.61	-0.95	-1.09	0.89	-1.28
Total agriculture	-3.51	1.10	-1.23	-0.34	-0.14
Food	-3.03	-0.68	-0.86	-0.34	0.22
Agricultural raw materials	-4.69	-2.40	-2.35	-2.10	1.51
Metals and minerals	-0.19	-0.85	-1.12	3.57	-4.64

Source: MacBean and Nguyen (1985), p. 33.

Table 5.6   Average annual percentage changes in primary commodity export prices of the LDCs, 1982–6

Year	Total Exports	Food	Non-food	Metals and minerals	Fuels
1982	-6.7	-8.5	-8.6	-10.2	-9.7
1983	-2.4	-5.3	5.5	2.1	9.0
1984	-1.0	1.9	-1.0	-3.0	-2.5
1985	-3.1	-9.5	-14.5	-5.5	-3.0
1986	-1.2	8.2	0.7	-4.6	-49.4

Source: World Bank (1987), p. 176.

primary commodity export prices has been downwards. This trend is attributed partly to endemic over–supply and partly to the switch in demand from natural to synthetic materials and other substitutes over the past two or three decades.

Another major problem of the LDCs is the instability of prices of primary commodities. This is also an old and enduring problem, of course, but there has apparently been a dramatic increase in the instability of commodity prices in the 1970s and the 1980s compared to two or three earlier decades. It is believed also that primary commodity prices have, over time, experienced shorter upswing and longer downswing periods than the prices of manufactured products. In any case, there appears to be a general consensus to the effect that prices of primary commodities have continued to be more volatile than prices of manufactured goods.

Primary commodity prices tend to fluctuate widely because of demand and supply conditions that are peculiar to commodity markets. In these markets, the combination of large shifts in supply and demand with low supply and demand price elasticities could result in unstable prices. Shifts in demand may reflect trade cycle and stocking policy changes in relation to market expectations. Rigidities emanating from unplanned variations in harvests may prevent immediate adjustment on the supply side.

Factors outside commodity markets also contribute, sometimes substantially, to commodity price fluctuations. Global economic conditions have become relatively less stable since the 1970s. The combination of rapid global inflation, wide fluctuations in interest rates, and severe recessions early in the 1970s and the 1980s, has had spill-over effects in terms of more unstable commodity markets. In the same way, exchange rate fluctuations, particularly of the dollar in which most commodity prices are quoted in long-term contracts, have transmitted additional instability to commodity prices.

Fluctuations in LDC export revenues constitute an important reason for the concern over instability of commodity prices. The inherent volatility of commodity markets is believed to cause export earnings instability, especially for those LDCs which are dependent on a single commodity or a small number of commodities for the majority of their foreign exchange requirements (Cuddy, 1985; UNCTAD, 1986).

Fluctuations in export earnings are, in principle, due to changes in prices, quantities exported or both. At the empirical level, however, export revenue instability seems to be caused primarily by fluctuations in quantities exported; the impact of fluctuating prices appears to be relatively small (Wahab, 1985; UNCTAD, 1986). This general result seems to be particularly robust for individual countries. Unstable export earnings among countries are due to the unusually high level of instability of their export receipts from one or more commodities. In addition, whenever the export earnings of a commodity are highly unstable for a particular country, the primary cause is usually the abnormally large swings in quantity exported. It would seem, therefore, that the major cause of export earnings instability emanates much more directly from domestic factors affecting supply than external events impinging upon world demand and prices.

The main reason why LDCs asscribe such importance to the issue of instability, whether of commodity prices or export earnings, is the belief that instability is harmful to the process, rate and/or level of economic development. To the extent that commodity price instability destabilizes export earnings, it contributes to the instability of government revenue and expenditures, imports and investments which in turn hinders economic growth.

MARKET ACCESS, MARKETING AND MARKET STRUCTURE

The concerns of the LDCs with respect to prospects for primary commodities touch also upon the interrelated issues of market access, marketing channels, and the market structure of primary commodities. Various difficulties associated with each of these constitute significant hurdles which hamper freer trade and deny the LDCs some of the benefits that should accrue to them as producers and exporters of primary commodities.

Primary commodities, particularly agricultural products, face problems of restricted market access in the industrialized countries. As these countries tend to protect their own agricultural sectors, they pursue a policy of stabilizing domestic prices of agricultural commodities at the expense of greater instability in international markets. By marginalizing world markets for many primary commodities, one of the effects of protectionism in the industrialized countries is to worsen price fluctuations (Valdes, 1986).

The strong protection of agriculture in the developed countries contrasts sharply with the taxing of agriculture in the LDCs. The progress made toward trade liberalization in manufactured goods through MTNs has not made a significant dent in agricultural protectionism in the developed countries. In many of the industrialized countries, average nominal protection rates actually increased over the 1960–80 period (Honma and Hayami, 1985). In addition, exports from LDCs also face many stringent NTBs in the developed countries. These barriers are implemented through instruments such as quantitative restrictions on imports, variable levies, 'voluntary' import quotas, subsidies to production and export and discriminatory procurement practices. The effect of these measures is to lower world prices as well as export volumes of the LDCs (Valdes, 1986).

The barriers against primary commodities in the developed countries are further increased through tariff escalation which occurs when tariff rates increase with the degree of processing, thus placing progressively higher trade restrictions on semi-processed and processed products. The escalating structure of developed country tariffs against LDC primary commodity exports has survived the

Tokyo Round of MTNs. This practice has the effect of discouraging if not preventing LDCs from processing their raw agricultural and mineral materials. The bias which this policy has introduced into the world trading system is partially captured in the radical differences in the export structures of developed countries as compared with LDCs with respect to resource-based products. Thus export of natural resources in raw form is more important in the LDCs, while the

Table 5.7   Merchandise exports by degree of processing

	Percentage share of exports by degree of processing, 1977*	
	Sub-Saharan Africa	Other developing countries
Food products		
Coffee		
Green, roasted	100°	95°
Essence, extracts	(–)°	5°
Cocoa		
Beans, raw, roasted	84	62
Powder and paste	15	29
Chocolate and products	1	9
Tobacco		
Unmanufactured	94	85
Manufactured	6	15
Ground nuts		
Green	24	53
Oil	76°	47
Non-food agricultural products		
Leather		
Hides and skins	77°	18°
Leather	22°	76°
Leather manufactures	1°	6°
Wood		
Rough logs	77	47
Shaped wood	15	25
Veneers, plywood	7	22
Manufactures	1	6
Cotton		
Raw	85	53
Grey yarn in bulk	1	18
Woven fabrics	14	29

(Table 5.7 continued)

	Percentage share of exports by degree of processing, 1977*	
	Sub-Saharan Africa	Other developing countries
Non-fuel minerals		
Copper		
Ores, excluding matte	3e	21o
Unrefined	11+	35o
Refined	85o	42o
Bars, wires	(–)o	2o
Tubes, pipes	(–)o	(–)o
Iron and steel		
Ore, concentrate	98	56
Pig Iron	(–)	17
Ingots, primary form	0	6
Worked in various forms	2	21
Aluminium		
Bauxite	35o	32o
Oxide, hydroxide	13	48
Unwrought	50	11o
Bars, wire	0	7
Plate, sheet, strip	3	2
Phosphate		
Natural	98	88
Chemical fertilizer	2	12

* Figures followed by an o are for years other than 1977.

Source: World Bank (1981), p. 153

export of natural resources in the form of complex finished products dominates in the case of the developed countries. A more detailed and product-specific analysis of the distribution of LDC exports of natural resources by degree of processing is presented in Table 5.7. This table confirms that the LDCs have not made much progress in exporting the processed forms of their natural resources. This failure is particularly noticeable in sub-Saharan Africa where, except for copper, close to 80 per cent and above of the natural resources exports is in raw or only slightly processed form.

LDCs could derive considerable benefits from processing their natural resources before export. Processing is a means of furthering their industrialization and promoting economic diversification. By adding value through processing, the benefits of more stable prices, higher income elasticity of demand, less producer competition and greater domestic income diffusion through backward and forward linkages could be gained. In addition, expansion of processing activities would increase and stabilize export earnings while enhancing faster growth of the GNP.

Tariffs and NTBs are not the only problems facing LDC exports in the developed countries. Other major obstacles against processed exports relate to marketing arrangements and market structures. Primary commodity markets are far from being perfectly competitive, and it is believed that some of the problems created by fluctuating prices and adverse price trends can be traced, partly, to some of the unsatisfactory features of these markets. It is widely recognized, for instance, that for mineral ores and concentrates, open and transparent world market transactions hardly exist; most transactions are internal, within vertically integrated transnational companies, based on transfer pricing systems. Raw materials are hardly ever traded on open markets and in any case, such markets tend to be rather thin; they often represent only a tiny proportion of the total value of the raw and semi-processed materials transacted. In the same way, markets for many agricultural commodities are characterized by very high degrees of concentration (Clairmonte and Cavanagh, 1983). The degree of concentration which characterizes the production, processing and marketing of natural resource commodities has the effect of reducing the bargaining powers of the LDCs substantially. Combined with tariff barriers and NTBs, the entry barriers constituted by unfavourable marketing arrangements and marketing structures restrict the ability of LDCs to increase their export earnings directly as well as through processing.

MULTILATERAL INITIATIVES ON PRIMARY COMMODITY TRADE PROBLEMS

The concerns of LDCs with respect to the problems of trade in primary commodities have led to various initiatives aimed at finding appropriate solutions. These initiatives can be grouped around two broad issues. One set of initiatives addresses problems related to terms of trade and instability questions such as commodity price stabilization schemes, broader international commodity arrangements and compensatory financing facilities. A second set of initiatives concerns general market access problems, including the various MTN rounds and the resulting special schemes designed to improve market access for the LDCs. Subsidiary to these are issues relating to marketing arrangements and market structure in which there has been much less activity.

Commodity Price Stabilization Schemes

Stability of export earnings can contribute significantly to the overall economic performance of the LDCs. The use of commodity price stabilization schemes to achieve this objective raises several important questions. A degree of consensus exists concerning the beneficial effects of minimizing price instability for both producers/exporters and importers/consumers (Schmitz, 1984). Price instability is thought to increase risks to producers, while stable prices would be beneficial to importers in the sense that they can base decisions on more reliable and predictable price trends.

The more critical question is the extent to which price stabilization schemes enhance export earnings stability (Wahab, 1985). Instability of commodity prices and export revenues are linked in discussions of commodity price stabilization schemes. The basic idea is that by stabilizing commodity prices, countries can be protected against violent fluctuations in their export earnings. The implicit assumption behind this is that fluctuating prices are the main causes of export earnings instability. However, there is some evidence indicating that export revenue instability is caused primarily by wide swings in quantities exported (UNCTAD, 1986) and hence that the impact of price stabilization may be rather small. There is some doubt therefore that a price stabilization scheme which is not combined with additional means of controlling supply can effectively reduce violent swings in primary commodity export revenues.

International Commodity Agreement

In spite of the reservation with respect to price stabilization schemes, ICAs to improve the prospects of commodity trade largely by stabilizing price levels have been popular among the LDCs. Although the idea was formally recognized in international discussions by the Havana Charter of 1948, attempts to regulate production, sale and prices of some primary commodities have a much longer history (Stone, 1984; Gardner, 1985). The principal objective of ICAs is price stabilization to achieve a more stable equilibrium between supply and demand for commodities traditionally subject to substantial fluctuations in both. Sometimes a subsidiary objective is implied: to stabilize prices at levels which will be remunerative to producers and equitable to consumers, without losing touch with long-term market trends. Price stabilization is, in general, approached by means of buffer stocks, buffer funds, and/or supply management via production or export quotas. Target or operational prices are usually defined in terms of a 'price band'; when prices fall below the floor or rise above the ceiling level, the buffer stock manager buys or sells the commodity, or export quotas are applied or removed, until the price returns to some pre-determined level. The range to be defended may be fixed for the term of the agreement or adjusted at some regular interval or at some defined price level.

Results achieved by existing ICAs have been mixed for a variety of reasons. A major problem is the conflict of interests between producing and consuming countries on issues relating to buffer stock acquisition, control and financing. In addition, differences often surface between producers themselves around the issue of quota allocation. For these reasons, some ICAs are established without the participation of some major producers and consumers. Furthermore, technical complications arise in allowing for types and grades of products according to quality, use, value and market. Hence ICAs have usually been difficult to negotiate and establish, and have often not achieved their objectives.

Compensatory Financing Facilities

Commodity price stabilization schemes may succeed in stabilizing prices, but this does not automatically ensure stabilization of export earnings. In any case, ICAs based on stocking cannot work for commodities which are not easily storable, while there are other commodities that are not amenable to price stabilization arrangements. Compensatory financing facilities, which provide for export earnings shortfalls, are thought to be more appropriate for dealing with wide swings in export revenues. It is argued that since such arrangements are divorced from the commodity markets, they do not impose the possible social costs of resource misallocation which market interventions (via ICAs) may involve.

The IMF's Compensatory Financing Facility, established in 1963, is the oldest of such schemes. It provides support to IMF members who are experiencing BOP difficulties which arise from temporary shortfalls in export earnings. Although liberalized in 1975 and 1979 to provide for more generous drawings, it continues to suffer from important limitations. Qualifications for compensation require the simultaneous existence of BOP problems, and maximum limits to drawings are related to quotas rather than the magnitude of shortfalls, with the result that compensation generally falls short of shortfalls. The STABEX scheme of the Lomé Convention provides for export earnings stabilization. The system compensates for shortfalls from individual agricultural commodity exports from ACP countries to the EEC. The poorest LDCs in this group receive compensation in the form of grants, while the rest receive interest-free loans. A separate scheme has been added to cover shortfalls in mineral export earnings.

These schemes have not solved the problem of export earnings instability. Beneficiaries under the schemes have generally not received full compensation, even in nominal terms, for their calculated eligible shortfalls. It appears also that compensatory financing has been most lacking precisely in those cases where the need was greatest: that is, in the lower-income countries facing the most difficult structural adjustment problems and experiencing the most severe impact of commodity price and export earnings fluctuations (Helleiner, 1986).

The UNCTAD Programme

UNCTAD has assumed the role of the principal international organ for cooperation in the field of primary commodity trade. This culminated in the adoption of its IPC, including the Common Fund in 1976. This was followed in 1979 by the adoption of 'developmental measures' aimed at increased participation of LDCs in the processing, marketing and distribution of the commodities they produce; and improvements in the systems of compensatory financing for shortfalls in export earnings from commodities.

UNCTAD sees compensatory financing as a globalized scheme for the stabilization of export earnings; it is a supplement to, rather than substitute for, ICAs (Cuddy, 1978, 1979; UNCTAD, 1986). Hence, compensatory financing should play a supporting role in market regulation because not all commodities can be covered by ICAs and, in any case, export earnings instability could be caused by factors other than price fluctuations. The Common Fund is to facilitate the conclusion and functioning of ICAs by providing prior assurance of the financial resources required for establishing and operating buffer stocks, contributing to the financing of buffer stocks and helping to finance measures in the field of commodities other than stock. The Common Fund would also be more economical than a series of individual funds, given that prices of different commodities would not rise and fall at the same time (Cuddy, 1978).

It has proved difficult, so far, to achieve the major objectives of the UNCTAD programme primarily because of the delay in ratifying the Common Fund and the lack of participation by the USA. This has impaired its mandate to facilitate the establishment of new ICAs.

Schemes for Improving Market Access

Major developments in terms of schemes to improve market access of LDCs have occurred in the form of special preferences. The most important of these is the GSP. The GSP schemes have several main features, some of which also constitute their principal drawbacks. Usually, preferences apply essentially to tariffs; these tariff concessions are not 'bound' and can therefore be withdrawn or modified unilaterally by the preference-granting country. They cover mostly manufactured and semi-manufactured products, although some include a few agricultural products. In any case, escape clauses (in terms of maximum allowable imports, 'sensitive' products and rules of origin) limit their coverage of, and benefits to, LDC primary commodity exports.

The second major preferential scheme is the Lomé Convention which provides some 66 ACP countries with preferential access to the EEC market. It grants tariff and some non-tariff concessions; it also covers relatively more primary commodities than the GSP schemes. In addition, it provides additional benefits in the form of an export earnings stabilization (STABEX) facility. The Convention was first signed in 1975 and has been renewed in 1979 and 1984. Various

assessments of the GSP and Lomé Convention preferential schemes
have shown mixed results (World Bank, 1987). Benefits from both
schemes have accrued largely to only a few LDCs which export
manufactured goods. While these established beneficiaries may
naturally wish to defend their gains, it seems clear that the LDCs as
a group would gain relatively more from less circumscribed and more
comprehensive trade liberalization by the developed countries.

PRIMARY COMMODITY ISSUES IN TRADE NEGOTIATIONS

Compared to previous MTNS, the Uruguay Round has attracted
increased LDC participation. Since one of its objectives is to carve
out a larger role for the LDCs in the global trading system,
the discussions and consultations preceding the Round generally
induced their enhanced participation, while the agenda issues are
more reflective of their interests than in the past. The increased
LDC participation may also reflect their general acceptance of the
legitimacy of the multilateral process.

Previous analysis shows that primary commodity exporting LDCs
face several major problems. Declining terms of trade and instability
of prices and export earnings create significant problems of economic
management. Market access difficulties, in terms of tariff and
non-tariff barriers as well as tariff escalation, combined with
entry barriers associated with non-competitive market structures
and marketing arrangements also create substantial problems. The
extent to which these problems are addressed in the Uruguay
Round is of considerable interest to the LDCs. A review of the
Round's agenda provide some clues. The demand by the LDCs that
commodity issues be included has been met somewhat. The agenda
explicitly recognizes the need to 'take account of serious difficulties
in commodity markets'. In concrete terms, however, this seems to
translate into the objective of substantial trade liberalization for
tropical and natural resource-based products through tariff and
non-tariff reductions, and the elimination of tariff escalation. In
addition, the agenda promises to impose more GATT discipline
on agriculture by bringing all measures affecting import access and
export competition under effective GATT rules.

Even if these objectives were achieved, several critical problems
facing primary commodity producers would remain unsolved. The
reduction or elimination of tariffs, NTBs and tariff escalation could

solve the market access problem. Imposing more effective GATT discipline on agriculture has basically the same effect. The LDC concerns regarding primary commodity trade extend well beyond the issue of market access. Improved market access could, of course, dampen price and export earnings instability, but it would largely ignore issues relating to declining terms of trade and entry barriers implicit in the prevailing marketing arrangements and market structures of primary commodities. These issues are not accommodated in GATT's current agenda of negotiations.

Thus, in spite of the increased LDC participation in the Uruguay Round, GATT as an institution has not moved away from its original narrowly defined set of responsibilities. Although it is often referred to as a successor of the Havana Charter, its mandate, institutional framework, negotiating format and operating procedures exclude certain issues of primary commodity trade encompassed within the broader sweep of the aborted ITO (Mark and Weston, 1987). GATT's provisions have been revised over time. One notable example of this is the addition, in 1965, of Chapter IV which accepts the need for ensuring stable, equitable and remunerative prices and improved market access for primary products. But the provisions also grant special treatment to agriculture and other primary commodities which has the effect of negating this objective.

As a result, the full range of primary commodity issues has never been seriously negotiated in GATT. Both historical development and prevailing practice within GATT are partly responsible for this. The structural weakness of the organization, in relation to its ability to handle primary commodity problems, is largely a reflection of the dominant interests of its designers and operators. The same developed-country coalition of interests has given domestic protection to the primary sector of the LDCs regarding primary commodity problems. The lack of active participation by the LDCs in previous MTNs has further weakened the chances of achieving significant reforms within GATT. The preoccupation of GATT with trade relations among Western industrialized countries and its lack of interest in those trade issues that are of paramount importance to the LDCs can probably be ascribed to this combination of factors.

What the LDCs want from the global trading system as far as primary commodities are concerned seems quite obvious. The fundamental objective is that primary commodity issues should be dealt with as part of the mainstream rather than as an adjunct of the international trading system. If GATT is to serve as the organization with primary responsibility for the management of this system, its institutional basis must be sufficiently strong, its mandate and focus sufficiently wide, and its operating procedures sufficiently flexible to accommodate trade issues of concern to both the developed and the developing world. The failure of GATT as currently structured to perform this role to the LDCs' satisfaction raises the question of the options available to them. At least three possibilities are suggested. The LDCs could ignore GATT and withhold their participation on the grounds that it does not pay adequate attention to the issues they consider important. The activities connected with the Uruguay Round imply that this option has not been embraced by the LDCs. A second option is to accept the current institutional structure and seek to change the rules within it. Some of the earlier revisions of GATT provisions reflect this type of option. A third option is to work toward changing the structure and the rules and broadening the negotiating framework so that issues important to the LDCs can be more fully accommodated and dealt with. The second and third options assume implicitly that the LDCs will continue to insist that primary commodities have special characteristics which should be recognized within either a modified GATT or an entirely different framework.

The enhanced LDC involvement in the ongoing negotiations would seem to imply that they consider a substantially modified GATT a more feasible objective than searching for an entirely different framework. Hence an emerging strategy for dealing with primary commodity trade is to treat the issues as multi-dimensional and thus beyond the mandate of any single forum. Those elements of the problem (such as market access) which lie within the scope of GATT can be pursued in the Uruguay Round. Other aspects of the problem should be tackled through other organizations. But the modifications to GATT should also include a strengthening of its links with other international organizations so that market access concessions on primary commodities negotiated in GATT can, for instance, be associated in a meaningful way with commitments made in another forum regarding the Common Fund. The feasibility of such changes depends on the willingness of the developed countries to accommodate LDC demands. The expressed desire of the developed countries to integrate LDCs more fully into the global trading system suggests that they may be willing to grant concessions regarding institutional changes. The increasingly rapid movement toward more liberal trade and payments regimes in many LDCs is likely to enhance their willingness to participate more effectively in the reciprocal exchange of concessions once both the type and range of admissible concessions are established in the suitably reformed GATT. The process of reforming GATT so as to transform it into a central body which manages the international trading system in an even-handed way in relation to the interests, rights and obligations of developed and developing countries is likely to involve difficult and protracted negotiations going well beyond the life of the Uruguay Round; but it should not be an impossible task.

Notes

1.   Comments and suggestions kindly offered by members of the project team, particularly John Whalley, as well as those provided by John Cuddy are gratefully acknowledged. Remi Ogun and Iyiola Raheem contributed valuable support.

References

Ali, L. (1984) 'Africa's Commodity Trade and Structure of Marketing and Distribution of Primary Commodities', *UNCTAD Reprint Series No. 58*, (Geneva: UNCTAD), December.

Bond, M. and Milne, E. (1987) 'Export Diversification in Developing Countries: Recent Trends and Policy Impact', *Staff Studies for the World Economic Outlook* (Washington, DC: IMF), August.

Brandt, W. (1980) *North–South: A Programme for Survival* (London: Pan).

Clairmonte, F. and Cavanagh, G. (1983) 'Corporate Power in Selected Food Commodities', *Raw Materials Report*, 1 (3), pp. 21–39.

Cuddy, J.D.A. (1978) 'Financial Savings from the Common Fund', *Review of World Economics*, pp. 499–514.

Cuddy, J.D.A. (1979) 'The Case for an Integrated Programme for Commodities', *Resources Policy*, pp. 16–25.

Cuddy, J.D.A. (1985) 'International Commodity Prices in the 1980s', mimeo (Geneva: UNCTAD), November.

Gardner, B. (1985) 'International Commodity Agreements', background paper to *World Development Report 1986* (Washington, DC: World Bank), October.

Helleiner, G.K. (1986) 'Primary Commodity Markets: Recent Trends and Research Requirements', mimeo (Washington, DC: Institute for International Economics).

Honma, M. and Hayami, A. (1985) 'Structure of Agricultural Protection in Industrial Countries', *Journal of International Economics*, 20, pp. 115–29.

MacBean, A.I. and Nguyen, D.T. (1985) 'Terms of Trade: The Facts', background paper to *World Development Report 1986*, mimeo (Washington, DC: World Bank), October.

Mark, J. and Weston, A. (1987) 'The Havana Charter Revisited', mimeo (Ottawa: North-South Institute), August.

Prebisch R. (1949) *The Economic Development of Latin America and Some of its Problems* (New York: ECLA).

Prebisch, R. (1959) 'The Role of Commercial Policies in Underdeveloped Countries', *American Economic Review, Papers and Proceedings*, May.

Schmitz, A. (1984) 'Commodity Price Stabilization: The Theory and its Application', *World Bank Staff Working Paper No. 668*, September.

Singer, H. (1950) 'The Distribution of Gains between Investing and Borrowing Countries', *American Economic Review, Papers and Proceedings*, May.

Stone, F. (1984) *Canada, the GATT and the International Trade System* (Ottawa: Institute for Research on Public Policy).

UNCTAD (1986) 'Commodities Earnings Shortfalls and an Additional Compensatory Financing Facility', Document No. TD/B/AC. 43/2, (Geneva: UNCTAD), April.

Valdes, A. (1986) 'Protectionism and Agricultural Trade: Issues of Interest to the Third World', (Washington, DC: IFPRI).

Wahab, I. (1985) 'The Effects of Price Stabilization on Export Revenue Instability of the Individual Countries', *Trade and Development*, 6, pp. 17–42.

World Bank (1981) *Accelerated Development in Sub-Saharan Africa: An Agenda for Action* (Washington DC: World Bank).

World Bank (1987) *World Development Report 1987* (Washington, DC: World Bank).

6 Market Access for Manufactured Exports from Developing Countries: Trends and Prospects[1]

Marcelo de Paiva Abreu and Winston Fritsch

This chapter discusses the main trade impediments facing developing countries' exports of manufactures to developed country markets and the prospects for improved market access. It is divided into two sections: the first describes the chief characteristics of the evolving structure of protection, and in the second the issues relating to market access for developing country exports of manufactures in the ongoing MTNs are analysed. It is argued (i) that no broad coalition with substantial participation of developing countries among its leading actors is likely to emerge, (ii) that the abandonment of S & D rights has very limited appeal to the vast majority of developing exporters of manufactures and, thus, is a very unlikely outcome, and (iii) that the prospects for improved market access through reciprocal bargaining basically depend on structural adjustment in the North Atlantic economies. The fact that the latter requires investment and, therefore growth, emphasizes the crucial importance of the Uruguay Round for leading the OECD economies to a higher growth path than that which can be envisaged under present macroeconomic policies in the North.

THE PATTERN AND COSTS OF PROTECTION AGAINST EXPORTS OF MANUFACTURES FROM DEVELOPING COUNTRIES IN INDUSTRIAL MARKETS

One of the most striking features of post-war developments in world trade has been the rise of a number of developing countries as exporters of manufactures on a significant scale. The growth of manufactured exports from developing countries accelerated from the 1960s to above the high growth rates of world trade in manufactures then prevailing and was not significantly affected by the severe dislocation experienced by the world economy after the first oil shock. In about two decades the share of developing countries in the global supply of manufactured exports rose three-fold, reaching 13.5 per cent in 1984. For some broad commodity groupings such as iron and steel, engineering goods and clothing the increase in LDC participation in world markets was particularly marked. This process also increased the diversification of developing country exports and today the value of their manufactured exports exceeds that of all their non-energy exports combined.

Access to OECD markets played a crucial role in this process of growth and diversification of developing countries' exports. During the early years of very rapid export growth before the first oil shock, the share of manufactured exports going to industrial country markets jumped from one-third to two-thirds where – after a period of diversion mainly towards fast growing OPEC markets – it still stands. There was also a steady change in the composition of the LDC export bundle going to industrial markets away from traditional items such as textiles and some semi-manufactures, and toward a variety of other goods, many of them more skill or capital-intensive.

The impressive growth and diversification of manufactured exports to industrial country markets by a small but growing number of developing countries has happened against the background of a continuously changing structure of protection in OECD countries. The outstanding characteristic of this change, as far as trade in manufactures is concerned, was the substitution of a number of NTBs for the traditional form of protection based on customs tariffs. In analysing the impact of the growth of protection in industrial markets on market access for developing country exports it is thus apt to distinguish those issues relating to the tariff structure of industrial countries from the more complex ones arising from the recent extension of new protectionist devices.

Regarding tariff protection, the post-war trend of rates applying to semi-manufactures and manufactures has unmistakably been one of decline in the OECD. From levels near 50 per cent in the immediate post-war years, average tariff rates on those products are now around 7 per cent in the main industrial markets (GATT, 1980). Comparison of average MFN tariffs, however, disguises the fact that, as developing countries enjoy a variety of preferential schemes – some of which, as with the GSP, are biased in favour of manufactured goods - actual *ex-post* average rates for their products in each tariff line enjoying such preferences are lower than MFN rates.

The most important tariff-related issues as far as South–North trade in manufactures is concerned would seem to be the withdrawal of the benefits of the GSP from the major developing exporters of manufactures – the graduation issue – and the inhibiting effect that higher tariff rates on products with a greater degree of fabrication have on the industrial processing of raw materials in developing countries – the question of tariff escalation (to be addressed in greater detail below).

Given this relatively favourable long-term trend in tariff protection against manufactures the growth in the use of non-tariff measures over the past few decades has deservedly received greater attention. Moreover, the changes in the structure of protection in industrial countries were not related simply to this shift in the nature of the instruments of trade policy. The overall incidence of NTBs has been growing over time[2] and is targeted against manufactures and semi-manufactures of great export interest to developing countries such as textiles, clothing and iron and steel products (UNCTAD, 1987).

Estimation of the aggregate trade effects of the various NTBs applied against developing country exports is plagued with a number of empirical difficulties. However, existing quantitative exercises show that trade losses entailed by existing non-tariff measures against developing country manufactured exports are greater than those caused by tariffs, in spite of the pronounced sectoral concentration of the former (see, for example, Sampson, 1986).

Tariff-Related Issues

The GSP and the Issue of Graduation

The GSP is a scheme through which preferential and non-discriminatory tariff treatment is unilaterally granted by industrial countries to their developing trade partners and was formally introduced in the GATT framework through a ten-year renewable waiver of the MFN clause in 1971. Implementation of individual schemes by donor countries took place gradually. The fact that the negotiation of these schemes within the donor countries took place in a period of rising protectionism and mounting fears of rapid developing country import penetration reduced, however, their expected impact. Notwithstanding its institutional limitations, the trade expansion effects of the GSP (see Karsenty and Laird, 1986) are not unimportant.

Even though developing countries have continuously pressed for the extension and improvement of the system, since the early 1980s the major donor countries – initially the USA and more recently the EEC – have instituted a policy of graduation, or 'differentiation' (in the Community's jargon), of beneficiary country products from preferential treatment previously granted under the GSP (for a more detailed discussion of the issue, see Abreu and Fritsch, 1986). The main practical arguments put forward to justify the discretionary withdrawal of benefits are two-fold: it is claimed that the losses entailed are small, and that graduation of the larger beneficiaries would produce a more equitable distribution of GSP benefits by increasing the imports of the least developed countries under the scheme.

As to the first point, it should be noted that although GSP benefits may be small as a proportion of total beneficiaries' exports, reflecting the limited product coverage of the GSP, the wide dispersion of gains accruing to different commodity classes shown above suggests that for some product–country pairs, losses are by no means negligible. As to the second argument, it is unlikely that graduation of an important GSP item from a major developing exporter will benefit the least developed, as the graduated supplier's trade shares would more likely be diverted toward industrial country or other advanced developing country competitors given the nature of the manufactures usually facing graduation. This is confirmed by a recent *ex-post* study of the behaviour of trade shares of 340 products affected by competitive need exclusions in the USA which shows that the least developed did not experience changes in their market shares, and in no instance were other LDCs the largest gainers (MacPhee, 1986, pp. 10–12).

Tariff Escalation

The increase in nominal tariff rates with the degree of processing of a particular primary input (that is, the 'escalation' of nominal tariffs with the stage of fabrication), is a well-known feature of the tariff structure in developed countries (for a comprehensive analysis of the issue, see Yeats, 1979). This tariff pattern has two negative implications for the processing of raw materials in developing countries. The first relates to the relatively high tariffs in the processed products *per se*, as there is ample evidence that demand import elasticities steadily increase with fabrication; the second and more directly related to escalation stresses its effect of amplifying rates of protection.[3]

The impact of tariff escalation in industrial countries on the global distribution of value added of a given processing chain is to some extent countervailed by the widespread application of export taxes on raw materials by the primary exporting developing countries. The joint operation of export taxes on unprocessed inputs and high tariffs on the processed goods raises the price of the final product in developed country markets with a depressing effect on demand and hence, on total value added in all stages of fabrication. It could thus be notionally possible to achieve a reduction of tariff escalation without contractionary effects on processing activities in industrial countries if a simultaneous reduction in developing countries' export taxes were implemented. This would 'give [developed country] policy makers an easier choice than is provided by suggestions that they unilaterally reduce their imports duties' (Golub and Finger, 1979, p. 570) and, by affording mutual gains, could be an important area for reciprocal bargaining in the multilateral negotiations. However, account should be taken of the fact that fiscal revenues in a great number of poor primary exporting countries are heavily dependent on trade taxes, and that MFN cuts in fabrication products may erode the present competitive edge of some 'offshore' processing plants which import less processed imports for processing and re-export to developed countries.

Non-Tariff Barriers

Restrictions on Textiles and Clothing: The MFA

The alleged rationale for the continued quota regulation of international trade in textiles and clothing is to avoid the dislocation of jobs in developed countries. It is, however, well known that only a small proportion of job contraction in textile and clothing industries can be attributed to increased imports from developing countries (Greenaway, 1983, p. 180; Silbertson, 1984, Chapter 7). Textile and clothing quotas, moreover, are an extremely expensive way of protecting jobs. There is massive evidence for major developed countries which underlines the very big gap between the social cost of maintaining jobs and the private gains of workers keeping their jobs (see Wolf *et al.*, 1984, Chapter 4, for work on Canada, the UK and the USA, as well as Greenaway and Hindley, 1985, Chapter 4, for more recent estimates of the cost of clothing protectionism in the UK). In spite of these extremely high costs to consumers and taxpayers it would be a mistake to underestimate the weight of the textile and clothing protectionist lobby, especially in the US.[4]

Costs of protection to developing countries stemming from the present restrictive arrangement are high. The heavy protection entailed by the MFA results in a very important contraction of trade if compared to the hypothetical alternative of a totally free market. UNCTAD computations of the cost of protection in terms of forgone imports show that the gains for textile and clothing exports by developing countries to the EEC, Japan and the US in the event of a total removal of trade and non-trade barriers would be no less than 50.8 per cent of total possible gains related to all trade. UNCTAD estimates suggest that textile exports would increase by 49.1 per cent and clothing exports by 128.9 per cent (UNCTAD, 1986, p. 25 and Annex II). Other aggregate estimates of the costs of protection to exporters roughly agree with these.[5]

The permanence or abolition of the MFA is, therefore, crucial in defining future trends for textile and clothing exports from developing countries. It can be argued that as some large NICs derive sizeable rents from the present quotas (Hamilton, 1986) there may be strong vested interests among developing exporters prepared to lend support to the maintenance of the arrangement. However, it is worth noticing that notwithstanding the revealed ability of some NICs to by-pass the maze of regulations and sustain high export growth rates through diversification into less restricted fibres and products, it will be progressively difficult to do that as MFA loopholes are progressively closed and the arrangement increasingly discriminates in favour of small suppliers.

From the negotiating perspective a crucial issue is, thus, how the benefits from reduced protectionism in the textile and clothing sectors would be distributed. This is an extremely difficult exercise for, as is well known, MFA regulations freeze the comparative advantage of different suppliers. Voluntary restraints have for so long regulated these markets that it is difficult to detect changes in comparative advantage positions. The comparison of quota utilization rates does not provide a sufficiently discriminating criterion to evaluate such possible developments as so many countries reach a high level of utilization (GATT, 1984, I, pp. 93–8). Information on comparative labour costs is difficult to obtain and not always easy to use. Moreover, as mentioned by Silbertson (1984, p. 27), low labour costs may mean little as they can be compensated for by productivity differences and exchange rate fluctuations which, since 1985, are likely to have made German and Japanese products much less competitive.

Other Voluntary Restraint Agreements

Quantitative limits affecting South–North trade in manufactures are not restricted to textiles and clothing. Of special concern to major developing exports of manufactures is the spread of bilaterally negotiated quota agreements between developed and developing country governments with a view to limiting exports of the developing trade partner: the so-called VERs or OMAs. This is usually achieved under the threat of unilateral imposition of a quota or other form of trade harassment by the importing country and has affected an increasing range of mostly non-traditional exports.

Costs to consumers resulting from the higher domestic prices implied by these supply restrictions as well as loss of revenue to exporting countries are extremely high (World Bank, 1985, Table 4; World Bank, 1987, Table 8.11). Although these arrangements are usually justified on the grounds of the employment effects of the dislocations caused by rapid import penetration, they have been shown to be very costly and ineffective. Costs of maintaining a worker employed in the US steel and automobile industries were estimated as being roughly equivalent to six times the average American industrial wage (Tarr and Morkre, 1984; Kalantzopoulos, 1986), and ten times the British wage in the case of protection of videocassette recorders in the UK (Greenaway and Hindley, 1985). On the other hand, as Baldwin (1986) noted, when non-rubber footwear quotas were applied by the USA against Taiwan and Korea in the late 1970s, imports from these countries fell by 9.4 per cent in volume terms but imports from other sources rose by 8.5 per cent.

In the light of the evidence presented above, to explain the continued application of VERs one has to resort to political arguments. It has been suggested that they only stand because of the political muscle of the protected oligopolies; because of the VERs' distributive effect which, as opposed to that of other restrictions (such as tariffs or global quotas), favours the exporter of the restrained product (for an estimate of Korea's rent gains from steel VERs see Tarr, 1987); and also because, as clandestine agreements, they allow governments to negotiate and implement them outside the reach of parliaments and GATT, thus reducing political costs (Jones, 1984; Frey, 1985). To these one should obviously add the asymmetry in trade power between the NICs and the major capitalist trading nations, reflected in the fact that the overall import coverage ratio for VERs applied to developing countries is 10.9 per cent as compared to 0.4 per cent for the industrial economies, a pattern replicated in every product line facing VERs (Nogues, Olechowski and Winters, 1986, pp. 195–6).

AD and CVD Actions

Rather old guns in the arsenal of trade policy measures, AD taxes and CVDs levied against foreign export subsidies – the so-called LFV measures in the jargon of protection – have been applied with increasing frequency since the mid-1970s by a small number of developed GATT signatories. Although initiations of CVD actions by Chile have increased dramatically in recent years, over the July 1983–June 1985 period the USA, the EEC, Canada and Australia alone were responsible for all but two of the 362 GATT-reported AD actions, and for 77 per cent of all CVD cases filed.

The rapid increase in LFV actions in leading OECD markets has an important bearing upon the question of market access for developing exporters. The two central trade policy issues in this connection are: (i) whether the pattern of such actions is generally biased against developing suppliers in terms of both initiations as well as the proportion of affirmative findings, and (ii) the extent to which those measures are being introduced as relief for competitive pressure and not, as is theoretically justified, as a countervail to distortive unfair trade practices and, therefore, differing in principle from sheer protectionist instruments such as VERs, or temporary relief measures taken under the umbrella of GATT Article XIX provisions.[6]

The data on LFV actions by the USA, the EEC, Canada and Australia also reveal that the frequency of initiations is not biased against developing country exporters. However, as far as the pattern of effective application of duties is concerned, this is only true of AD actions and there is a clear bias against developing

countries in the application of CVDs by the USA, as shown in
Table 6.1.

Table 6.1   Affirmative countervailing actions* as a proportion of initiations:
1 July 1980–30 June 1985 (%)

Target group+	Initiating Country				
	USA	*EEC*	*Canada*	*Australia*	*Total*
Industrial countries	33.0	50.0	37.5	5.9	31.7
Developing countries	64.0	40.0	–	–	63.1
Eastern trading area	–	–	–	–	–
Total	46.4	42.9	33.3	5.9	43.1

* Actions terminating with the application of duties or suspended through
agreement.
+ Groups defined as follows; (i) *Industrial countries*: Australia, Belgium,
Canada, Switzerland, Fereral Republic of Germany, Spain, Finland, France,
UK, Ireland, Italy, Japan, Luxembourg, the Netherlands, New Zealand,
Norway, Portugal, Sweden, South Africa, USA, Yugoslavia; (ii) *Developing
countries*: Argentina, Brazil, Chile, Colombia, Dominican Republic, Hong
Kong, Israel, India, Indonesia, Korea, Malaysia, Mexico, Philippines,
Singapore, Thailand, Trinidad and Tobago, Taiwan, Turkey, Uruguay,
Venezuela, Pakistan, Panama; (iii) *Eastern trading area*, China, Czecho-
slovakia, Demorcratic Republic of Germany, Hungary, Poland, Romania,
USSR.

Source: GATT, *Report of the Committee on Subsidies and Countervailing
(Several Issues) (Geneva: GATT).*

This high frequency of CVD initiations by the USA and the
higher concentration of affirmative cases on developing suppliers
merits some comments. It is hard to believe, as suggested by Nam,
that this much higher frequency of CVD action can be accounted
for either by longer US tradition in the legislation and practice of
anti-bounty rules or by an allegedly higher American attachment 'to
the free market enterprise system with less government intervention'
than that existing in other industrial countries (Nam, 1986, p. 25).
Both hypotheses are irreconcilable with the explosive increase in
the initiations and applications of CVDs since the mid-1970s by
the US government. Only 17 cases ended with the application of
duties between 1959 and 1974 and in the first half of the 1970s
just 11 cases were initiated (Balassa and Sharpston, 1976). A more

plausible cause of the high number of US cases against developing countries in the pattern of CVD application may be the combination of export incentives and targeting of the American market as central pieces of export promotion strategies in a large number of developing countries since the late 1960s.

As to the higher incidence of affirmative cases, the reason may lie in the fact that as the unconditional MFN clause does not apply to the Subsidies Code, non-signatories (among which there are many developing countries) are not guaranteed the right to an injury test. Thus, while all CVD actions against industrial countries in the USA during 1980–5 generated injury tests, this was true of only 40 per cent of developing country cases (Nam, 1986, pp. 27–8).

The high concentration of LFV cases against the more dynamic developing exporters (see Table 6.2) suggests the existence of a strong element of import relief in the motivation of their initiation. This impression seems, in fact, to be confirmed by the analysis of the pattern of industry incidence of AD and CVD actions in the USA and EEC which tend to be concentrated in textiles and semi-manufactures such as metals (especially iron and steel) and chemicals. These are sectors in which the large developing exporters have demonstrated an increasing competitive edge. The high coverage ratios for iron and steel products among developing exporters indicate a rapidly changing industry–country pattern of application of LFV action, for this sector was not reported as one of high incidence of complaints

Table 6.2   Industry incidence of AD and CVD initiations against the leading developing exporters of manufactures in the USA and EEC in 1983 (coverage ratios in %)

Product class	Brazil	Mexico	Korea	Hong Kong	Taiwan
Iron and steel	33.6	37.9	16.9	–	28.4
Non-ferrous metals	4.4	–	4.2	–	–
Chemicals	14.7	17.3	1.7	–	34.9
Manufactures	6.6	3.7	4.8	6.4	2.8
Leather	–	–	–	–	–
Textiles	5.2	65.8	–	–	–
Clothing	5.4	7.2	–	–	–
Footwear	8.6	–	–	–	–
Other manufactures	6.7	2.5	7.8	0.6	3.6

Source: UNCTAD Data Base on Trade Measures.

against developing countries in studies of LFV incidence in the 1970s (cf. Finger, 1981, p. 269).

In practice, therefore, the pattern of product and country incidence of LFV actions displays strong similarities with that of other forms of administered protection: actions are concentrated in some industries of great export interest to developing countries and affect, to a disproportionate extent, the leading developing exporters of manufactures. Unlike VERs, however, LFV actions can, within limits, be by-passed by the affected exporter if margins are lowered and, in the case of CVDs, by the affected country devaluing the exchange rate or granting other legal forms of subsidy. Thus, it seems that in the presence of severe structural adjustment problems, LFV actions may tend to be replaced by more robust quantitative limitations, as indeed was the case with steel. Nevertheless, barring a profound reform of multilateral trade rules, LFV actions are likely to continue to be widely used as a protectionist device.

PROSPECTS FOR THE GROWTH OF MANUFACTURED EXPORTS FROM DEVELOPING COUNTRIES

The launching of a new round of multilateral trade negotiations in Punta del Este in September 1986 created the possibility of reversing the protectionist trends described above thus improving market access for manufactured exports in OECD markets. As far as developing country participation is concerned this new round was hailed by many observers in the North as having two historically distinctive features which could positively influence the negotiating process. First, it was to bring forward a host of negotiating issues likely to give rise to new coalitions outside the traditional North–South divide. Second, it was likely to witness greater participation of the more advanced developing countries for which market access for manufactured exports has become an increasingly important issue.

A closer analysis of the extent to which developing GATT members are presently affected by each of the barriers reviewed in the first section tends to suggest, however, that the likelihood of the formation of NIC-led coalitions or coalitions with strong participation of a large number of developing exporters of manufactures to lower these barriers or, where appropriate, subject their use to improved multilateral rules and surveillance is, perhaps, greatly exaggerated.

GSP graduation is not, by the very unilateral nature of the GSP offer, to provide a basis for broad coalition formation. Unilateral self-graduation proposals may be issued in isolation by a few large NICs, especially if this symbolic gesture can be translated into gains in the context of bilateral relations with the USA or, in the case of the Asian NICs, Japan. Barring this alternative the likely approach by the leading beneficiaries would be the rather indirect one of pressing for a further reduction of OECD countries' MFN tariffs, which would have the added advantage of eroding the competitive margins of Lomé and other arrangements' beneficiaries without straining G77 solidarity. However, the explicit preservation of S & D in the Uruguay ministerial declaration and the great country concentration of GSP benefits make developing country pressures for improving these benefits towards the least developed among them the most likely outcome of the MTNs in this area.

Tariff escalation is and will remain largely an issue involving the larger group of developing primary exporters and thus will be negotiated along traditional North–South lines. This is a question of no export interest to many of the top Asian exporters of manufactures which are net importers of raw materials.

The reform of the Anti-Dumping and Subsidies Codes is also an issue in which broad, cohesive, developing country participation is unlikely. On the one hand, AD actions are not something of specific interest to developing exporters of manufactures as their abuse as an instrument of protection severely affects intra-OECD trade. Some leading developing exporters of manufactures will certainly actively join in the negotiations for AD rule reform as they have indeed done in the past, but are not likely to shape the outcome of these discussions.

CVD application, on the other hand, tends to be disproportionately concentrated on a small number of leading developing exporters of manufactures. However, there is a tendency for these countries to deal bilaterally with this issue for, as a recent study put it, it 'is not a multilateral, but a bilateral issue, with the United States on one side and its trading partners on the other' (Finger and Nogues, 1987, p. 709). Moreover, developing country interest on this issue differs as the importance of border subsidies for an individual country's trade performance largely depends on the degree of neutrality of its trade and exchange rate policy, which greatly varies even among the leading developing exporters of manufactures.

Safeguarding (that is, the improving of Article XIX so as to provide the basis for the elimination of VERs) is usually considered a key issue around which significant developing country coalitions could be built. This would affect the MFA (a special case of a multilateral VER), the abolition of which is basically conditional to the achievement of a successful accord on safeguards in the Round.

There are, however, two main stumbling blocks on the way to the formation of developing country coalitions over the safeguards issue. The first is that VERs, albeit growing in application, affect as yet a very small number of products and developing country exporters. According to the UNCTAD Data Base on Trade Measures these restrictions (as applied by the USA, EEC and Japan) are concentrated almost exclusively on Korean miscellaneous manufactures and steel exports and on the exports of steel of the three major Latin American economies. This is not to say that the potential threat to market access for latecomers represented by existing VERs could not make for a broadening of developing countries' support for the strengthening of GATT's safeguards clause. The problem is that the small number of 'injuring' suppliers makes unlikely a wide support for the application of GATT's *non-discriminating* safeguards. Although selectivity in the application of Article XIX as proposed by the EEC during the Tokyo Round (that is, the targeting of 'disruptive' trade partners by the injured country) has been resisted in principle by a large number of developing countries as a dangerous departure from the principle of non-discrimination, the fact that the number of developing countries facing VERs is very small is certainly a factor which greatly weakens the political will toward the formation of broad developing country coalitions to strengthen GATT safeguards application.[7]

The second and by no means less important stumbling block is that, as discussed earlier, VERs are not without interest to the injured country since they result in the generation of rents appropriated by exporters. Moreover, since periodical revision of quota allocations is not the rule in the existing agreements as the political costs involved in the negotiations are large, changing competitive advantage among suppliers in favour of latecomers creates a vested interest among traditional large suppliers against liberalization, as is the case with the MFA today.

This negative assessment of the likelihood of a decisive participation of developing countries in grand coalitions formed around

the crucial issues relating to market access for manufactures in t,
OECD should come as no surprise. The diversity of developin
countries' interests stemming mostly from structural heterogeneity
among even the leading NICs, the fact that the major NTBs to
trade in manufactures are not a unique feature of South–North
trade and that in GATT the division between developing and
developed countries is not as clear as in other multilateral fora
and last but not least, the lack of retaliatory power of developing
countries *vis-à-vis* their developed trade partners are major factors
accounting for that.

It should be noted, however, that current conventional wisdom
among mainstream economists and government officials in the North
about the prospects for improvement of market access for the leading
developing exporters of manufactures has centred less on arguments
about coalition formation than on likely benefits to be derived from
their 'fuller participation'.[8] Academic support for this view seems
to be derived from a combination of two main arguments. First,
there is the belief in the advantages of more liberal trade and
exchange rate regimes for developing countries, and a genuine fear
that the growing tide of neo-protectionism in industrial countries
may impair trade performance and lead to 'export pessimism' and
scepticism as to the effectiveness of 'outward-oriented' trade and
industrialization strategies and, eventually, to their abandonment
in developing countries. These presuppositions, combined with a
somewhat simplified account of the historical reasons for the uneven
spread of trade liberalization in the post-war years as deriving from
limited developing country participation in GATT and their revealed
preference for free-riderism based on the benefits of S & D conceded
in the 1960s, provide a strong case for fuller participation based on
self-interest. Translated into the multilateral trade policy framework
this means advising developing countries to be prepared not only
to bind their tariffs but, more importantly given the high rate of
tariff redundancy in developing countries, to give up the exemption
from strict GATT discipline they are entitled to by reason of BOP
difficulties or infant industry protection under Article XVIII-B and
Part IV.

From the more mercantilist viewpoint of government officials
in the North, this self-graduation argument seems to provide
valuable negotiating chips for their otherwise bare agenda for talks
with their more industrially advanced developing trade partners.
From the equally mercantilist viewpoint of Southern negotiators,

rather more problematic. Although it is certainly ⟨adv⟩antages of greater neutrality of incentives in trade ⟨⟩ rate policies are now much more widely recognized ⟨de⟩veloping country policy-makers than 20 years ago, there ⟨⟩l widespread doubts as to the wisdom of self-graduation and ⟨ful⟩ler participation'. The crucial question here is by no means GSP graduation, as the GSP is now seen by most leading beneficiaries as a mixed blessing, given the extent to which the withdrawal or reduction of the offer has been used as a bargaining weapon by the main donors. The issue is whether unilaterally to give away the right granted by GATT's S & D clauses to administer protection for development purposes with much greater discretion than their developed partners, and there is no compelling reason why they should so act. The case against infant industry protection, especially in the larger, resource rich and more diversified developing countries, cannot be made on purely theoretical grounds as very little can be said *a priori* on the patterns and velocity of change in comparative advantage; and the case against relaxing GATT-approved discretionary trade and payments controls for short-term BOP motives in the present uncertain international economic outlook is overwhelming, especially in debtor countries.

It should be noted, therefore, that unless the traditional GATT practice of reciprocity at the margin is to be replaced by the so-called 'level playing field' approach – which under present conditions is tantamount to asking developing countries for a substantial amount of unilateral liberalization – the basic determinant in the Round is the possibility of *increased* market access in the North. The simple political economy of fuller participation by the more advanced developing countries in the Uruguay Round is that the structural adjustment required by trade liberalization efforts in the South must be matched by structural adjustment in the manufacturing sector in the North. This will require substantially lowering labour adjustment costs in the latter which, because they tend to be concentrated both in time and space while the benefits from lower prices are diffuse, have been the source of not inconsiderable political opposition to trade liberalization in most of the leading North Atlantic economies.

An important step in this direction is the re-establishment of active labour adjustment and industrial policies in developed countries. It has been convincingly argued that resistance to trade policy reform in the USA has been increased by the demolition of government-sponsored labour adjustment programmes in the early 1980s (Aho, 1985). However, as structural adjustment requires investment, the crux of the matter is OECD growth. It is undeniable that high growth and investment rates in the central countries were essential factors in the relatively frictionless adjustment to rapid growth in manufactured exports in Japan and in the leading NICs before the first oil shock. The worldwide economic dislocation of the 1970s and early 1980s – the collapse of Bretton Woods, severe oil and commodity price shocks, wide interest rate fluctuations – increased the pressure for structural adjustment, but the slowing down of OECD growth and investment made this task immensely more difficult and increased the strains on the multilateral trade system.

This dependence of the achievements of multilateral trade policy on the global economic environment cannot be underestimated. Its recognition is an essential ingredient in any realistic assessment of the short-term prospects for market access for manufactured exports from developing countries owing to the global effects of the inevitable adjustment of the massive US trade deficit. It is widely acknowledged that the levels of current account disequilibrium in the US BOP are unsustainable and represent a real threat to the stability of world financial markets (Marris, 1985). Adjustment to a sustainable path – after the large dollar depreciation since the Plaza agreement reached what seems to be its maximum politically acceptable extent – requires a fall in US demand growth rates relative to that of the leading OECD surplus countries. This could be done either unilaterally, through demand contraction in the US, or by a combination of coordinated policy action between the American and surplus countries' governments, the latter expanding domestic demand in tandem with the slowing down of demand growth in the USA.

The impacts of each of these two possibilities upon the growth of world trade would, however, be quite different. Although the superiority of coordinated action has been repeatedly recognized in G-5 formal policy agreements and summit meetings since at least 1985, very little has been effectively done. Not only does the USA seem unable to break the long-standing political deadlock between Congress and the White House which prevents needed action to reduce the large fiscal stimulus, but in addition the West German, and to a lesser extent, the Japanese governments seem unwilling to reflate domestic demand either by fiscal or monetary means. Even setting aside the negative effect of the recent stock market crash, the prospects for the growth of manufactured imports in OECD markets are rather poor, as can be seen in Table 6.3.

This poor outlook for world trade in manufactures could be made much worse in the event of unilateral American adjustment, with especially damaging effects on developing countries as the USA is currently absorbing not less than two-thirds of their sales of manufactures and semi-manufactures. Moreover, there is a high probability that with continued anaemic domestic demand growth and historically high levels of unemployment in the EEC, the lagged effects of the recent appreciation of the leading European currencies against the dollar may flare up protectionism in Europe.

Table 6.3   Rates of growth of real GDP and manufactured import volume in the OECD and the USA, 1983–8 (%)

	1983	1984	1985	1986	1987*	1988*
Real GDP						
OECD	2.9	4.8	3.1	2.5	2.3	2.3
USA	4.0	6.7	3.0	2.5	2.3	2.3
Manufactured import volume						
OECD	7.0	15.3	8.2	8.5	3.8	4.5
USA	14.8	30.1	11.7	9.0	2.3	1.5

* Forecasts

Notes: Forecasts for 1987 and 1988 are made under assumptions of no change in actual and stated policies and exchange rates as of April 1987 and OECD f.o.b. oil import prices of US$ 18 per barrel.

Source: OECD, *OECD Economic Outlook*, December 1985 and June 1987.

Thus, low OECD growth rates and the ensuing deterioration of the conditions for easier structural adjustment are the real threat to the prospects of developing country export growth and diversification and, indeed, to the multilateral trading system in the near future. Failure to lead the industrial countries to a higher aggregate growth path during the period of the inevitable massive external adjustment of the US economy means allocating the current American trade deficit through beggar-my-neighbour policies. The result, as the lessons of the interwar years teach us, is equilibrium only at a much reduced level of world trade and, most likely, the disintegration of the multilateral trade system.

Notes

1. The authors wish to thank Michael Finger, Clodoaldo Hugueney Filho, Jerzy Rozanski and René Vossenaar for help in obtaining unpublished data and other information, the research assistance of Claudio Alves Goncalves da Silva and the comments from participants of the several of this project's workshops in which earlier versions of this chapter were presented.

2. The proportion of total world manufactured exports to industrial countries affected by non-tariff measures (excluding technical and sanitary regulations and excise taxes) rose from 18.6 per cent to 20.5 per cent between 1981 and 1986 (UNCTAD, 1987).

3. Effective rates of protection measure the effect of protection in value added per unit of output in the importing country, and are better indicators of protection in incomes in industries using large amounts of dutiable inputs. On this, see Corden (1971).

4. Cline (1987) contains a very useful discussion of trends of textile and clothing protectionism in the USA as well as of recent work on its costs.

5. Kirmani, Molajoni and Mayer (1984) estimated rates of growth of 81.8 per cent and 92.6 per cent for textiles and clothing respectively; OECD (1985) suggested 100 per cent for the aggregate based on a somewhat objectionable econometric exercise. These estimates do not take into account terms-of-trade losses as implied by the existence of quota premia but also ignore the dynamic benefits to exports (Cable, 1986). The estimates of Choi, Chung and Marian (1985) seem extremely conservative when compared to the others mentioned above.

6. As reported by Finger (1981), an IMF study included AD and CVD cases as protectionist devices, but a World Bank tabulation excluded them. For a discussion of the welfare implications of dumping and export subsidies see Dale (1980) and Bryan (1980).

7. The MFA poses a different situation in that the status quo generates dissatisfaction in latecomers for whom textiles represent a large share of their total, or more dynamic, exports. This could broaden the basis for safeguards-reform coalition. However, the recent renewal of the MFA makes the Uruguay Round debate on safeguards much more related to the larger VER issues.

8. 'The Uruguay Round . . . is unique from the viewpoint of the developing countries. It marks a sufficiently radical departure from the earlier GATT rounds in that, more than ever, it calls for the developing countries to engage actively in the negotiations' (Bhagwati, Krueger and Snape, 1987, p. 540).

130   *Market Access for Manufactured Exports*

References

Abreu, M. de P. and Fritsch, W. (1986) 'GSP Graduation: Impact on Major Latin American Beneficiaries', *Texto para Discussão 150* (Rio de Janeiro: Department of Economics, Catholic University).

Aho, M.C. (1985) 'US Labor Market Adjustment, Import Restrictions and Trade Policy Formulation', in E. Preeg (ed.), *Hard Bargaining Ahead: US Trade Policy and Developing Countries* (New Brunswick, NJ: Transaction Books for the ODC).

Balassa, B. and Sharpston, M. (1976) 'Export Subsidies by Developing Countries: Issues of Policy', World Bank Working Paper 238, (Washington, DC: World Bank).

Baldwin, R.E. (1986) 'Fashioning a Negotiating Package Between Developing and Developed Countries', mimeo, paper presented to the Study Group on the Integration of Developing Countries in the World Trading System, Council on Foreign Relations, Washington.

Bhagwati, J.N., Krueger, A.O. and Snape R. (1987) 'Introduction', *World Bank Economic Review*, Symposium Issue, September.

Bryan, G. (1980) *Taxing Unfair International Trade Practices* (New York: Lexington Books).

Cable, V. (1986) 'Textiles and Clothing in a New Trade Round', paper prepared by the Commonwealth Secretariat, mimeo (London).

Choi, Y.P, Chung, H.S. and Marian, N. (1985) *The Multi-Fibre Arrangement in Theory and Practice* (London: Pinter).

Cline, W. (1987) *The Future of World Trade in Textiles and Apparel* (Washington, DC: IIE).

Corden, W.M. (1971) *The Theory of Protection* (Oxford: Clarendon Press).

Dale, R. (1980) *Anti-Dumping Law in a Liberal Trade Order* (New York: St. Martin's Press).

Finger, J.M. (1981) 'The Industry-Country Incidence of 'Less than Value' Cases in US Import Trade', in W. Baer and M. Gillis (eds), *Export Diversification and the New Protectionism: The Experiences of Latin America* (Champaign, Ill: NBER/University of Illinois).

Finger, J.M. and Nogues, J. (1987) 'International Control of Subsidies and Countervailing Duties', *The World Bank Economic Review*, September.

Frey, B. (1985) 'The Political Economy of Protection', in D. Greenaway (ed.), *Current Issues in International Trade* (London: Macmillan).

GATT (1980) *The Tokyo Round of Multilateral Trade Negotiations* (Geneva: GATT).

GATT (1984) *Textile and Clothing in the World Economy* (Geneva:GATT).

Golub, S.S. and Finger, J.M. (1979) 'The Processing of Primary Commodities: Effects of Developed-Country Tariff Escalation and Developing-Country Export Taxes', *Journal of Political Economy*, June, pp. 559–77.

Greenaway, D. (1983) *International Trade Policy: From Tariffs to the New Protectionism* (London: Macmillan).

Greenaway, D. and Hindley, B. (1985) 'What Britain Pays for Voluntary Export Restraints', Thames Essay 43 (London: TPRC).

Hamilton, C. (1986) 'An Assessment of Voluntary Restraints on Hong Kong's Exports to Europe and the USA', *Economica*, August, pp. 339–50.

Jones, K. (1984) 'The Political Economy of Voluntary Export Restraint Agreements', *Kyklos*, 37 (1), pp. 81–101.

Kalantzopoulos, O. (1986) *The Cost of Voluntary Export Restraints for Selected Industries* (Washington, DC: Industrial Policy and Strategy Division, The World Bank).

Karsenty, G. and Laird, S. (1986) 'The Generalized System of Preferences: A Quantitative Assessment of the Direct Trade Effects and of Policy Options', UNCTAD Discussion Paper 18 (Geneva: UNCTAD).

Kirmani, N., Molajoni, P. and Mayer, T. (1984) 'Effects on Increased Market Access on Selected Developing Countries' Export Earnings: An Illustrative Exercise', DM/84/85 (Washington, DC: IMF).

MacPhee, C.R. (1986) 'Effects of Competitive Need Exclusions and Redesignations under the US Scheme of Generalized Preferences', UNCTAD/ST/MD/29 (Geneva: UNCTAD).

Marris, S. (1985) *Deficits and the Dollar: The World Economy at Risk* (Washington, DC: IIE).

Nam, C. (1986) 'Export Promoting Policies under Countervailing Threats: GATT Rules and Practice', Discussion paper, Development Policy Issues Series (Washington, DC: The World Bank).

Nogues, J., Olechowski, A. and Winters, L.A. (1986) 'The Extent of Non-Tariff Barriers to Industrial Countries' Imports', *The World Bank Economic Review*, 1 (1).

OECD (1985) *Costs and Benefits of Protection* (Paris: OECD).

Sampson, G.P. (1986) 'Protection in Agriculture and Manufacturing: Meeting the Objectives of the Uruguay Round', mimeo.

Silbertson, Z.A. (1984) *The Multi-Fibre Agreement and the UK Economy* (London: HMSO).

Tarr, D. (1987) 'The Effects of Restraining a Nation's Exports', *World Bank Economic Review*, 1 (3).

Tarr, D. and Morkre, M. (1984) *Aggregate Costs to the United States of Tariffs and Quotas on Imports: General Tariff Cuts and Removal of Quotas on Automobiles, Steel, Sugar and Textiles* (Washington, DC: Federal Trade Commission, Bureau of Economics).

UNCTAD (1986) *Protectionism and Structural Adjustment*, report by the UNCTAD Secretariat, Restrictions on Trade and Structural Adjustment, TD/B/1081 (Part 1) (Geneva: UNCTAD), January.

UNCTAD (1987) *Problems of Protectionism and Structural Adjustment: Restrictions on Trade*, report by the UNCTAD Secretariat, TD/B/1126 (Part 1), (Geneva: UNCTAD).

Wolf, M., Glismann, H.H., Pelzman, J. and Spinanger, D. (1984) 'Costs of Protecting Jobs in Textiles and Clothing', Thames Essay 37 (London: TPRC).

World Bank (1985) 'Trade and Development', Development Committee Paper 6, (Washington, DC: World Bank).

World Bank (1987) *World Development Report* (Washington, DC: World Bank).

Yeats, A.J. (1979) *Trade Barriers Facing Developing Countries* (London: Macmillan).

7 Developing Countries and the Liberalization of Trade in Services

Gary P. Sampson[1]

INTRODUCTION

We are currently experiencing a marked change in the thinking of professional economists, government officials, business leaders and others as to the role of the service sector and its contribution to national economic development.

In OECD countries, policy debates relating to matters such as employment creation have tended to polarize around the relative merits of Keynesian theories of aggregate demand stimulation, monetarist theories involving changes in the money supply or interest rates, and neo-classical approaches to 'getting the prices right'. The 'new' interest in services constitutes more of a Schumpeterian approach: technological developments in services creating possibilities for entrepreneurial initiatives, thereby providing a stimulus to production, demand and employment. From an international perspective, the counterpart is a realization that the domestic growth in some service activities could be accompanied by growth in employment and production of 'traded' services. The case is sometimes made that some countries perceive themselves as being at a marked disadvantage in producing many manufactured goods and look to some of the 'new' services exports to bolster export earnings and improve their current account position.[2]

The focus of this chapter is on developing countries. Here too, there has been a profound change in thinking. In the development literature over the past half century, the role ascribed to the services sector – if indeed there has been a role at all – has at best been a passive one. In discussions of economic growth, the development of the services sector has frequently been treated as a result of economic development rather than a contributor to it. Services entered the discussion as a stage of economic development. Famous growth economists - Allan Fisher, Walter Rostow and Colin Clark – espoused a theory where the process of development consisted of three main phases:[3] first, the pre-industrial phase in

132

which the economy is primarily extractive, based on agriculture, mining, fishing, timber and other natural resources; second, the industrial phase where manufacturing plays the dominant role (in this phase there is a significant shift from agriculture to industry); third, the post-industrial stage, in which the economy becomes a service economy. In other development literature the services sector has played no role at all. The traditional growth models of Harrod and Domar concentrated on macroeconomic variables such as investment and savings and ignored the services sector. Theories of import substitution normally considered only manufactured goods. Input–output models and linear programming models have rarely, if ever, specified the services sector. Indigenous development models based on the notion of autonomous development, collective self-reliance and related concepts, neglected the services sector.

The change in thinking has come through the realization that the many activities in the service sector provide a crucial input into the process of economic development itself.[4] First, there are key activities that may or may not be traded – commercial services such as banking, marketing and distribution – and infrastructural services (such as health, education, local communications and local transport). Second, there are these and other services which are important in determining the export supply capacity of goods: maritime transport, freight insurance and international finance. Third, there are services that are currently traded (exported and imported) or could be exported (or replace imports) in the future; these include tourism, international transport and labour services.

Closely related to the interest in services and development is an interest on the part of some countries in a multilateral liberalization of trade in services. Multilateral discussion of specific international service activities is not new. There are, for example, intergovernmental sectoral arrangements to maintain and develop the technical, legal and economic environment for international civil aviation (International Civil Aviation Organization), maritime transport (Intergovernmental Maritime Organization) and telecommunications (ITU). The focus of these arrangements has not been on the services sector, and neither has it been on the multilateral liberalization of trade in services. Today it is. While the origins of this new interest and focus cannot be clearly identified, it is probably fair to say that it at least partially derives from the US move to liberalize international services activities within the framework of the GATT in the November 1982 Ministerial Session of the GATT contracting parties. This initiative provoked considerable research on the part of GATT contracting parties as they carried out 'national studies' and 'exchanged information' (a result of the GATT ministerial meeting).

At the time of the meeting and subsequently, there has been a well-publicized resistance on the part of some developing countries – most notably Brazil and India[5] – to bringing services within the ambit of GATT.[6] Other countries (EEC and Japan) did not receive the US initiative with unreserved enthusiasm but came to offer varying degrees of support as time progressed. The heavily negotiated compromise text which emerged from the Punta del Este ministerial meeting placed trade liberalization in services squarely on the negotiating agenda, albeit with services on a different track from goods, and heralded the start of the Uruguay Round of MTN.

Given the new interest in the contribution of services to development, the commitment to liberalize trade in services has provoked considerable introspection in developing (and developed) countries as to the impact of government intervention in the services sector. Whether or not liberalization is a 'good thing' requires first an assessment of the contribution of the services sector to national development – economic, social and cultural - and then an evaluation of whether national goals would be better met if trade in services were more liberal. From an institutional perspective, the agreement to liberalize trade in services through multilateral negotiations raises a number of important considerations, not the least being that GATT does not (in general) cover trade in services. During all the seven rounds of trade-liberalizing negotiations little or no attention was paid to liberalizing trade in services. There are therefore no general GATT rules (for example, safeguards) and procedures (for example, dispute settlement) for the services sector. All countries are identifying the issues that are relevant for them in the Uruguay Round negotiations. While this is far from simple, it is a precondition for serious negotiations.

This chapter outlines the principal issues, and then turns to the topic of how this translates into concrete negotiations in GATT. Not surprisingly, a crucial consideration for the purposes of negotiations is that many governments protect certain services activities for non-economic reasons. The implications of this for negotiations are addressed directly in this chapter. Here, as elsewhere, special attention is paid to the interests of developing countries.

While this chapter contains some discussion of the current negotiation positions of countries, it does not attempt a comprehensive review.[7] The purpose is rather to address some of the more lasting economic problems that will have to be faced by developing country officials in the coming years in determining their national strategies toward the liberalization of services.

PROBLEMS OF ANALYSIS

To have a well-developed negotiating strategy it is important to have a clear idea of the contribution of services to economic development and the role of the government in this process. This requires detailed quantitative analysis. Unfortunately, there is a dearth of disaggregated information in the national accounts of most countries (and in particular developing countries) relating to production and trade in services. It is not surprising that the availability of statistics (the first of the five items on the 1987 negotiating agenda) has emerged as an important issue in the negotiations; some developing countries have argued that a good information base is a precondition for serious negotiations.[8]

Perhaps the principal problem facing negotiators stems from the need to deal with services as a sector. The search for a 'multilateral framework' (as it is called in the Punta del Este Declaration) encounters the problem that the service sector encompasses a heterogeneous set of economic activities which often have very little in common. Trading insurance internationally is different from leasing equipment. Supplying legal services across national frontiers is quite distinct from operating a restaurant chain on a franchise basis. Educating foreign students or employing foreign teachers involves quite different skills from engaging in maritime transportation. Furthermore, some services, such as air and maritime transportation, are by their very nature exported and imported. Computer programs are supplied internationally and are traded in the form of magnetic disks. Other services, such as hotel accommodation, must be produced in the locality where they are consumed. Some internationally traded services can be produced either in the country of the provider or the country of the purchaser. Many construction plans, for example, can be prepared equally well in either the country importing or the country exporting the services.

As services encompass such a heterogeneous group of economic activities, the formulation of a definition of the services sector – another item on the 1987 negotiating agenda – is conceptually difficult. One approach has been to define services residually as being activities that are neither manufacturing, mining nor agriculture. Sometimes, services are described as non-storables or intangibles. While service industries generally do deal in intangibles, there are exceptions. A number of economic activities with tangible outputs such as construction, publishing, films or public utilities are, none the less, commonly considered as being services. The residual and intangible nature of services is, however, quite unhelpful in attempting to find a multilateral framework within which to identify issues for negotiators.

Given the sensitive nature of some services and the lack of a natural scientific definition there are a number of key questions which confront negotiators in defining trade in services. Are traded services only those that actually cross the frontier or do they include those produced outside the exporting country, perhaps within the boundaries of the country of import? Otherwise put, will factor movements be part of the negotiations? What will be the sectoral coverage of the services negotiations? The importance of these questions becomes more apparent when service activities are classified according to how they enter into international trade.

THE ISSUES

The issues relating to liberalization in service transactions relate to the need for the means of production of services to move internationally or for the recipient of the service to be internationally mobile. Deciding on the international service transactions that are to be considered as trade in services will determine the nature and scope of the future negotiations. The narrowest definition would include the 'just like goods' category. If one takes a broader definition of trade in services, however, the following issues emerge as being of key importance.

Foreign Investment and Work Permits

As some services can only be exported if there is a presence by the exporter in the importing country, the issue is the permission to establish in the purchasing country. If permission is not granted, there can be no international service transaction. Clearly the issue relates to controls on the flow of investment and skilled and unskilled labour. In such cases, the link between the attitude of the host government to foreign investment and work permits and the possibility of exporting the service is crucial.

There may also be services that can be produced either in the country from which the service is exported or in the country in which the service is consumed. These are cases where a domestic presence may be desirable, but not always crucial. Once again, the liberalization issue relates to the permission to establish business and the attitude of the government to foreign investment and work visas. In these instances restrictions on factor movement may not be a total barrier to trade in services, but they make it more costly to provide a service, and/or lower quality.

National Treatment

Foreign investment policies often take the form of measures relating to both initial establishment and operations after establishment. Thus, an issue that has emerged is national treatment (that is, treatment no less favourable than that received by national firms) after permission has been granted for a foreign firm to establish. Differential treatment for non-rational firms can come about in a variety of ways. Most governments, for example, practise discrimination in favour of national producers in their purchases of services as they do in the procurement of manufactured goods and other products.[9] For instance, procurement policies often give preference to local construction and engineering firms for government contracts. Regarding the banking sector, governmental and semi-governmental entities may be under the 'implied directive' not to transact business with foreign bank affiliates. In the same way, procurement policies can oblige government authorities to purchase their insurance only from national companies. Discriminatory government procurement also affects the maritime transportation sector; procurement policies may require that government purchases and sales of goods and government-financed imports and exports be reserved for national flag vessels. Similarly, procurement policies may oblige government employees and industries to use national air carriers. Dissimilar treatment also derives from the fact that governments commonly grant subsidies to a number of services activities. Maritime and air transportation, the film industry and computer services industries are among the services sectors often benefiting from government aid. Support measures include operating subsidies, low-interest finance, official loan guarantees and special tax and depreciation regulations.

Discriminatory taxes can affect foreign enterprises in the services and the manufacturing sectors. Thus affiliates of overseas companies may be required to pay higher corporate income taxes than locally-owned enterprises. Profits, fees and other earnings remitted abroad can be subject to taxation not faced by indigenous enterprises which keep their earnings in the national economy. Home office overhead costs may not be deductible expenses in tax payments by overseas affiliates. Restrictions on the employment of non-nationals are common in services industries. In many countries, banking regulations require that management positions in foreign banks be filled by citizens of the host country.

Receiver Mobility

As noted, some services can only be sold by the receiver of the service moving to the place of production of the service. The entry by foreigners into some countries to purchase services (for example, tourists) is regulated by the issuing of visitor's visas. There can also be restrictions on the exporting country side; foreign exchange can be restricted for nationals travelling abroad. There are other related issues that arise when considering receiver mobility. If, for example, the exporting country is selling services to foreigners (such as, education or medical care) that are provided by the state as part of a welfare programme, how to price these services (which are not produced in the market) can be an issue.

LIBERALIZING TRADE IN SERVICES: THE MAJOR ISSUES AND GATT

If the contracting parties to GATT did not see advantages in liberalizing trade in goods, phasing out the production of internationally uncompetitive lines of production and permitting domestic resources to flow to areas where they are internationally competitive, they would not be contracting parties to GATT. The obvious corollary of this process of liberalization and phasing out of domestic production is that goods that were produced domestically will be imported following the removal of trade barriers. Applying the same principles to services in an unrestricted manner, however, has implications that far transcend those for goods. This lies at the heart of the debate on the competence – and desire on the part of the governments – for GATT to deal with trade in services. The different implications of liberalization are primarily due to the fact that for many international services transactions, the services that are sold are not 'just like goods'. This in turn follows from the manner in which services are produced, and therefore the way they enter into international trade. The phasing out of internationally uncompetitive services activities and their replacement by foreign-supplied services often means the importation of foreign capital and labour and this can be contrary to national provisions. This raises many questions that are quite different from those associated with the importation of more competitively-priced goods, and the issues are more akin to those relating to foreign investment. Thus, for the developing countries opposed to GATT negotiations on services at Punta del Este and wishing to maintain domestic regulations, the wording that 'such a framework shall respect the policy objectives of national laws and regulations applying to services' has a special significance.

Developing (and other) countries have been hesitant to enter services negotiations in GATT because opening such negotiations could lead to a shift in priorities on the negotiating agenda. Due to the sensitive nature of services negotiations, it is clear that any discussions (regardless of what is considered to be traded services) will be protracted. Recognizing this, some countries have been of the view that entering into time-consuming discussions in this new area while old issues remain unresolved (particularly the work programme of the 1982 GATT Ministerial Meeting) would shift attention away from the outstanding issues. Outstanding matters relating to trade liberalization in tropical products, agriculture and the return of trade in textile goods to normal GATT disciplines, for example, may move to the background.

Some developing country governments have also insisted that there be a 'two-track' approach to the negotiations. They consider concessions based on the opening up of their services markets in return for improved market access for goods in the developed countries to be unacceptable. Developing countries consider that much of what they are asking for in the area of goods constitutes nothing more than a fulfilment of outstanding commitments already made by developed countries and the return of a number of derogations from GATT to the normal workings of the Agreement (for example, returning textile trade to the normal workings of GATT). They consider that no price should be paid for countries to stop breaking the law.

In a substantive sense (that is, quite apart from the procedural agreement to negotiate), it is not yet clear what is to be covered by the negotiations, and some developing countries are hesitant to enter into serious negotiations until this is established. If factor services are to be included, labour flows will be discussed. This service can only be traded internationally if there is a presence of the 'factor of production' (labour) in the importing country. While there have been very considerable flows of labour from developing to developed countries as part of 'normal business',[10] it is not yet clear that all developed countries are prepared greatly to modify national laws and allow the import of labour services from developing countries. Similarly (labour-abundant) developing countries may not be prepared to modify national laws and offer unrestricted rights of establishment and national treatment for foreign businesses in services activities that are still in their infancy.

It would be erroneous, however, to consider that it is only unskilled-labour-intensive activities that developing countries can export abroad. In 1978–9, multinational banking institutions which had a developing country of origin accounted for 20 per cent of branches and 6 per cent of subsidiaries throughout the world. There is a particularly strong presence of Brazilian and Indian banks. In 1984, Indian commercial banks had 141 branches operating in 25 countries.[11] Furthermore, in 1985, some 15 developing countries had travel income in excess of US$ 500 million. Mexico, Singapore, Thailand and India are counted among the top 20 income earners in 1985 and multinational hotel chains operate from Colombia, Hong Kong, India and Mexico.[12]

DEVELOPING COUNTRIES' INTERESTS IN TRADE LIBERALIZING NEGOTIATIONS

Developing countries, or any other group of countries for that matter, will only engage in trade liberalizing negotiations in international trade in services if they can identify clear national benefits flowing from such negotiations. Identifying developing countries' interests in the negotiations is difficult for at least two reasons. First, the diversity of their economic structures, policies (for example, openness of the economy), and perceptions of what is in the economic, political and social interests of the country is perhaps more pronounced in the services sectors than in the goods sectors. Second, very little information exists about the functioning of the services sectors (and even less about trade in services) in most developing countries.

There is a further consideration. Trade liberalizing negotiations in services are extremely complex for many well-known reasons (for instance, the specialized nature of some of the sectors under consideration). These complexities are exacerbated by other difficulties (such as inadequate statistical coverage and a lack of information generally). Furthermore, many of the activities that fall in the realm of internationally-traded services are very sensitive (perhaps for security and cultural reasons). All this taken together means that the formulation of a national negotiating position is resource intensive and takes time. To presume that all developing countries have come to grips with this problem would be an error. In fact, it is clear that some developed countries with substantial resources and highly sophisticated bureaucracies have only recently put in place the necessary governmental infrastructure (for example, interdepartmental committees that represent the various services interests such as shipping, insurance, civil aviation, and so on) to formulate a national negotiating position. It seems fair to say that most developing countries do not yet have a clear idea of where their interests lie. This may well be translated into a negotiating brief where the objective is to secure a holding operation where no agreement is struck that could foreclose options which may be in the national interest in the future. Should this be the case, the surest way for those interested in furthering the negotiations would be to provide technical support to those developing countries attempting to determine whether net benefits would flow from an open and liberal trade regime in services.

Notwithstanding the lack of detailed knowledge, a number

of general comments can be made. For example, whether or not the government of a developing country considers that the national interests are best served by an open and liberal rules-based multinational trading system for services depends on the perception it has of the contribution of traded services to the national economy. This far transcends the idea of imported services as inputs into the process of national production and consumption, and includes considerations such as the contribution of the disciplines of international competition, the efficiency of domestic production, the impact of international trade on domestic relative prices, the structure of production and the allocation of national resources. The presumption of those favouring an open rules-based system is presumably that world trade in services will grow if certain concepts apply, just as world trade in goods grew during the decades following the Second World War. For those that hold this view, a 'mutuality of interests' will be achieved, providing the system is built on the 'right' sorts of concepts. What should the elements be that provide the intellectual foundation of such a system? Whether comparative advantage, MFN treatment, non-discrimination, transparency and other principles that underlay the Bretton Woods system are considered to be supportive of national development, however, depends on the perception on the part of the government as to whether these principles are in practice supportive of economic development and whether or not services are just like goods.

Regardless of whether governments pursue inward- or outward-oriented development strategies, it would appear that there are at least five not unrelated areas of potential interest for developing countries in the current services negotiations.

First, it may be possible that a negotiated liberalization of trade in services would improve the market access for those activities which are of current and potential export interest for developing countries. By way of example, it is clear that construction, tourism and labour-intensive services would fall into this category for many countries. Identifying the specific national interests for individual sectors requires intensive 'grass roots' research.

Next, it may not be inconceivable that multilateral negotiations could lead to an improved supply capacity on the part of some developing countries for a number of service activities of current and potential export interest. While this may more naturally be considered as a technical assistance exercise, imaginative negotiators may find a way of writing such conditions into an agreement.

Third, negotiations of this nature may prove useful for developing countries wishing to improve their import procurement policies for services. There may be the possibility of producing more services for the same outlay or improving the quality of services purchased for the same sum.

Fourth, potential benefits could include the possible benefits of multilateral obligations in strengthening the hands of governments that are looking for a lever to implement reforms at home that may not be in the interests of some powerful lobby groups. For those countries committed to an outward-oriented development strategy, this area is perhaps the most significant.

Finally, for developing countries, as with all medium-sized trading countries, there are benefits to be had by the adherence of governments to rules that promote an efficient, equitable and well-disciplined trading system in goods or services. In the creation of trading systems, it is in the interests of developing countries to ensure that concepts which underpin the system are supportive of the process of economic development. The challenge before developing countries at this time is to identify those concepts which would lead to the creation of a development-oriented multilateral trading system for services.

PROTECTING NATIONAL SERVICE ACTIVITIES FOR NON-ECONOMIC REASONS

As in the case of goods trade, whether or not to protect and provide public assistance to certain activities involves a national choice with implications for the whole economy. Protecting some economic activities by restraining foreign competition means that some part of the community pays more for the domestically-produced service than they would in the absence of protection. There are trade-offs to be made. For governments faced with this national choice, it is useful to recall some recent reports – all of which relate to goods trade – which stress the need for protection to be evaluated in terms of whether protection is in the interest of the community at large. They also point to the advantages of a full public awareness of the costs and benefits of protection.

This is the conclusion of the well-publicized *Costs and Benefits of Protection* study – and other studies – of the OECD.[13] Similarly, according to the Leutwiler Report presented to the Director General of GATT,[14] national institutions are needed to provide a 'magnifying glass' which highlights 'the domestic distribution of the costs and benefits of protection. Organizations like these should be developed in all countries.' According to the Report of the Secretary-General of UNCTAD to the Seventh UNCTAD Conference in Geneva in 1987,[15] if policy

> is to be seen as to be impartially administered and to be primarily concerned with serving the general well being of the community . . . it seems necessary for its operation to be subject, to the maximum possible extent, to public scrutiny and accountability . . . it is necessary to examine the implications of protection for the domestic economy as a whole and for this to be the basis for governmental decision making. (p. 143)

It is worth noting that it is rare to see this degree of agreement on how to evaluate the merits of government intervention across institutions with sometimes different philosophies.

Bearing in mind the characteristics of services discussed above (in particular the crucial role in the process of national development), this conclusion is perhaps even more important than for goods. For present purposes, it translates into the following prescription. Countries wishing to protect their national services activities certainly have the right providing they have not undertaken international commitments to do otherwise. This is a national choice that only national governments can take. If governments do protect certain services activities, however, this should be done with a clear idea of the costs and benefits of their policies and the implications for the national development of the economy as a whole.[16] This has important implications for developing countries.

The debate pertaining to the desirability of protecting key services activities in developing countries – at its deepest level – is a manifestation of the assessment in individual countries of the contribution that can be made to the national economy of imported services. Countries favouring outward-oriented development strategies will import the services from the cheapest possible source. The alternative approach is to attempt to build a domestic capacity for providing services and to emphasize the autonomous process of economic growth and development, even if this means a loss of efficiency. What governments therefore face is a trade-off in deciding between the choices before them. In this process, the crucial question is how to ascertain the relative long- and short-term costs and benefits of different strategies. Is there anything economists can say about this process of decision-making in developing countries? In answering this question it seems important to note a crucial distinction between goods and services. First, some services activities have a higher propensity to be protected for non-economic reasons than goods. Second, given the crucial nature of many services activities in the production process and national development generally, there is even more of a need to have information as to the economy-wide implications of protection. For many service activities, it is difficult to evaluate both costs and benefits; the objectives of government regulation of service activities are often non-economic and it is therefore difficult to evaluate quantitatively the benefits of protection. Normally, however, it is possible to assign an economic cost to various policies. This may not be precise, but a good idea can be obtained.[17]

A concrete example of what is meant above can be found by referring to a report by the Industries Assistance Commission in Australia which notes that the cabotage requirements of the Navigation Act of Australia add 15 per cent to the final selling price of some chemicals in Australia. According to the Act, coastal trade must be carried in Australian bottoms.[18] The question is not whether governments can or cannot pass such legislation, it is rather whether the government was aware of the economy-wide implications – or economic costs – of the decision taken.

CONCLUSION

The diverse (and sensitive) nature of service activities is such that the service sector is technically (and politically) very difficult to deal with. The characteristics that permit the grouping of service activities for the purposes of negotiations may well relate more to the manner in which they enter into trade (and therefore are controlled by governments) rather than to their physical characteristics. Services are more prone to regulation for non-economic reasons than goods. Because of their crucial role in economic development, the consideration of the implications of this regulation for the economy as a whole is even more important than for goods. The more underdeveloped the country, the more important is the need to be aware of the resources forgone by protecting for non-economic reasons. Concern about the evaluation of public assistance to services activities should be inversely related to the level of economic development.

Notes

1. While currently Senior Counsellor, GATT, the chapter was written while employed by UNCTAD in Geneva. Helpful comments from Richard H. Snape are gratefully acknowledged. The views expressed in this chapter are the sole responsibility of the author.
2. For a statement of the argument see UNCTAD (1985b, 1987). For a rebuttal, see Nayaar (1986).
3. See Fisher (1935) and Clark (1940).
4. While governments naturally pay attention to key activities (banking, insurance, transport, and so on) as do various intergovernmental organizations (UNCTAD and shipping, and so on), it is the interest of the services *sector* to economic development that is new. See UNCTAD (1985b, 1987).
5. The Group of Ten developing countries which offered the strongest opposition to GATT negotiations on services - particularly at the time of the 1986 GATT ministerial meeting and Punta del Este – included also Argentina, Cuba, Egypt, Nicaragua, Nigeria, Peru, Yugoslavia and Tanzania. Not all developing countries – or developed for that matter – were unhappy with the opposition. There was also the Group of Twenty developing countries which was prepared to accept GATT negotiations on services but only when the conditions were clearly specified.
6. The US negotiators did not take the opposition lying down. The US Trade Representative Clayton Yeutter is reported as saying: 'We simply can't afford to have a handful of countries responsible for 5 per cent of world trade, dictate the destiny of a large number of countries who deal with 95 per cent of that trade.' ('Yeutter Hits Blockers of Trade Talks', *Washington Post*, 15 November, 1985). Also: 'As part of their counter-attack, US officials began to suggest that it might prove difficult to renew the Generalized System of Preferences if the LDCs and NICs continued to block the new round'; see US Congress (1987, p. 300).
7. For a detailed discussion of events leading up to Punta del Este, the formation of coalitions (national and international), how services are dealt with in various organizations (OECD, and others) and other institutional matters, see Sauvant (1986). For a comprehensive commentary on negotiating positions and issues in the Uruguay Round, see Grace and Miller (1986).
8. For a very comprehensive discussion of the availability and shortcomings of the existing data on services, see UNCTAD (1985a).
9. Indeed, the GATT Government Procurement Code relates to both goods and services.
10. By way of example, it was recently reported that there was

a shortage of between 300 000 and 500 000 temporary farm
workers in the USA, and that the President of the Chinese
Agricultural Manpower Centre of New York planned to move
toward filling this gap by importing Chinese agricultural workers
under a programme known as H-2A by the US Department of
Labor. While these are just plans, almost 25 000 temporary farm
labourers had been admitted to the US in the early part of 1987.
See 'US Company to Recruit Chinese for Farm Work', *International
Herald Tribune*, 26-7 September, 1987, p. 3.

11. See Modwel, Mehrotra and Kumar (1984).
12. See GATT (1985a).
13. See OECD (1986).
14. See GATT (1985b).
15. See UNCTAD (1987).
16. For a discussion of the need for an economy-wide perspective
of public assistance to industries, see Laird and Sampson (1987).
17. Brian Hindley makes the point that 'an essential piece of information
for any attempt to estimate the costs of protection in the service
sector is some idea of the price and quality of the service within
the protected economy as compared with the price and quality that
would be available to its residents under other circumstance'. Due
to the nature of the barriers to international transactions, these
data are not available. He nevertheless concludes that this does
not impede judgements as to whether the costs are large or small,
and concludes that in many cases the costs are very considerable.
See Hindley (1987).
18. This is data provided by private representatives of the chemicals
industry to a public inquiry held into the chemicals sector in
Australia. See the Industries Assistance Commission (1986) p. 34.

References

Clark, C. (1940) *The Conditions of Economic Progress* (New York:
Macmillan).
Fisher, A.G.B. (1935) *The Clash of Progress and Security* (London:
Macmillan).
GATT (1985a) 'Services: Summary of Information made Available by
Relevant International Organizations', MDF/17/Add.3, (Geneva: GATT)
7 November.
GATT (1985b) *Trade Policies for a Better Future: Proposals for Action*
(Geneva: GATT), March.
Grace, B. and Miller, A. (1986) 'The Future of World Trade: The
GATT and the Uruguay Round', *UFSI Reports*, Number 31.
Hindley, B. (1987) 'Protection in the Services Sector: Methods and Effects',
paper presented at The World Bank Conference on Developing Countries'
Interests and International Transactions in Services, Washington, DC,
15–16 July.

Industries Assistance Commission (1986) *Regulatory Impediments to Industry Adjustment* (Canberra: Australian Government Publishing Service).

Laird, S. and Sampson, G.P. (1987) 'Case for Evaluating Protection in an Economy-Wide Perspective', *The World Economy*, 10 (2), pp. 177–92.

Modwel, S.K., Mehrotra, K.N. and Kumar, S. (1984) *Trade in Services* (Indian Institute for Foreign Trade), November.

Nayaar, D. (1986) *International Trade in Services: Implications for Developing Countries*, Exim Bank of India Commencement Day Annual Lecture.

OECD (1986) *Costs and Benefits of Protection* (Paris: OECD).

Sauvant, K.P. (1986) *International Transactions in Services*, The Atwater Series on the World Information Economy (Boulder, Col., and London: Westview Press).

UNCTAD (1985a) *Production and Trade in Services: Policies and their Underlying Factors bearing upon International Services Transactions*, TD/B/941/Rev.1, (New York: UN).

UNCTAD (1985b) *Services and the Development Process*, TD/B/1008/Rev.1, (New York: UN).

UNCTAD (1987) *Revitalizing Development, Growth and International Trade: Assessment and Policy Options*, Report to UNCTAD VII (New York: UN).

US Congress (1987) *International Competition in Services: Banking, Building, Softwear, Knowhow . . .* , (Washington, DC: Office of Technology Assessment, US Government Printing Office).

8 Developing Country Coalition-Building and International Trade Negotiations

Miles Kahler and John Odell

For much of the post-war era, the stance of developing countries towards international trade negotiations has encompassed two somewhat contradictory strategies: on the one hand, considerable energy in maintaining the unity of a developing country bloc that vocally expressed concern over the existing trading system and demanded changes in it; on the other, a relatively passive attitude toward the negotiation rounds themselves.[1] This strategy has long been criticized by Northern sceptics, and preparations for the Uruguay Round demonstrated discontent among some of the developing countries themselves. Arguments for a more active participation by developing countries in trade negotiations have seldom dealt specifically with the other strategies that could be pursued more successfully, however. Our examination of possible coalition strategies for the developing countries in the Uruguay Round and other international economic negotiations is motivated by an awareness of both the existing criticisms of the bloc strategy previously endorsed by G-77 and the underlying logic of that strategy: individually, the developing countries are not major powers in the international trading system. For those with less power, skilful strategies of coalition formation are a major implement for increasing success in such negotiations.

In examining coalition formation, a coalition is defined as two or more actors with shared interests that influence their bargaining behaviour toward other actors. This 'loose' definition of a coalition recognizes that in trade and other international economic negotiations, coalitions are often fleeting and not exclusive. A coalition partner on one issue may not remain a partner on others. The level of organization of coalitions will also vary: few of the potential coalitions described below are likely to approach the level of institutionalization found in military alliances, for example. Finally, the coalitions that have been prominent to date in the Uruguay Round of trade negotiations have often been directed towards agenda setting; their success at the much more difficult task of formulating a common negotiating position remains to be seen.

Each developing country will need to weigh the opportunities and risks presented by possible coalitions that it could join. This study is meant primarily to illuminate both the opportunities and obstacles to a more activist and innovative attitude toward coalition formation.

SOUTHERN BLOC ON THE SIDELINES: TRADE NEGOTIATIONS BEFORE THE URUGUAY ROUND

As Gilbert Winham describes in his account of the Tokyo Round negotiations, the developing countries played a somewhat larger role in those negotiations as compared to their 'wholly marginal' participation in the Kennedy Round. Their efforts were concentrated on such exercises as the framework negotiation, however, which was designed to embed preferential status within the GATT regime. Efforts to construct developing country coalitions on more concrete measures, such as tariff reductions, foundered on divisions within the group.[2]

Three principal explanations can be offered for the peripheral role of the developing countries in past GATT negotiations. First the structure of the negotiations themselves suggested that a relatively passive stance made sense. Trade negotiations, particularly tariff negotiations on a reciprocal basis, do not offer many incentives for smaller economies to participate actively: they have little to offer, since they are not principal suppliers or large markets and, given the extension of MFN status, they could obtain the resulting benefits in any case.[3] Since the developing countries did not accept the principle of reciprocity, incentives for active participation were further diminished. Alternative fora for negotiations also beckoned to the Third World. Instead of negotiating for benefits with the existing post-war regimes, the G-77 sought extensive changes in those regimes through negotiations that included a broad spectrum of issue areas. Those negotiations, and the North–South cleavage that they presupposed, also hardened the dominant, Southern bloc model of coalition formation. Finally, and related to the appeal of the NIEO, the benefits of liberalization and non-discrimination in the trading system, (two key norms of the GATT regime), were reduced by the strategy of economic development endorsed by many developing countries, particularly the largest ones (China, India and Brazil). Until the 1980s, international trade was viewed at best as an ancillary engine of growth by many developing countries. If trade and exports were not critical to economic development, then negotiations within the existing trade regime would receive less attention.

Each of these obstacles to enlarged participation by the developing countries has been lowered, if not removed, during the 1980s. In contrast to the Kennedy and Tokyo Rounds, developing countries were actively involved in the discussions that led to the Uruguay Round; the large number of accessions or requests for accession to GATT (including such major trading countries as Mexico and China) indicate that the issues on the table are regarded as important by the developing countries. Heightened interest in the latest round of trade negotiations has also been stimulated by the decline of global negotiations and the agenda of the NIEO. The GATT round is one of the few games in town, in large measure because of the hostility of the USA regarding the global negotiations arena. Finally, the economic circumstances of the 1980s have also moved the elites of the developing countries towards greater interest in export expansion and hence the international trade regime. The debt crisis has had a mixed impact (discussed below), forcing import contraction far more than export expansion and lowering the perceived ability of many developing countries to liberalize their commercial policies. The successive shocks of the last decade and pressure from the North have produced an acceptance, sometimes grudging, of more outward-oriented policies. (Such policies need not include import liberalization, however.)

In shaping the agenda for the Uruguay Round, the new importance of developing country actors was clear, as was the erosion of the previous bloc model of interaction. The coalition model that will dominate during the Uruguay Round remains uncertain, however. There are four basic options (or some of these could be combined)

1. In the event that the trade negotiations stall or fail, an accentuation of bilateralism or minilateralism within (or outside) the multilateral GATT framework is likely.
2. A pattern of coalitions across the North–South divide could develop in the Uruguay Round.
3. A looser Southern coalition could develop in which the first- and second-generation NICs would take a leadership role.
4. The previous pattern of a broad developing country bloc could

be re-established, concentrating its negotiations on questions of regime change and pursuing a joint programme with linkages to other issue areas, such as international finance.

These patterns are dependent not only on perceived developing country interests, but also on the strategies of the major industrialized country participants. They are also highly dependent on the agenda issues in question: as described below, certain issues (such as agriculture) point towards coalition formation across the North–South divide, while others (safeguards) are more likely to produce a predominantly Southern coalition. Each strategy has certain benefits and costs for particular groups of developing countries as a result; what follows is an analysis of the clusters and coalition building blocks that might result.

BILATERALISM AND MINILATERALISM: A LIKELY SECOND-BEST?

Given the circumstances of the 1980s, and particularly the absence of a dominant economic power, bilateral or minilateral approaches to trade negotiations may be more successful than multilateral negotiations at the Uruguay Round.[4] Certainly such options could grow in importance if current trade negotiations stall or fail. These less-than-multilateral outcomes describe two distinct scenarios, however. Bilateral or minilateral fragmentation of the GATT system could grow from an accentuation of the trend towards managed trade, following such existing models as the MFA, or 'grey area' measures of voluntary export restraint. Rather than organized protectionism, a second scenario views these possibilities as a means of preserving and extending islands of liberalization in a global system tending toward greater closure. The arrangements might be discriminatory, but between partners greater liberalization would result. It is worth examining each of these scenarios for its impact on developing countries.

A system of managed trade is usually held up as a commercial nightmare for developing economies: confronting their far larger industrialized partners in an unequal contest with little or no international surveillance. The pronounced interest of many developing countries in strengthening certain norms of the GATT multilateral system (at least as applied to OECD countries) suggests that they have dreamed this nightmare. Yet one could also point to certain sectors – textiles and apparel in particular – that are already intensively managed on a bilateral basis, with little GATT oversight, which represent considerable successes for developing country exports.

The textiles and apparel case offers substantiation for minority arguments that managed trade between North and South is inevitable and that it need not be disastrous. Considerable evidence exists that any 'new protectionism' directed against the dynamic exporters of the developing world has been ineffectual in restraining the growth of their exports.[5] For the NIC, managed trade affords some of the same benefits perceived by the OECD countries – a stable market share protected from more competitive suppliers – as well as offering a substantial portion of the rents. By forcing suppliers into more sophisticated lines of production, it could be argued that such arrangements also provide a beneficial industrial policy for adaptable developing countries.[6] Finally, some of the NICs do have bargaining strengths: either a security relationship with a major industrialized market (for example, Korea or Yugoslavia) or a large potential market that can be used in retaliation for protectionist measures (for example, Brazil or China).

These short-term advantages for some of the NICs may have implications for coalition-building in such sectors as textiles, since the impact of liberalization in the textiles and apparel sector may be uneven in its benefits.[7] Nevertheless, most developing countries are not convinced of the advantages of a more managed system of trade, with the possible exception of commodities. Even the skilful Asian NICs have discovered that the import-competing industries in their major markets are capable of learning as well, and that bilateral regimes can be tightened. For the second and later generation industrializers, market sharing agreements may temporarily stimulate 'quota seeking' manufacturing exports but, in general, they are particularly damaging for new and more competitive suppliers.

Should the trading environment deteriorate, particularly because of failure at Geneva, another variant of bilateralism and minilateralism could beckon. Developing countries could seek liberalizing agreements with industrialized countries or, in an effort to expand South–South trade, with other developing countries. Such arrangements have become a theme of American commercial diplomacy in recent years – for instance, the Caribbean Basin initiative, or proposed free trade agreements with Canada and Israel - but have also been employed by other countries, most notably Australia and New Zealand in their Closer Economic Relations Agreement, negotiated in 1983. The Lomé Convention is an earlier example with roots in colonial ties between European states and the ACP group of developing countries. Developing country preferential trading arrangements have a different lineage. Strongly backed by UNCTAD in the 1960s and 1970s, they have been seen as a means not only of benefiting from economies of scale, but also of increasing the bargaining leverage of developing economies with both the industrialized world and multinational corporations. Few have been very successful at increasing intra-regional trade; even ASEAN, which has had the goal of a free trade arrangement for ten years, still remains mired in highly resistant domestic politics of protection.[8] Most Northern observers are sceptical of their benefits, but many developing countries remain impressed by their prospects for market expansion, particularly as a liberalization 'half-way house' for relatively inefficient manufacturers.[9] Such arrangements pose risks for both the global trading system and for individual developing countries. They could serve as building blocks for a larger, liberalizing multilateral system, but preferential agreements could easily become inward-looking rather than outward-looking. External liberalization may fail to keep pace with internal freeing of trade; indeed, the latter may distract attention from the importance of the former. In addition, this 'à la carte' approach to trade negotiations and liberalization produces even greater fragmentation in the world trading system and both a psychological and a real undermining of the MFN principle.[10]

Individual developing countries would have to calculate their long-term bargaining advantages within such a bilateral or minilateral relationship and, given the availability of government attention and personnel, the opportunity costs for participation in the global trading arena. Larger developing countries that are highly dependent on particular industrial country markets and that have attractive internal markets to use as a bargaining resource may find bilateral arrangements attractive; Mexico is a possible case in point. For smaller and less diversified economies, even collective bargaining may not yield significant gains: the experience of the ACP states in their bargaining with the EEC provides a caution to other, similar economies.[11]

The popularity of bilateralism and minilateralism as liberalizing (rather than management) strategies is likely to be affected by the success or failure of the GATT negotiations. Some fraction of developing country interest in the new trade round derives from a certain disenchantment with South–South regional trading arrangements. In pursuing an activist course at the multilateral level, however, choice among alternative strategies remains.

NORTH–SOUTH COALITIONS WITH MULTILATERAL NEGOTIATIONS: COMMON INTERESTS OR COOPTATION?

In the wake of failed efforts at global North–South negotiations, many Northern observers have suggested that developing countries must form coalitions across the North–South divide if their negotiating goals are to be achieved. Sewell and Zartman (1984), for example, argue that: 'perhaps the most important single innovation needed in North–South relations is ways and means to develop coalitions between Northern and Southern countries on various specific issues without undermining the unity of the Third World'.[12] Arguing the benefits of such coalitions does not produce them, however; embarking on this strategy requires an analysis of latent coalitions that the developing countries might bring into being and a clear assessment of the risks to Southern interests that such a course poses.

In analysing this alternative and the succeeding NIC-led model, economic interests of the developing countries are assumed to determine their behaviour in trade negotiations. As noted below, ideological or political goals could incline the Third World to a resurrection of the bloc strategy, but here economic aims are awarded dominance. In examining the heterogeneous interests of the developing economies in trade negotiations, several overlapping issue clusters emerge, as illustrated in Figure 8.1. The principal groups are competitive exporters of manufactures (the NICs, the ASEAN countries, and other second-generation industrializers); exporters of temperate agricultural products; exporters of other commodities; and those countries with serious international debt repayments constraints (indicated by rescheduling).[13] These clusters may not capture all the divisions within the developing group, but

Figure 8.1 Developing countries' interests in international trade negotiations

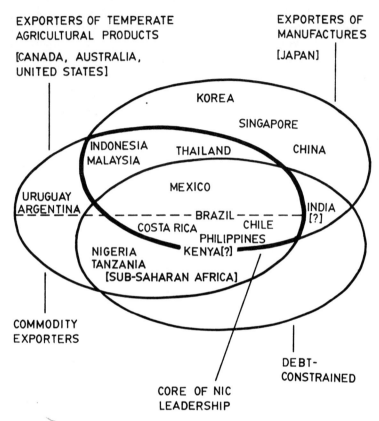

EXPORTERS OF TEMPERATE
AGRICULTURAL PRODUCTS

[CANADA, AUSTRALIA,
UNITED STATES]

EXPORTERS OF
MANUFACTURES

[JAPAN]

KOREA

SINGAPORE

INDONESIA   THAILAND   CHINA
MALAYSIA

MEXICO

URUGUAY   INDIA
ARGENTINA   BRAZIL   [?]
                COSTA RICA   CHILE
                        PHILIPPINES
        NIGERIA   KENYA[?]
        TANZANIA
        [SUB-SAHARAN AFRICA]

COMMODITY
EXPORTERS

DEBT-
CONSTRAINED

CORE OF NIC
LEADERSHIP

porters of manufactures in the USA and EEC
they highlight certain features that have already determined the coalition behaviour of some developing countries.

Certain likely alliances across the North–South line become apparent using these criteria for divisions. Agriculture has already witnessed an incipient coalition in the Cairns Group, formed in response to the damaging European–American agricultural subsidies war. The group is notable in that it includes not only exporters of foodstuffs, North and South, but also current exporters of tropical commodities who are concerned over indirect damage to their exports and also have hopes of future diversification (Malaysia and Indonesia, for example).

Two risks emerge from North–South collaboration on this issue. First, although the EEC agreed to the inclusion of agriculture in the Uruguay Round, it promises to be an issue of major conflict. The experience of the Tokyo Round, in which stalemate over agriculture stalled the talks for four years, could be repeated.[14] A second risk is the opposition of developing countries which have depended on imports of foodstuffs (India, China) or which protect their agricultural sectors (Korea). This potential conflict among developing countries is likely to be reduced by the substantial progress that has been made in China, South Asia and Indonesia in increasing agricultural production. From being substantial importers of foodstuffs, they have in some cases become self-sufficient and could potentially become exporters.

The power of a North–South coalition in agriculture should not be overestimated. The EEC and Japan will not dispense with their cosseted agricultural sectors lightly; despite the free-market rhetoric of the USA, its farm lobby is as powerful as any. Outside agriculture and the Cairns Group, North–South coalitions-in-formation are more difficult to discern. For selfish reasons, the USA may support developing country exporters of manufactures in their push for less managed trade, particularly in restraining the use of safeguards: the United States sees an opening of the Japanese and European markets as a means of relieving some of the pressure on its own market from the dynamic exporters of Asia. The USA also has an interest in strengthening the GATT system to avoid a system of managed trade in which it would be at a comparative political disadvantage: as compared to Japan, the USA is relatively inept at managing trade to secure competitive gain.

The developing countries share common interests with Japan in tightening the use of CVDs and the definition of subsidies, in circumscribing the use of safeguards, and in strengthening the GATT system, since Japan remains the subject of discriminatory NTBs at the hands of the USA and the Europeans. (Smaller industrialized countries, such as Canada and the Nordic countries, would also be interested in this issue.) Should resolution of the debt problems of the developing countries be linked to the trade negotiations, Japan could well smooth a resolution through contributing to its financing. With the Europeans there may also be a joint interest in resolving the debt crisis, but, given their lack of enthusiasm so far, it is not clear on what issues the developing countries might form a firm coalition with the EEC. Given Europe's interests in Sub-Saharan

Africa, commodities might be one such issue but, in general, the African states may be the least involved of the participant developing countries.

Overall, a strategy of seeking alliances and coalitions across the North–South divide could offer gains on particular issues, but the risk in this strategy is that the developing countries would find themselves confronting their giant trading counterparts in asymmetric bargaining situations within the coalitions or joining battles, in agriculture for example, that may serve the interests of one or another industrialized country but not their own. Most important, the value of concessions made by the developing countries increases if they are made in a coordinated fashion by at least the largest country exporters. This positive value in coordination (and the fact that the more industrialized developing countries have the most to offer in bargaining with the industrialized countries) points to a third strategy.

LEADERSHIP BY THE NICS, FOR THE NICs?

A strategy in which the NICs, the developing countries with the greatest stake in a liberalized trading system, took an active lead in bargaining on behalf of a looser Southern coalition is the strategy of choice for most Northern observers.[15] This approach concentrates on the common interest of those developing countries seeking more secure access for their manufactures in Northern markets, using their own combined internal markets as an inducement.[16] NIC leadership in making a constructive proposal to the OECD would at least put Northern protection on the defensive and could achieve reductions in barriers that would benefit less-industrialized developing countries as well.

The strategy is appealing, but it immediately confronts an important question: which NICs? In fact, two leadership groups emerged in the negotiations preceding the Punte del Este meetings: those resisting the new agenda proposed by the USA, especially Brazil and India, and a group (with ASEAN at its core) that was willing to break with the traditional Southern stance and support the new round. (The latter group was apparently supported by several smaller Latin American states and by the Francophone African states.) In examining Figure 8.1, it is clear that two groups – the

largest Latin American exporters (Brazil and Mexico) and ASEAN
– are the hinges of any Southern bloc and the likeliest candidates for
leadership, given their exporting records, their diversified interests in
the negotiations and the size of their domestic markets. Since Brazil
opposed the agenda and has been sceptical of the talks, the question
of how the principal exporting countries could unify to lead is a
pressing one.

A second issue is the outline of a NIC-led strategy. The answer
is complicated by the fact that how the developing countries bargain
– whether by reciprocal bargaining or not – is one of the issues on
the table. Once again, a chorus of Northern observers has argued
that S&D treatment has meant little of benefit in economic terms
(though the benefits have disproportionately accrued to the NICs)
and has had the more important political and legal effect of
undermining the GATT regime, to the detriment of developing
country interests.[17] Although uniform in their assessment, these
critics are not in agreement on whether a move toward greater
reciprocity or 'graduation' will result in significant gains for the
developing countries.

At least three 'NIC-led' bargains seem possible: these are
strategies which focus on the constitutional, the instrumental and
the substantive. At the constitutional level – dealing with the
structure of the trade regime – the NICs could trade a 'reasonably specific program for integrating their trade regimes into the
GATT system of open trade and non-discrimination',[18] including
graduation from the provisions of Part IV, for a strengthening of
the GATT regime in ways desired by the developing countries,
particularly in restraining CVDs, AD penalties and safeguard
measures, and in strengthening procedures for dispute settlement.
S&D treatment would be reserved for the poorest developing
countries (although they too could be encouraged to liberalize
their trade regimes), which does pose problems of definition
(perhaps those countries eligible for IDA lending from the World
Bank).

Such a bargain displays symmetry; at other levels of bargaining
the knotty question of reciprocity might be circumvented by the
same concept or by using the idea of 'unequal reciprocity'. A
second bargain – the instrumental one – would focus on exchanging
concessions on QRs affecting trade in manufactures. For North
and South, QRs are perhaps the most salient trade barriers, and
certainly are squarely within the existing GATT regime. The NICs

could propose that the OECD states commit themselves to a phased elimination of existing quantitative restrictions affecting manufactures, perhaps including 'grey area' measures. (Such a bargain could be coordinated with safeguards negotiations to improve control over the emergence of new, equally restrictive barriers.) In return the NICs could offer to bargain over their own QRs on the basis of unequal reciprocity, making concessions clearly smaller in magnitude than those they would receive. For example, they could offer a code that would place some limits on their future use of GATT exceptions permitting the use of QRs for BOP reasons, infant industry promotion and development needs. The proposed limits could be quite loose, but OECD governments might value an agreement that did little more in the short run than establish principles covering NIC markets. NIC governments that would reap most of the benefits of greater market access could consider side deals with neighbours and others in the G77 to obtain their political support.

A third, substantive bargain concerns the sectoral scope of GATT and would probably be the most controversial. The NICs and the other developing countries have been highly sceptical of America's strenuous efforts to bring services into the new round. (All participants seem to have some difficulty estimating their interests in this diffuse set of industries and sectors.) While the specific outlines of a services agreement or code remain obscure, the NICs could certainly demand that sectors of interest to them be brought within GATT once again, particularly textiles and apparel. This prospective trade has been rejected by some of the NICs as asymmetric, equating existing violations of GATT rules with the expansion of GATT into uncharted territory highly favourable to the OECD countries. The bargain could be made more attractive for the NICs, however, by emphasizing labour-intensive services of interest to the developing countries and by designing a graduated (unequally reciprocal) code that would impose few immediate constraints on the NICs.[19] Given the political interests of either side of this goods-for-services bargain, it would be very difficult to negotiate. NIC unity might be difficult to achieve, given their own mixed interests in the MFA regime and in any future services code.

While NIC leadership may result in bargains that benefit them more than the rest of the developing countries (particularly those whose exports are still overwhelmingly based on a small number of commodities), enough common interests exist between the NICs and these other countries to expect that their interests would not be harmed by such bargaining. (Figure 8.1 demonstrates that many exporters of manufactures remain significant commodity exporters, for example.) The poorest and least industrialized developing countries are not likely to gain very much from reciprocal bargaining, indeed, their gains from the trade negotiations are likely to be small. Phasing out the MFA might help (though it would probably benefit China and India most of all), negotiations to end tariff escalation on processed raw materials have been on the agenda for some time, and linkage to issues of debt and development assistance, considered below, could well be of more interest than commercial issues *per se*. The NICs, in reserving S&D treatment for these economies and attempting to win certain concessions that would benefit them, would be exercising leadership in the strict sense, giving the less industrialized developing countries the chance of a free ride on their bargaining strengths. But the bargain between the NICs and the other developing countries might not be so one-sided: Southern unity may still produce benefits in bargaining with the North.

A UNIFIED AND PRAGMATIC SOUTH

If Northern critics are uniform in their scepticism concerning the gains derived from S&D treatment, they are even more unanimous in their disregard for the bloc strategy that has sought that goal. Robert Rothstein has offered a detailed account of the way in which the developing countries, throughout the NIEO negotiations, maintained a high degree of unity at the cost of bargaining inflexibility and ultimate lack of success.[20] The heterogeneity of the South produced a unity based on ideological principles and the simple addition of one group's demands to those of the others; as Rothstein observes, 'procedural unity without substantive unity diminishes the possibility of achieving viable settlements'.[21]

The bloc strategy was not irrational, however: it grew out of a particular perception of Southern economic weakness, and a belief that only through Southern unity could negotiating concessions be obtained from the Northern countries. That fundamental perception remains to be disproven by the critics; as Hudec declares, the main obstacle to improved market access is lack of economic power on the part of the developing countries: opposition to demands for protection 'requires having enough economic power to create, or threaten, equally important economic interests, in an equally sharp and immediate manner'.[22]

A NIC-led strategy may not amass enough economic power to force concessions from the industrialized countries. Would retaining a framework for coordinating developing country actions add substantially to developing country leverage? The non-NIC developing countries are likely to add little in a process of reciprocal bargaining, but they do add legitimacy, in the form of universality, to the norms of the trading system and to the claims of the NICs to represent the developing countries. While legitimacy has a value that is hard to assess, it does have value. It is that increment that the NICs should seek to retain in their bargaining on behalf of the other developing countries, one additional barrier to wholly self-interested deal-making.

ISSUE LINKAGE: DEBT AND COMMODITIES

The strategies of coalition formation outlined here have been limited to the arena of trade negotiations. For many developing countries in the 1980s, however, other international economic issues have been of equal or greater importance. One of the principal causes of import compression by the developing countries during the 1980s has been persistent BOP crises, aggravated by debt servicing obligations and a decline in external finance. The links between trade and finance have been underlined by the IMF and the World Bank in their calls for open markets in the OECD countries for developing country exports. There are also more specific links to trade negotiations in the phasing of any agreed liberalization in accord with BOP considerations and the possibility of developing country 'credit' for liberalization already undertaken in the course of an adjustment programme.

A broader linkage has also been suggested: connecting developing country participation in the Uruguay Round with negotiations directed toward a resolution of the debt crisis. As Figure 8.1

demonstrates, another division between prospective developing country leaders is that of the debt constraint: Latin America has been deeply affected by the debt crisis since 1982, while Asia, with the major exception of the Philippines, has largely been spared.

That division suggests a major shortcoming in any attempt at linkage between trade and debt: it would serve to fragment the developing countries further. The major Latin American debtors themselves have been unable to agree on a joint strategy *vis-à-vis* their creditors; linkage is not likely to solve the problem of coordination. Also, it is not clear that linkage in this case would strengthen the position of the developing countries: the debt 'weapon' could prove as short-lived and illusory as the oil 'weapon' of the 1980s. The reverse linkage – from trade to debt - overestimates the bargaining leverage of the developing countries within the trade negotiations.

Although a global negotiation linking debt and trade seems of dubious benefit to the developing countries, two more limited connections between the two issue areas could be put on the table during trade negotiations. First, developing countries could ask that unilateral trade liberalization undertaken during adjustment programmes be accepted as part of their concessions during the trade round. In addition, for those countries under a very tight BOP constraint, international financial assistance could be earmarked (as it has been in the past) to support liberalization measures that are negotiated.

A second issue area that is more closely tied in its substance to trade is that of commodities. Despite more than a decade of negotiation, the situation confronting commodity producers among the developing countries is as bleak as it has been at any time since the 1930s. Despite the recent upturn in certain commodity prices and the agreement of the Soviet Union to join the CFC, no solution to the plight of commodity producers is in sight. The trade round can deal directly with such barriers to processing as tariff escalation and can remove the remaining trade barriers (relatively minor) to commodity exports, but additional efforts would be required to link these negotiations to a broader attempt to assist the commodity producers, through an expanded CFC and diversification for markets and products. Here once again, it is not clear that the developing countries, following any of the strategies outlined above, can reopen the issue on more favourable terms.

CONCLUSION

While the past experience of the developing countries in trade negotiations provides some hint of their future behaviour, the choices in coalition formation, international and domestic, remain wide and possibilities for surprise, especially for academic observers, is great. Nevertheless, this review does suggest certain practical conclusions for the developing countries as they confront the Uruguay Round.

Two particular problems stare out at those who advocate a more activist stance in trade negotiations. The first is achieving substantive unity, at least among the key trading states (and we have noted the large Latin American economies and ASEAN as focal groups). The possibilities for division on issues such as services or debt is great, and the other options - disaggregated deal-making or a return to an ideological and unprofitable bloc strategy – are likely to offer fewer rewards in bargaining with the industrialized countries. Equally important is the question of representation: although the largest traders must lead, much of the leadership to this point has come from smaller economies, North and South, which perceive strong national interests in a strengthened multilateral system (Colombia is a case in point). How to couple the realities of economic power with the need for adequate representation is far more difficult for the developing countries than for the industrialized countries, where three trading powers so clearly outweigh the others. In part, the problem can be resolved by existing groups, such as ASEAN, but additional innovation may be required.

In general, among the coalition strategies examined, an NIC-led strategy appears potentially the most rewarding for the developing countries and one that seems to fit best within the existing pattern of (unequal) reciprocal bargaining within GATT. Coalition-building across the North–South divide appears promising in certain sectors, but problems of coordination in formulating a common negotiating position would probably be greater, and the shared interests outside those sectors weaker. Various bilateral and minilateral alternatives outside the multilateral bargaining could provide the arena for focused bargaining between key trading partners, but the advantages appear limited for smaller developing countries, which could offer neither a large internal market nor some strategic benefit to their Northern partners. Finally, this menu of coalitional strategies should not exclude maintenance of Southern unity on certain issues in which legitimacy provides an additional bargaining resource for the South.

Notes

1. Hamilton and Whalley (1987), p. 8.
2. Winham (1986), pp. 272–7. While the Latin American countries pushed for preferential tariff cuts, they were opposed by the African states, which resisted a reduction in the preferences that they already received from the EEC.
3. The position of the developing countries resembled that of smaller industrial economies such as Canada in this regard (Winham, 1986, pp. 272–3).
4. This argument is made in Yarbrough and Yarbrough (1987).
5. A review of this literature is given in Anjaria, Kirmani and Petersen (1985), pp. 23–4 and 81–2. On the key question of whether exports would have been significantly higher in the absence of bilateral management, the evidence is mixed.
6. Perhaps the strongest argument of the beneficial side-effects of such protectionism, and the abilities of the developing countries to circumvent the restraints, is Yoffie (1983), especially pp. 167–8, 196–7, 234. See also Nau (1985), p. 72.
7. One estimate of the effects is given by Vincent Cable in Finger and Olechowski (1987), p. 185.
8. A recent analysis of intra-ASEAN trade suggests a substantial increase over ten years, but closer analysis reveals its dependence on trade in petroleum products among Indonesia, Malaysia and Singapore (Rieger, 1985).
9. For one harsh judgement, see Wolf (1984), pp. 214–5. A sceptical view of African efforts at economic integration is given in Mazzeo (1984). Nevertheless, a large number of authors in Whalley (1987) award a large place to such regional arrangements in their national commercial policies.
10. On these risks, see Hufbauer and Schott (1985), pp. 92–4.
11. See the conclusions of Ravenhill (1985), pp. 309–40.
12. Sewell and Zartman (1984), p. 115. They argue this point particularly in the area of trade.
13. The countries that are part of this trade project have been used to represent certain groups (Costa Rica is a proxy for other Central American countries); certain other significant participants have also been added.
14. On the treatment of agriculture in the Tokyo Round, see Winham (1986), Chapter 4.
15. For example, see Wolf (1984, p. 222) and Nau (1985, p. 78) who argues that 'NIC diplomacy seeks a fluid pattern of alignments with other developing countries that avoids NIC isolation from the 'Group of 77' developing countries yet discards for good the rigid, lowest-common denominator solidarity with the South that in the 1970s sacrifices real NIC interests to ideological symbols.'
16. For example, in 1985, combined imports of South Korea, Hong Kong, Singapore, Taiwan, India, Brazil, Mexico and Malaysia amounted to US$ 162 billion, or 8 per cent of world imports.

Even if some of this list did not join the group, other smaller traders probably would. For reference, imports of West Germany and Japan in that year totalled US$ 158 and US$ 128 billion respectively (GATT, 1985–6).

17.   See, for example, Wolf (1984), pp. 212–5; Behrman (1984), p. 248; Hamilton and Whalley (1987), pp. 12–13; Hudec (1987), Part II.
18.   Preeg (1985), p. 13.
19.   In arguing for Southern participation in negotiations over services, Jagdish Bhagwati notes in Finger and Olechowski (1987, p. 214) that the Uruguay Round 'is unlikely to yield anything more concrete than a code or an agreement of principles'.
20.   Rothstein (1979), pp. 121-2, 150.
21.   Rothstein (1979), p. 196.
22.   Hudec (1987), p. 215.

References

Anjaria, S.J., Kirmani, N. and Peterson, A.B. (1985) *Trade Policy Issues and Developments*, IMF Occasional Paper No. 38 (Washington, DC: IMF).

Behrman, J.R. (1984) 'Rethinking Global Negotiations: Trade', in J.N. Bhagwati and J.G. Ruggie (eds) *Power, Passions and Purpose* (Cambridge, Mass.: MIT Press).

Finger, M.J. and Olechowski, A. (eds) (1987) *The Uruguay Round* (Washington, DC: World Bank).

GATT (1985-6) *International Trade* (Geneva: GATT).

Hamilton, C. and Whalley, J. (1987) 'A View from the Developed World', in J. Whalley (ed.), *Dealing with the North: Developing Countries and the Global Trading System* (London, Canada: CSIER, University of Western Ontario).

Hudec, R.E. (1987) *Developing Countries in the GATT Legal System* (London: Macmillan, for TPRC).

Hufbauer, G. and Schott, J.J. (1985) *Trading for Growth: The Next Round of Trade Negotiations* (Washington, DC: IIE).

Mazzeo, D. (ed.) (1984) *African Regional Organizations* (Cambridge University Press).

Nau, H. (1985) 'The NICs in a New Trade Round', in Preeg (1985).

Preeg, E.H. (1985) 'An Agenda for US Trade Policy', in E.H. Preeg (ed.), *Hard Bargaining Ahead* (New Brunswick, NJ: Transaction Books).

Ravenhill, J. (1985) *Collective Clientelism: The Lomé Conventions and North-South Relations* (New York: Columbia University Press).

Rieger, H.C. (1985) 'ASEAN Cooperation and Intra-ASEAN Trade', ISEAS/ASEAN Economic Research Unit, Research Notes and Discussion Paper No. 57 (Singapore: Institute of Southeast Asian Studies).

Rothstein, R.L. (1979) *Global Bargaining: UNCTAD and the Quest for a New International Economic Order* (Princeton University Press).

Sewell, J.W. and Zartman, I.W. (1984) 'Global Negotiations: Path to the Future or Dead-End Street?', in J.N. Bhagwati and J.G. Ruggie (eds), *Power, Passions and Purpose*, (Cambridge, Mass: MIT Press).

Whalley, J. (ed.) (1987) *Dealing with the North: Developing Countries and the Global Trading System* (London, Canada: CSIER, University of Western Ontario).

Winham, G.R. (1986) *International Trade and the Tokyo Round* (Princeton University Press).

Wolf, M. (1984) 'Two-Edged Sword: Demands of Developing Countries and the Trading System', in J.N. Bhagwati and J.G. Ruggie (eds) *Power, Passions and Purpose* (Cambridge, Mass.: MIT Press).

Yarbrough, B.V. and Yarbrough, R.M. (1987) 'Cooperation in the Liberalization of International Trade: After Hegemony, What?', *International Organization* 41, 1 (Winter), pp. 1–26.

Yoffie, D. (1983) *Power and Protectionism* (New York: Columbia University Press).

Part III

Barriers, Trade and Sector Issues

9 Non-Tariff Barriers Facing Developing Country Exports

Gary P. Sampson[1]

INTRODUCTION

The post-war period up to the early 1970s was one where trade liberalization, based principally on the dismantling of QRs and the reduction of tariff barriers, permitted substantial growth rates of international trade flows. The past decade has seen a proliferation of barriers to trade and despite general advocacy of governments for an improved and strengthened trade regime coupled with further liberalization, protectionism and other forms of trade intervention have tended to increase.

Recent experience has reinforced the political economy rationalization of how trade 'policy' is formed; governments have intervened to prevent what they perceive to be unacceptable trade-related changes in the distribution of income. An obvious manifestation of these developments is that the international trading system is under severe pressure. There is a lack of adherence to the existing rules of the GATT-based system with a neglect of the MFN commitments; discriminatory trade measures have been applied and other concepts developed to circumvent traditional GATT procedures. Furthermore, actions taken within the system provide evidence that the system itself is operating poorly; there is a lack of a multilateral commitment to an adequate disputes settlement mechanism, no consensus on the safeguard provisions and an inability on the part of governments to translate multilateral rules and principles into national laws and regulations.

There are also external pressures placed on the international trading system with which it was never expected to cope. Exchange rates fluctuate widely, massive amounts of speculative capital flow around the world and debt payments for a number of developing countries have become crippling. Fiscal imbalances have poured over into trade imbalances and added to forces claiming that the 'playing field is not level', and trade surpluses have not led to demand stimulation and growth in trading partners. These and

171

many other factors outside the system have served to create additional strains.

The gravity of the problems confronting the trading system has been realized and at Punta del Este in September 1986 the Uruguay Round of MTN was launched by Ministers of the 95 GATT contracting parties. But while both the realization that the international trading system is functioning poorly and the political commitment to strengthen the open and liberal multilateral trading system are evident, much of this is based on *ad hoc* and anecdotal pieces of evidence as there is no comprehensive and official intergovernmental information system that describes the nature and the level of the current barriers to international trade.

The purpose of this chapter is to attempt to go at least part of the way towards filling that gap by quantitatively addressing three important questions of relevance to any discussions on reform of the international trading system. First, what quantitative evidence is there of discrimination in the international trading system? Second, what is the nature of the barriers to trade as they exist today? Third, how is the incidence of protection changing over time? In addressing these questions, special attention will be paid to barriers to trade in developed market economy countries which restrict the market access of developing countries.

THE DATA

Unlike national tariff schedules, there are no official and comprehensive national inventories of non-tariff measures affecting world trade. It is therefore not possible to compare the frequency of incidence of formally notified non-tariff measures across countries and sectors at the international level. In an attempt to know more about non-tariff measures on a global basis, the secretariat of UNCTAD constructed an inventory of governmental non-tariff measures having the potential to distort international trade. A nomenclature was devised by UNCTAD for recording and classifying non-tariff measures to trade and information on over 50 countries was collected. All non-tariff measures which were identified were documented with their governmental sources and entered into a computerized data base.[2] This chapter draws on the contents of this inventory for the basic raw material on non-tariff measures.

The information included in the data base could be considered conservative. For example, only official governmental measures which are registered in national legislation have been included; 'unofficial' government action (for instance, unnecessarily demanding health and quarantine standards for imports) and restrictive business practices and other restraints by private corporations (such as market sharing arrangements) are not included. Also, there is a conservative bias to the extent that it is simply not possible to identify all governmental measures which restrict trade. While the inventory contains over 2 000 000 entries, it is simply not possible to identify all governmental trade restrictions in each of the countries.

The information is less conservative, however, in the sense that governmental actions relating to AD and CVDs have been included. While many would argue that these measures are used unnecessarily to restrain trade, many would also argue that they are legitimate measures designed to adjust for unfair trading practices elsewhere. A further point is that while some administrative procedures (for example, import licencing and surveillance) are trade barriers for some products (for instance, footwear in some countries), these same measures are used by other countries for reasons unrelated to import control. In particular, most countries monitor the import of petroleum, even though the intention is not to restrict trade. These administrative measures have been included as it is not possible to ascertain the true intention of governments. To the extent that imported fuels represent the major problem, results have been shown with and without fuel imports.

As with tariffs, non-tariff measures are recorded at the tariff line level of product aggregation. While this information has many uses (for instance, identifying barriers to very specific export items for the purposes of market analysis by traders), the volume of the information is unmanageable for analytical purposes as many tariff schedules contain some thousands of tariff line items with most countries having dozens of trading partners. As with tariffs, it is necessary to summarize the information. In doing this, one of two types of summary statistics is normally employed: (i) a frequency index of the use of the measures, or (ii) a trade coverage ratio. The frequency index indicates the total number of tariff items in any product group subject to NTBs expressed as a percentage of the total number of items in the product category. It has its counterpart in an arithmetic tariff average and as such has similar merits and shortcomings. An advantage is that if a particular measure prohibits trade, it is still recorded in the index. One of the shortcomings is that all tariff line items receive the same weight in the index. The trade coverage ratio is the value of imports in any product group subject to NTBs expressed as a percentage of the total value of imports of the same product group. It has its counterpart in a trade-weighted average tariff; while trade weights are assigned to imported items, those goods for which the non-tariff measure severely restricts trade receive little or no weight. Neither measure is perfect and, in this chapter, the trade-weighted average has been employed.

DISCRIMINATION

It has long been appreciated that tariffs in some major developed countries tend to be biased against manufactured goods in which developing countries are internationally competitive. The bias in the use of non-tariff measures would appear to be even more accentuated. The MFA provides a vivid example of this, as the bilateral quotas negotiated under the Arrangement have restricted imports from over 30 developing countries. No developed countries face quantitative restraints under the MFA. This is despite the fact that developed country exporters – individually and collectively – frequently have a greater share in the markets of the restricting countries.

In fact, only four developing countries (all restrained under the MFA) provide more than 1 per cent of the imports of textile goods to the collective market of the developed country signatories. The USA, on the other hand, supplies over 40 per cent of Canadian imported textile products; the EEC supplies 70 per cent of the Austrian market, 65 per cent of the Swiss market and over 40 per cent of Swedish and Finnish imported textiles. None of this textile trade is quantitatively restrained under the MFA. Sri Lanka supplies 0.22 per cent of Swedish imports of textiles, Peru 0.49 per cent of US imports, and Argentina 0.05 per cent of the EEC market. All are restrained under the MFA.[3]

The question that arises is why has there been this discriminatory treatment of developing country exports. One answer frequently given is that competitive exporters simply serve as a scapegoat for the economic problems of other countries.[4] Apart from the obvious convenience of throwing the blame on some external factor, discriminatory treatment often has the advantage of corresponding to a wide range of public perceptions regarding external competition.

For example, the fact that the exporter is a 'low-cost' supplier is often believed to provide sufficient reason to justify restrictions. This is indeed the case with the MFA.[5] The explicit connection drawn between 'low-cost' production and 'unfair' competition is as old as protection itself and, of course, one of the fallacies long exposed by economic science.

A second important aspect of the public perception is the belief that the exporting countries themselves do not fully adhere to the rules of the game and that restrictions on their exports are therefore more acceptable than they would be in the case of those countries that play by the rules. Supporters of this proposition frequently point to the protectionist barriers erected by the competitive exporting countries themselves in order to shield their home markets in certain products,[6] and the 'unfair' (low) wages paid by the producers.

However, discriminatory treatment clearly has much to do with relative bargaining strengths. The liberalization of trade among the developed countries in the post-war period has taken place largely on the basis of reciprocity between trade partners of roughly equal negotiating and bargaining strength. This type of reciprocity has seldom characterized the relations between the developed and developing countries. Relatively larger countries may perceive the smaller countries as not possessing the means to make an effective threat of retaliation when protectionist measures are erected against them.

The bargaining disadvantage is aggravated when the international rules prescribe bilateral agreements between exporting and importing countries. In the case of the MFA, the link between the multilateral agreement – which is supposed to provide the discipline for the bilateral arrangements – and the bilateral agreements themselves is particularly loose, since the multilateral mechanism established for the purpose of surveillance and ensuring discipline in the conclusion of bilateral agreements contains terms which are vaguely defined, hence enabling them to be interpreted in an almost unilateral fashion.[7] Such bilateral negotiations highlight the differences in the power of the two parties, and the tendency to push trade negotiations into a bilateral framework denies weaker exporting countries the bargaining leverage they could best exercise collectively.

Aside from the bargaining issue, there are indications that discriminatory treatment may be attributable to certain economic reasons as well. These are usually connected with the industry or product characteristics of the goods traded. One argument is that industries in which certain exporters are competing may exhibit intrinsically higher adjustment costs or more visible distributional implications.

This argument is frequently put within the context of inter- versus intra-industry trade. The theory of comparative advantage has traditionally envisaged trade among countries as occurring in different products. From Ricardo's example of trade in cloth and wine down to the factor-endowments theory's espousal of trade in goods with divergent factor intensities, the traditional theory of international trade has concerned itself almost exclusively with trade across industries: that is, interindustry trade. However, for some 25 years, some economists have recognized that the most dynamic segment of world trade in the post-war era was that part of trade which took place within industries.[8]

Among the chief characteristics of intra-industry trade is that it takes place in differentiated products with economies of scale in production and heterogeneous demand features. It characterizes trade primarily among countries at similar levels of development. The distributional implications of intra-industry trade are rarely as blatant as those associated with interindustry trade. Unlike the case of trade based on factor proportions (interindustry exchanges), the gains and losses associated with such trade are not distributed strictly along factor lines. In other words, there is no clear-cut distinction between the losing (scarce) factor and the gaining (abundant) factor.

If with intra-industry trade there are lower adjustment costs and hence less resistance to liberalization than with interindustry trade it would go some way towards explaining the discriminatory treatment of developing countries. It has been shown that trade between developed and developing countries is overwhelmingly interindustry in character.[9] It could well be, then, that imports from developing countries have more visible distributional implications and higher adjustment costs for a number of developed market economy countries.

Table 9.1 has been prepared to provide some quantitative evidence of the extent to which discrimination exists between different country groupings. The table shows the share of trade affected by non-tariff measures for various product groupings in 1986. The importing markets are all major developed market economy countries (as defined in the table), and imports into these markets have been classified according to origin: total imports from the world, from other developed market economy countries, imports from developing countries and imports from the socialist countries of Eastern Europe.

In this table (as elsewhere in this chapter), the trade-weighted average has been used to show the share of trade affected by the non-tariff measure. Correspondingly, the results should be read bearing in mind that a low coverage ratio may mean that the non-tariff measures have a prohibitive effect on some of the items in the product group. In these cases, while only a small share of trade is affected, the value of trade is lower than it would be in the absence of the measures.

NATURE OF INTERVENTION

There is a very considerable body of literature that sets out the preferred options for trade intervention.[10] The unanimous conclusion of this literature is that the policy intervention should be made as close as possible to the source of the distortion which is hampering adjustment. In other words, if the problem is one of inadequate sectoral mobility of labour, the appropriate policy is one of subsidizing the movement of workers across industries and regions. In almost all cases, direct restrictions on trade are far removed from being first-best policies.[11] But theory and practice have diverged significantly on this score. Indeed, it has been argued that from the point of view of what theory would prescribe as the optimal policy, much of the trade intervention has been not first, second- or third-best options, but nth-best options.[12]

An example is provided by subsidies which have often been considered by economic theorists as an optimal form of intervention. They are, however, frequently granted on an *ad hoc* basis with little consideration given to economic efficiency. In fact subsidies, as a first-best measure, are passed over as other protectionist measures project an image of immediate effectiveness. Subsidies designed to increase factor mobility may take a considerable time to have the desired impact on the affected factors of production whereas quantitative import restrictions, by instantly eliminating the symptoms of the problem – that is, by reducing the import-penetration ratio - often appear to have dealt effectively with its sources as well. Moreover, unlike the granting of subsidies, some protectionist measures of a non-tariff type (for example, some administered protection) usually do not require lengthy recourse to legislative processes.[13]

Table 9.1   Import coverage ratios * of non-tariff measures applied by selected developed market economy countries+ (%)

SITC	Product coverage	NTM Coverage in imports from:							
		World		Developed countries		Developing countries		Socialist countries	
		1981	1986	1981	1986	1981	1986	1981	198●
0+1+22 +4	All food items	40.8	42.6	44.7	47.6	32.2	33.1	51.9	52.●
0	Food and live animals	47.1	49.0	56.2	59.1	35.0	36.0	54.0	54.●
22	Oil seeds and nuts	7.5	11.0	2.4	6.9	20.8	19.7	50.3	50.?
4	Animal/vegetable oils	9.1	12.5	7.5	17.9	7.1	7.0	37.0	36.●
2 less (22+27 +28)	Agricultural raw materials	2.8	8.4	2.3	10.2	2.8	3.9	7.2	12.
27+28 +67+68	Ores and metals	12.7	24.7	13.1	29.4	8.6	12.8	26.2	30.●
67	Iron and steel	29.0	64.2	26.8	65.2	24.8	54.6	58.1	68.?
68	Non-ferrous metals	3.8	6.4	1.9	6.0	6.1	6.4	7.9	8.●
3	Fuels	42.4	15.5	57.7	20.5	40.1	12.5	46.6	43.?
5	Chemicals	13.2	12.7	13.8	12.9	11.4	12.6	10.5	13.?
6–8 less (67+68)	Manufactures (not chemicals	18.6	20.5	15.4	17.8	31.3	31.0	41.3	43.●
61	Leather	8.2	13.9	5.5	17.9	9.9	9.9	3.9	8.?
65	Textile yarn and fabrics	37.3	39.6	18.6	21.2	57.6	61.4	74.3	75.●
84	Clothing	67.3	67.4	40.2	38.9	77.1	77.9	74.8	74.●
85	Footwear	71.3	32.5	65.1	24.1	71.0	27.0	81.5	62.●
0–9 less 3	All items (excluding fuels)	19.6	22.7	17.2	21.1	25.3	26.2	30.9	33.?
0–9	All items	27.3	20.3	20.9	21.0	34.7	17.5	38.4	38.

* Ratios have been computed using 1981 import trade weights. Computations have been made at the tariff-line level and results aggregated to relevant product group levels.
+ Austria, Canada, EEC (10), Finland, Japan, New Zealand, Norway, Switzerland and the USA.

Source: UNCTAD Data Base on Trade Measures.

There are a number of important characteristics of the current trade restrictions as they have evolved in recent years. In the past decade there has been both a hardening in commercial policy and greater recourse to bilateral procedures. There has been a proliferation of voluntary restraint arrangements (that is, country-specific quotas). Also, there has been an increasing degree of government involvement in the market; greater responsibility appears to have been taken by some governments in deciding which industries should flourish or survive, and a wide variety of industries now appear to be considered by governments to be in their realm of responsibility.[14]

Furthermore, a characteristic common to many of the recently imposed protection measures is that they have proved difficult to negotiate away within the existing institutional framework established for MTNs. Indeed, it has long been argued that this may be an indication of a changing preference for non-tariff forms of protection. In an increasingly interdependent world, governments may feel the need to compensate for their loss of autonomy in areas such as international trade by taking measures less conducive to international negotiation.[15] Tariffs, the traditional protectionist tool, may not be considered as providing adequate insulation, particularly since, in successive tariff-cutting rounds of negotiations, considerable success has been achieved in reducing MFN tariff rates. This is a practical consideration for those proposing retariffication *en route* to a negotiated reduction of other trade barriers in the Uruguay Round.[16]

The case for retariffication usually rests on the grounds that in purely economic terms, tariffs are preferable to QRs for a number of reasons.[17] In particular, QRs such as OMAs and VER arrangements can introduce greater uncertainty in world trade than do tariffs. Tariff rates are recorded in national schedules, so import prices are known in advance. To the extent that they are applied in an MFN fashion, all countries face the same barriers and can assess their competitive position. Similarly, tariff changes are traditionally negotiated multilaterally, so changes in competitive positions are common knowledge. To the extent that a country participates in a bilateral quota, price certainty is replaced by quantity certainty. Non-participating countries, however, have neither price nor quantity certainty, and the trading arrangements of competitors are not always common knowledge.

Furthermore, QRs may introduce greater price instability into world markets than tariffs. Under certain assumptions, tariffs have their exact counterpart in quantitative restrictions.[18] But while equivalence may exist in a static sense, should the import demand or export supply curve shift, the impact on world price is not the same for the tariff as for the quota. Regardless of whether exports or imports shift, and the direction of the shift, world price fluctuations are greater with the quota than with the tariff. It has therefore been argued that, as countries move to isolate themselves from world price fluctuations by using quantitative controls, they may well exacerbate future world price fluctuations: thereby perhaps increasing the 'case' for further protective measures.[19]

An additional feature of QRs such as VERs and OMAs is that these arrangements encourage firms in the exporting country to cartelize. After a sharing of the export market has taken place, the entry of new firms may be extremely difficult. This may have undesirable implications for the state of competition in the exporting country. Neither does future market growth necessarily offer hope for the entry of new firms, as some export growth for the exporting firms may be a condition of the VER. Thus, because VERs cater to the interests of established firms, they frequently prove to be acceptable to exporters, importers, import-competing firms and even governments wishing to increase autonomy without facing multilateral discipline. It is also worth noting that VERs and OMAs may encourage cartelization in the importing country as well.

However, what is perhaps most important for weaker trading partners is the fact that it may be bargaining power which determines whether a claim for export restraint receives government approval in the importing country or not. It can be argued that government support tends to depend on the political clout of industry leaders and on the importance for the importing country of the exporters concerned. The latter may influence the way in which individual countries fare in securing a share of the import market.

Table 9.2 has been prepared to give some idea of the incidence of VERs and the importing and exporting countries involved. While it is difficult to have comprehensive information on bilateral export restraint arrangements, the GATT secretariat has identified 96 such arrangements operating in the second half of 1986 which are inconsistent with GATT.[20] Among these, 53 protected the markets of the EEC or its individual member states and 32 the US market. All other countries combined accounted for only 11 restraint arrangements. Almost one-third of these arrangements were directed toward developing countries: more than the total restraints facing Japan, the US and the EEC combined (that is, 29 restraint arrangements). Korea, in turn, was found to be the object of almost half of the restraint arrangements directed toward developing countries. There were only four cases where the exports originated in the EEC or the USA.

Table 9.2 Incidence of VERs: importing and exporting countries *

	Importing			
Exporting	*EEC*	*USA*	*Other*	*Total*
Japan	18	5	2	25
EEC+	0	4	0	4
USA	0	0	0	0
Developing countries	11	10	9	30
(of which: Republic of Korea)	5	2	7	14
Centrally planned economies	11	6	0	17
Other	12	7	0	19
Total	52	32	11	95

* As of September 1986.
+ Includes country-level arrangements which apply irrespective of arrangements concluded at the EEC level.

Source: Basic information drawn from GATT (1986); also presented as Table 19.2 in Sampson (1987a).

Another development in recent years has been the growth in so-called 'administered' protection (for example, misused AD and CVD provisions). This constitutes what some international trade lawyers describe as contingent protection or made-to-measure protection; protection which is 'legitimate' providing certain legal or administrative conditions are met.[21]

In the Tokyo Round, in the absence of a comprehensive information base on NTBs, codes of behaviour were negotiated. Some have argued that while the intention of the codes was to discipline the use of non-tariff measures, they have in fact served to define situations in which trade restrictions can be legitimized in terms of GATT. Thus, rather than controlling the spread of non-tariff measures, the codes have given rise to increasing use of administered protection (for instance, misused AD and CVD provisions) which apparently meet the 'political' needs of government.[22]

The idea of made-to-measure protection, however (a term coined by Max Corden almost 20 years ago with respect to the tariff) is certainly not new.[23] There is, however, an important difference between made-to-measure tariff protection as described by Max Corden and the more recent administered protection. Made-to-measure protection relied on the tariff and as such was objective. Administered protection, on the other hand, needs interpretation on the part of government officials and therefore opens the door to what is frequently a high degree of bureaucratic discretion in its application.

A final observation is that for their own reasons, most of the more popular recent forms of trade barriers are such that they are difficult to negotiate away in a multilateral context. In the past, for example, an important characteristic which was often considered to be peculiar to agricultural trade was that trade policies were inextricably linked to domestic policies pertaining to the agricultural sector. The traditional position of the EEC *vis-à-vis* the CAP and the subsidization of EEC farmers has for many years been that the CAP has as its objective the meeting of the special requirements of the Community and its 'principles and machinery cannot be called into question' and are 'not a matter for negotiation'.[24] It would appear that this is no longer peculiar to the agricultural sectors and is evident in many other sectors: motor vehicles, steel, textile products and, now, machine tools and high technology products. As such, trade policy merely accommodates domestic industry policies which are frequently directed at non-economic objectives and the 'principles and machinery cannot be called into question'.[25]

A further consideration which complicates the negotiating process relates to QRs; for technical reasons, QRs are hard to negotiate away. As a practical consideration, it is difficult (if not impossible) to calculate the *ad valorem* equivalence and therefore exchange concessions in traditional multilateral negotiations.[26]

Table 9.3 indicates the relative importance of different forms of non-tariff measures. The importing countries are as in Table 9.1, imports are from all sources, and a trade coverage index has been calculated. A distinction has been made between total non-tariff measures and non-tariff measures net of non-tariff charges, AD and CVD and import surveillance (that is, the 'softer' measures). The share of trade affected by QRs has been shown and, within this, the share covered by OMAs and VERs.[27]

The information in Table 9.3 on total incidence of non-tariff

Table 9.3   Import coverage ratios * of selected non-tariff measures (NTMs), applied by selected developed market economy countries+ (%)

SITC	Product coverage	NTM Coverage							
		All NTMs		Subgroup of NTMs‡		Quantitative restrictions		VERs and OMAs§	
		1981	1986	1981	1986	1981	1986	1981	1986
0+1+22 +4	All food items	40.8	42.6	35.0	35.1	27.3	27.4	0.8	1.8
0	Food and live animals	47.1	49.0	40.2	40.3	30.5	30.7	0.1	1.3
22	Oil seeds and nuts	7.5	11.0	6.8	6.2	6.8	6.2	0.0	0.0
4	Animal/vegetable oils	9.1	12.5	5.0	7.6	4.6	7.3	0.0	0.0
2 less (22+27 +28)	Agricultural raw materials	2.8	8.4	1.8	1.8	1.8	1.8	0.0	0.0
27+28 +67+68	Ores and metals	12.7	24.7	9.0	17.6	4.5	16.8	2.1	14.4
67	Iron and steel	29.0	64.2	21.7	49.7	7.8	47.3	6.6	45.2
68	Non-ferrous metals	3.8	6.4	0.4	0.4	0.4	0.4	0.0	0.0
3	Fuels	42.4	15.5	12.5	12.5	12.5	12.5	0.0	0.0
5	Chemicals	13.2	12.7	8.1	8.6	8.1	7.6	0.0	0.0
6–8 less (67+68)	Manufactures (not chemicals	18.6	20.5	11.7	12.2	11.7	12.2	9.2	9.7
61	Leather	8.2	13.9	0.9	0.9	0.9	0.9	0.0	0.0
65	Textile yarn and fabrics	37.3	39.6	34.1	33.9	34.1	33.9	23.1	23.5
84	Clothing	67.3	67.4	60.0	60.0	60.0	60.0	53.0	54.4
85	Footwear	71.3	32.5	24.1	7.6	24.1	7.6	16.3	0.9
0–9 less 3	All items (excluding fuels)	19.6	22.7	13.8	15.2	12.2	14.4	5.6	7.7
0–9	All items	27.3	20.3	13.8	14.3	12.3	13.8	3.8	5.1

* Ratios have been computed using 1981 import trade weights. Computations have been made at the tariff-line level and results aggregated to relevant product group levels.
+ Austria, Canada, EEC (10), Finland, Japan, New Zealand, Norway, Switzerland and the USA.
‡ All selected NTMs, excluding para-tariff measures, AD and countervailing actions and import surveillance.
§ Including restraint agreements under MFA.

Source: UNCTAD Data Base on Trade Measures.

measures duplicates that in Table 9.1 but has been shown for purposes of comparison. The product categories most severely affected by the subgroup of non-tariff measures are clothing (60 per cent), iron and steel (50 per cent), food and live animals (40 per cent) and textile yarn and fabrics (33.9 per cent). This pattern is also followed if only QRs are considered. As far as VERs and OMAs are concerned, the most severely affected sectors are clothing (54.4 per cent), iron and steel (45.2 per cent) and textile yarn and fabrics (23.5 per cent).

CONCLUSION

Far from the integration of trade practices into a comprehensive set of rules accepted by all governments, the past decade has seen a fragmentation of the trading system, with an ever-increasing number of trade issues being treated outside the framework of GATT, and a large and growing number of GATT rules themselves being circumvented. Commitments by developed countries on standstill and roll-back have not been realized in overall terms and the share of imports covered by non-tariff measures has increased.

The recent developments have been of particular concern to developing countries. Non-tariff measures, particularly VERs and OMAs, have become a principal instrument of protection applied in a discriminatory manner to manufactured exports of current and potential export interest to developing countries. Detailed analyses of tariff and non-tariff measures certainly create doubts about the notion that developing countries as a group receive in practice differential and more favourable treatment. Especially in the 1970s, protectionist measures were directed disproportionately against them. Estimates presented in this chapter reveal that over 30 per cent of developing countries' exports of manufactures to developed countries were subject to non-tariff measures in 1986. The corresponding coverage ratio for trade in manufactures between developed countries was less than 18 per cent.

Moreover, there has been a general growth in the application of trade measures by developed countries. Figures show that trade measures affected 22.7 per cent of non-fuel imports of developed countries in 1986, a 16 per cent increase over the 19.6 per cent coverage ratio in 1981. This is attributable to the maintenance of traditional restrictions on textiles, clothing and food products, and

the rapid increase in new types of restrictions (such as VERs) in
iron and steel and other sectors, including certain high technology
goods.

Notes

1. Until 1985, Professorial Fellow, Centre of Policy Studies, Monash
    University, Australia, and Senior Fellow in Economic Policy
    (Reserve Bank of Australia). While currently Senior Counsellor,
    GATT, the chapter was written while employed by UNCTAD,
    Geneva. Assistance from René Vossenaar of the UNCTAD sec-
    retariat for the preparation of the tables on non-tariff measures is
    gratefully acknowledged. The views expressed in this chapter are
    the sole responsibility of the author.
2. For a description of the non-tariff measures included along with
    other matters concerning the data base, see UNCTAD (1983).
3. The product categories are SITC 65 plus 84. EEC intra-trade
    is included in the value of total trade. See UNCTAD (1984).
4. See Wolf (1979) and Krueger (1978).
5. See the discussion of low cost suppliers in Sampson (1986).
6. For an indication of the nature and extent of barriers to trade
    in developing countries, see UNCTAD (1987).
7. See Sampson (1987b).
8. See Balassa (1963), Grubel and Lloyd (1975) and Caves (1981).
9. See Laird (1981).
10. A relatively recent – and excellent – paper on this subject
    is Corden (1986). Other classic works include Corden (1974),
    Bhagwati and Ramaswami (1963) and Bhagwati, Ramaswami and
    Srinivasan (1969).
11. The exception, of course, is when the distortion exists in trade
    itself. In particular, when a country faces less than a perfectly
    elastic demand for its export, an 'optimum tariff' is called for.
12. See Meier (1978).
13. The Code of Subsidies and Countervailing Duties negotiated
    at the Tokyo Round of MTNs (see GATT, 1979) recognizes
    the need for subsidies to assist in restructuring industry in line
    with changes in trade flows. More generally, it allows signatories
    to use subsidization for certain policy objectives, as long as benefits
    accruing to other signatories are not thereby impaired. However,
    by recognizing broadly that subsidies can be used for a wide range
    of social and economic objectives, the Code fails to distinguish
    explicitly between subsidies designed to facilitate change and those
    that make change more difficult by aggravating structural rigidities.
    Improving the Code is one of the objectives of the Uruguay Round
    and a negotiating group has been established for this purpose.
14. This has, for decades, included sectors such as textiles and clothing

and agriculture. Motor vehicles and steel are among many others
that have been added to the list, but more recently a number of
high technology goods have been added, and, even more recently,
services using high technology.

15. See Lindbeck (1977).
16. For proposals on retariffication, see Hufbauer and Schott (1985),
and with special reference to the MFA, see Wolf (1985).
17. See Murray and Walter (1977).
18. The most rigorous requirements are a single tariff rate which would
have the same effect as an import quota on the volume and value
of imports, on the domestic and foreign price, and on the volume
of domestic output, with the extent of the difference depending on
the elasticities of the curves.
19. A good example is provided by agricultural import quotas made
possible by the use of sliding-scale tariffs. They isolate a country
from world price fluctuations while exacerbating these fluctuations.
See Sampson and Snape (1980).
20. See GATT (1986).
21. See Grey (1986).
22. See Finger, Hall and Nelson (1982).
23. Corden (1967).
24. See Commission of the European Communities (1976).
25. Given the proposal that has been tabled by the European Commission in the Agriculture Committee of GATT (created for the
Uruguay Round), there is tangible evidence that the position of
the Community is changing in this respect.
26. The same is true of minimum import pricing. In fact, given the
domestic demand and supply schedules for a product, a fixed import
set below the domestic market-clearing price (but above the world
market price) has the effect of establishing a quota. Such minimum
import prices have long been applied to many agricultural imports,
and more recently, to steel products.
27. Note that unlike Table 9.2, GATT 'consistent' measures (such
as the MFA restraints) have been included.

References

Balassa, B. (1963) 'European Integration: Problems and Issues', *American
Economic Review, Papers and Proceedings*, May, pp. 175–84.
Bhagwati, J.N. and Ramaswami, V.K. (1963) 'Domestic Distortions, Tariffs
and the Theory of Optimum Subsidy', *Journal of Political Economy*, 71 (1),
pp. 44–50.
Bhagwati, J.N. Ramaswami, V.K. and Srinivasan, T.N. (1969) 'Domestic
Distortions, Tariffs and the Theory of Optimum Subsidy: Some Further
Results', *Journal of Political Economy*, 77 (6), pp. 1005–10.
Caves, R.E. (1981) 'Intra-industry trade and market structure in the
industrial countries', *Oxford Economic Papers*, July, pp. 203–23.

Commission of the European Communities (1976) *Newsletter on the Common Agricultural Policy; Extract from the 1975 Report on the Agricultural Situation in the Community* (Brussels and Luxembourg: EEC).

Corden, W.M. (1967) 'Australian Tariff Policy', *Australian Economic Papers*, December, pp. 131–54.

Corden, W.M. (1974) *Trade Policy and Economic Welfare* (Oxford: Clarendon Press).

Corden, W.M. (1986) 'Policies towards Market Disturbances', in R.H. Snape (ed.), *Issues in World Trade Policy: GATT at the Crossroads* (London: Macmillan).

Finger, J.M., Hall, H.K and Nelson, D.R. (1982) 'The Political Economy of Administered Protection', *American Economic Review*, 72, June, pp. 452–66.

GATT (1979) *Agreement on Interpretation and Application of Article VI of the General Agreement on Tariffs and Trade* (Geneva: GATT).

GATT (1986) *Developments in the International Trading System* (Geneva: GATT), 28 November.

Grey, R. de C. (1986) 'The Decay of the Trade Relations System', in R.H. Snape (ed.), *Issues in World Trade Policy: GATT at the Crossroads* (London: Macmillan).

Grubel, H.G. and Lloyd, P.J. (1975) *Intra-Industry Trade* (London: Macmillan).

Hufbauer, G. and Schott, J. (1985) *Trading for Growth: The Next Round of Trade Negotiations* (Washington, DC: IIE) September.

Krueger, A.D. (1978) 'Effects of Exports from New Industrial Countries on US Industries', in W. Kasper and T.G. Parry (eds), *Growth, Trade and Structural Change in an Open Australian Economy* (Kensington, NSW: Centre for Applied Economic Research, University of New South Wales).

Laird, S. (1981) 'Intra-Industry Trade and the Expansion, Diversification and Integration of the Trade of the Developing Countries', *Trade and Development: An UNCTAD Review*, 3 (Winter), United Nations Publication, Sales No. E.82.II.D.3.

Lindbeck, A. (1977) 'Economic Dependence and Interdependence in the Industrialized World', Seminar Paper No. 83 (Stockholm: Institute for International Economic Studies), June.

Meier, G.M. (1978) 'The Safeguard Negotiations and Developing Countries', in *Trade Policies Toward Developing Countries: The Multilateral Trade Negotiations* (Washington, DC:).

Murray, T. and Walter, I. (1977) 'Quantitative Restrictions, Developing Countries and GATT', *Journal of World Trade Law*, 11 (5), September–October, pp. 391–421.

Sampson, G.P. (1986) 'Market Disturbances and the MFA', in R.H. Snape (ed.) *Issues in World Trade Policy: GATT at the Crossroads* (London: Macmillan).

Sampson, G.P. (1987a) 'Safeguards', in J.M. Finger and A. Olechowski (eds.) *A Handbook on the Multilateral Trade Negotiations* (Washington, DC: World Bank), November.

188   *NTBs Facing Developing Country Exports*

Sampson, G.P. (1987b) 'The Pseudo Economics of the MFA: A Practical Proposal for Reform', *The World Economy*, December, pp. 455–68.

Sampson, G.P. and R.H. Snape (1980) 'Effects of the EEC's Variable Levies', *Journal of Political Economy*, 88 (5), pp. 1026–40.

UNCTAD (1983) *Introductory Note on Methodology Employed and the Problems of Definition*, Report prepared by the UNCTAD Secretariat, TD/B/AC.42/2 (Geneva: UNCTAD).

UNCTAD (1984) *International Trade in Textiles With Special Reference to the Problems Faced by Developing Countries*, Report by the UNCTAD Secretariat, TD/B/C.2/215 (Geneva: UNCTAD).

UNCTAD (1987) *Handbook of Trade Control Measures of Developing Countries* (New York: UN), UNCTAD/ST/ECDC/33.

Wolf, M. (1979) 'Adjustment Policies and Problems in Developed Countries', World Bank Staff Working Paper No. 349 (Washington, DC: World Bank), August.

Wolf, M. (1985) 'How to Unravel the MFA', *The World Economy*, 8 (3), September, pp. 235–47.

10 South-South Trade: Building Block or Bargaining Chip?

Manmohan Agarwal

INTRODUCTION

In this chapter we examine the two usually-mentioned rationales for encouraging SST: namely, to enlarge the size of markets and permit LDCs to take advantage of economies of scale, and to act as a bargaining chip in North–South negotiations. The chapter examines the argument that SST is not in the interest of LDCs as it will be trade diverting and will mainly help the inward-looking LDCs to export their capital-intensive products. Though free trade may be the first-best policy for developing countries (although even this is controversial), the chapter argues that the reality is that given the BOP problems which most LDCs face, they are more likely to try to develop their industries behind protectionist barriers rather than forgo industrialization since export-led industrialization may be difficult because of the developed countries' protectionist policies. In these circumstances, SST may permit some specialization and exploitation of economies of scale to reduce inefficiency. Exploitation of economies of scale is particularly stressed in the newer theories of trade. Furthermore, it is argued in this chapter that the current extent of SST is not optimal since for historical reasons transport, credit and information links are between developing and developed countries. In addition, Northern monopolies often control trade in primary commodities reducing Southern gains from such trade. If SST became more competitive this source of welfare loss would be avoided.

In this chapter we show that there is no reason to suppose that inward-looking countries would benefit from SST and export the products of their inefficient capital-intensive industries as those countries which have been most successful in penetrating markets in developed countries have also been most successful in SST. Furthermore, there is evidence that SST helps development of skill intensive industries and that exporting to LDCs is often a first step in enabling skill-intensive goods to compete in the world market. SST would be efficient in terms of theories of international trade which lay greater stress on economies of scale or product differentiation.

The chapter, however, finds that the actual extent of SST has been influenced much more by market forces such as the growth of demand in different markets, overall trade policies and the state of the international economy than by various preferential trading arrangements among LDCs. SST grew rapidly in the 1970s when economic growth was more rapid in LDCs than in developed countries and as developed countries became more protectionist while LDCs liberalized their trade regimes and relied less on overvalued exchange rates. The debt crisis seems to have resulted in cuts in competitive imports from LDCs and channelling of exports to developed countries to obtain the hard currencies needed for debt servicing, and has resulted in a decline in the share of SST in the exports of LDCs.

The chapter argues that a fundamental constraint to SST has been the unequal growth effects which such trade is alleged to generate, but it also argues that a major problem is the difficulty of judging how much growth and industrialization would have occurred in the absence of a preferential trading arrangement among LDCs. This leads to subjective judgements regarding the effect of regional preferences on growth and it is difficult either to argue against a country that claims it is not gaining enough or to compensate satisfactorily the country which is gaining less. None of the various schemes which have been devised to distribute more equally the growth benefits of regional schemes have satisfactorily resolved the problem. Broader preferential trading arrangements among LDCs have been sought under GATT auspices. An agreement has been reached in the current attempt called the Global System of Trade Preferences (GSTP), but has still to be ratified. The chapter notes that one limitation with regional and more general LDC preferential trading arrangements has been their concentration on tariff cuts, ignoring the role of other trade inhibiting policies such as QRs. The negotiations for the GSTP among LDCs also suffer from this drawback.

Apart from the question of the distribution of gains, successful operation of a preferential trading arrangement requires an administrative machinery to analyse policy choices and recommendations to the governments: recommendations which are recognized to be reasonable and fair. Furthermore, it is necessary that member countries have a broad similarity in their approach to economic issues. Personal compatibility among the political leaders and a senior government figure having responsibility for regional trading issues would also help.

This chapter is pessimistic about the use of SST as a bargaining chip at either the global or sectoral level in North–South negotiations. Imports by LDCs from developed countries are mainly of non-competing capital goods which cannot be supplied by other LDCs. Increased production following larger SST may require greater imports of capital goods from the North and worsen the balance of payments position of LDCs *vis-à-vis* the North.

In a few sectors, such as textiles and steel products, LDCs both export to and import from developed countries and access of developed countries to the markets of LDCs could be made conditional on easier access for exports of LDCs. The chapter concludes that such sectoral bargains may not be feasible. The important exporters are rarely the importers or they import from countries different from those they export to so that they could not directly engage in negotiations. Moreover, it is not clear what incentive the LDCs who would benefit from improved market access could offer the other LDCs to form a negotiating coalition.

THE ROLE OF SST IN ECONOMIC DEVELOPMENT

In this section we examine the role of SST in fostering economic growth by critically examining the debate that has centred around the role of SST in economic development. The proponents of SST argue that SST would contribute to economic development of LDCs by enabling them to exploit the economies of scale which would come about when the size of the market was increased.[1] Against this viewpoint other economists argue that since LDCs produce primary products there is not much scope for trade among them. Preferential trading arrangements among LDCs would just enable them to continue with inefficient import substitution policies. SST, in the view of such economists, would only benefit large inefficient producers of capital-intensive products in which they do not have a comparative advantage.[2] Furthermore, if economies of scale are important such economies can also be reaped through trade with the industrialized countries. We, however, argue in this section that SST can play an important role in the economic development of LDCs which NST cannot.

The traditional analysis of customs unions through the concepts of trade diversion and trade creation has been conducted within the framework of the Heckscher–Ohlin model and does not take account of the newer theories of trade.[3] But even within the Heckscher–Ohlin framework preferential trading arrangements among LDCs can be supported on economic efficiency grounds. Traditional customs union analysis starts from the assumption of given prices and full information and all the other requirements for markets to operate efficiently. But we think that there are significant market impediments to SST based on the historical evolution of these economies. The links of LDCs have generally been with specific metropolitan countries, very often those who initially colonized the LDC. Trade among LDCs has been hindered by the lack of adequate transport facilities, finance, information, and so on. For instance, goods and passengers can often move more conveniently from one LDC to another LDC when the route lies through a developed country.[4] Lack of transport facilities might also explain why trade in many regional schemes is basically bilateral.[5] Standard indivisibility of social overhead capital would justify measures to remove these infrastructural constraints. The minimum scale of such infrastructural requirements may be larger than that which can be profitably utilized immediately so that the private sector would not provide it. The question really is whether the public sector should provide merely the infrastructure even though it may remain relatively underutilized for a while or try to encourage SST so that the infrastructure is more fully used. This is the standard problem of the appropriate rate of provision of overhead capital when there are indivisibilities.

There is another form of significant market failure in NST. Very often monopolies in the North control NST and this reduces Southern gains from such trade. If SST is more competitive LDCs could gain even if SST is relatively inefficient as compared to NST. It is well established that Northern monopolies control trade in many primary commodities, apart from the distortions created by Northern policies regarding trade in agricultural products.[6] But no studies have been carried out to see whether SST occurs under more competitive market conditions.

One's evaluation of SST also depends on the alternative to which one compares it. If LDCs were in a position to follow free trade policies then that might be the first-best choice. But this is controversial. Recent work by Taylor (1986), Pack and Westphal (1986) and others has cast serious doubt on the proposition that free trade, or at least equal effective exchange rates for export and import competing activities is the appropriate policy rule.[7] In our opinion the comparison is not between SST and more liberal overall trade policies. Few developing countries have had such a long history of following an outward-oriented policy as the Pacific Asian countries and their experience with liberalization attempts suggests that in the initial stages the BOP is likely to deteriorate.[8] But what is more significant is that in the current state of the world economy LDCs are finding it extremely difficult to depend on exports to the indus-trialized countries for managing their BOP deficits. BOP problems have persisted despite the substantial increase in recent years in the volume of exports by many LDCs as prices of primary imports have deteriorated and debt servicing burdens have become worse. In these circumstances, these LDCs have turned toward more inward-oriented policies to curtail imports and manage their BOP.[9]

The Indian case seems to suggest that worsening of the BOP position leads to a slowing down of the liberalization process. Indian exports have grown rapidly in 1987–88 while the trade deficit has not appreciably worsened, and this seems to have encouraged the government to liberalize imports further, whereas in the previous few years no significant liberalization occurred. In the current international environment, we think that SST is a halfway house to freer trade.

The question of whether SST is a halfway house to general freer trade is also tied in with the question of whether benefits of economies of scale can be equally well reaped from NST as with SST. Evidence seems to suggest that SST is different from NST. For instance, Lall, Ray and Ghosh (1985) found that exports to LDCs were more skill-intensive than exports to developed countries. They conjectured that there was a learning process involved in SST which was not available in NST. Agarwal (1988a) also found evidence to suggest that there is a learning process in trade. It seems that coun-tries move from intra-regional to extra-regional but intra-LDC trade and then to competing in the world market. Also countries often seem to start by producing simpler products and gradually move up the ladder towards producing more sophisticated products. This was suggested as countries moved from exporting general manufactures to exporting chemicals and then to exporting machinery. Examples also exist at the micro level.[10] A study of Brazil's capital goods exports found that these were first sent to LDCs and then to developed countries. South Korean exports of motor cars were initially destined mainly for markets in developing countries. It is not that NST does not lead to skill formation in LDCs; as described by Lall, Ray and Ghosh (1985):

> S–S trade exploited accumulated skills and learning to a greater extent than S–N trade. However, this does not imply that exporting to the N does not generate skills and capabilities of a different sort within the product categories exported . . . What is likely is that S–S trade builds upon the learning edge of the dynamic comparative advantage of the larger NICs.

Empirical work does not support the contention of Havrylyshyn and Wolf (1988) that SST would benefit mainly the large inward-oriented LDCs and that SST would consist of more capital-intensive products than NST. While Khanna (1983) in his study for the World Bank found that Indian exports to developing countries were more capital intensive than to the developed countries, Lall, Ray and Ghosh (1985) found no significant difference in capital intensity between exports to the North and to the South.[11] Furthermore, Agarwal (1988a) found that those countries which have done well in SST have also been successful in penetrating markets in developed countries. For instance, Brazil, Hong Kong, Korea, Singapore and Taiwan accounted for almost 60 per cent of manufactures exported by LDCs to other LDCs in 1980 and this was an increase from their share of about 40 per cent in 1965. India's share on the other hand declined from about 15 per cent in 1965 to only about 3 per cent in 1980 and India is obviously a large country following inward-oriented policies. A study of the pattern of trade in the Arab Common Market found that most intra-regional trade was accounted for by labour-intensive manufactures such as furniture and fixtures, wearing apparel and footwear.[12]

The newer theories of trade give greater importance to factors such as learning effects and economies of scale. They show that a country which can get a start would gain and obviously the larger market provided by SST would assist in the development of such industries.[13] These theories also suggest the importance of intra-industry trade and that trade occurs among countries with similar consumption tastes, with these being dependent on income levels.[14] This would suggest that there might be considerable scope for intra-industry trade among LDCs and that similarity of production structures is not a bar to efficient trade any longer. Whereas if two developing countries produce and export the same primary commodity, say wheat, there may be little scope for trade among them, this is not necessarily the case if both are producing and exporting textiles or other manufactures. The significant increase in manufacturing activities in LDCs during the past two to three decades has in our opinion laid the foundation for efficient intra-industry trade among LDCs.[15]

In conclusion, we find reason to believe that, because of infrastructure constraints, the existing level of SST is less than optimal. Furthermore, Northern monopolies reduce Southern gains from NST. We also find significant learning effects from SST and do not find that SST is likely to occur in capital-intensive products in which LDCs do not have a comparative advantage. The growth of manufacturing in LDCs increases the scope for intra-industry trade which might further help LDCs to exploit economies of scale. Similarity of production structures does not seem to us to be as great a barrier to SST now as it was earlier when LDCs were more specialized in primary production.

CONSTRAINTS TO SST

Despite the contribution that SST could make to economic development as discussed in the previous section, and despite numerous attempts at regional trading arrangements, limited progress has been made in fostering SST.[16] In the late 1970s only 12 per cent of imports by LDCs of chemicals and 7 per cent of their imports of machinery and transport equipment came from other LDCs. Only in the case of SITC 6 and 8 did collective self-reliance reach as high as 20 per cent.

Trends in SST have been more in response to market forces than to government attempts to foster it. The faster growth of LDCs than of developed countries in the seventies and the increasing openness of LDCs in contrast to the protectionism in the developed world meant that demand grew more rapidly in LDCs. Furthermore, in the 1970s LDCs paid greater attention to export promotion and also generally had more realistic exchange rate policies. The relative collective devaluation by LDCs in relation to the currencies of the developed countries made LDC goods more competitive. In the 1980s SST has tended to decline in importance in contrast to the situation in the 1970s. The BOP problems of many LDCs has led them to export to the developed countries in order to earn hard currencies to service their debt.

As a result of the above–mentioned factors, exports by LDCs as a percentage of world exports increased from about 18 per cent in 1970 to over 27 per cent in 1980, reversing the declining trend of earlier years (see Table 10.1).[17] But by the mid-1980s the share of LDCs in world exports had declined to under 25 per cent. This decline is misleading, however, as it is largely due to the declining importance of petroleum exports. The share of LDCs in exports of agricultural products and, even more importantly, in exports of manufactures increased. The share of LDCs in world exports of manufactures which had increased from 5.3 per cent in 1970 to about 9.7 per cent in 1980 (see Table 10.3) further increased to 13 per cent in 1984. The increase in share was particularly large in SITC 6, 7 and 8. But the share of SST in world exports has been relatively stagnant in the 1980s in contrast to the experience of the previous decade. In the 1970s SST as a percentage of total world exports almost doubled from 3.6 per cent to 7 per cent at which level it has remained in the 1980s (see Table 10.1). This is also true for SST in manufactures which accounts for only 3.9 per cent of world exports of manufactures in 1984 as against 3.5 per cent in

Table 10.1   Share of LDCs in world exports (%)

To	World				LDCs			
From	1955	1960	1970	1980	1955	1960	1970	1980
World					24.4	22.4	18.7	18.8
LDCs	24.2	21.5	17.8	27.4	5.8	4.8	3.6	7.0
Africa	5.2	4.7	3.9	4.5	0.7	0.6	0.4	0.6
Latin America	8.3	6.8	5.4	5.4	1.5	1.2	1.1	1.4
Middle East	3.9	4.0	3.8	10.4	1.0	0.9	0.7	2.6
Asia	6.8	5.9	4.7	6.9	2.6	2.1	1.4	2.2

Table 10.2   Share of LDCs in world agricultural exports (%)

To	World				LDCs			
From	1955	1960	1970	1980	1955	1960	1970	1980
World					20.3	20.4	18.1	22.9
LDCs	40.9	35.7	30.9	29.5	7.6	6.5	5.2	7.9
Africa	9.8	8.9	7.0	5.2	1.0	0.9	0.9	0.7
Latin America	20.2	16.6	16.1	15.2	2.0	1.5	1.7	2.3
Middle East	1.8	1.6	1.5	1.4	0.8	0.6	0.5	2.0
Asia	9.2	8.6	6.0	7.5	3.9	3.5	2.1	2.9

Table 10.3   Share of LDCs in exports of manufactures (%)

To	World				LDCs			
From	1955	1960	1970	1980	1955	1960	1970	1980
World	0.0	0.0	0.0	0.0	32.3	27.9	20.7	25.7
LDCs	4.7	4.2	5.3	9.7	2.4	1.8	1.8	0.5
Africa	0.7	0.6	0.5	0.5	0.2	0.2	0.1	0.1
Latin America	0.7	0.5	1.0	1.9	0.2	0.1	0.4	0.8
Middle East	0.3	0.4	0.2	0.6	0.1	0.1	0.1	0.3
Asia	3.0	2.7	3.6	6.7	1.9	1.3	1.1	0.2

Table 10.4 Share of LDCs in exports of raw materials of agricultural origin (%)

To	World				LDCs			
From	1955	1960	1970	1980	1955	1960	1970	1980
World					12.0	11.5	12.9	17.9
LDCs	40.3	36.2	29.9	26.8	7.7	6.3	6.0	7.6
Africa	8.6	9.2	7.8	4.4	1.2	1.1	1.0	0.5
Latin America	8.9	7.0	6.1	4.4	1.2	0.7	1.5	1.1
Middle East	1.5	1.0	2.3	1.2	0.2	0.2	0.3	0.3
Asia	21.3	19.0	13.8	17.0	5.1	4.3	3.2	5.8

Table 10.5 Share of LDCs in exports of raw materials of industrial origin (%)

To	World				LDCs			
From	1955	1960	1970	1980	1955	1960	1970	1980
World					14.4	13.0	12.0	14.8
LDCs	21.1	17.9	18.0	21.2	1.2	1.1	1.6	3.4
Africa	8.1	6.4	6.0	4.0	0.1	0.3	0.2	0.3
Latin America	9.2	7.9	8.1	9.3	0.3	0.2	0.7	1.3
Middle East	0.3	0.2	0.3	0.9	0.0	0.0	0.1	0.3
Asia	3.5	3.4	3.5	6.9	0.6	0.5	0.7	1.5

1980, whereas the 1970s saw vigorous growth in SST from 1.8 per cent in 1970 (see Table 10.3). The share of LDC imports coming from other LDCs has also been relatively constant in the 1980s except in the case of manufactures. The situation can be illustrated by the experience of trade in category SITC 7. The share of exports by LDCs in total world exports increased from 5.4 per cent in 1980 to 8.7 per cent in 1984 but the share of SST in world exports grew only marginally from 2.5 per cent to 2.7 per cent during this period as most of such exports went to developed countries. However, world exports of SITC 7 items to LDCs declined sharply from 29 per cent of total world exports to 25 per cent so that the share of LDC imports supplied by LDCs increased from about 7 per cent to about 11 per cent.

In this section we now discuss the problems that have led to only a limited realization of the potential for SST despite government attempts to encourage it. We first discuss the political and administrative difficulties in organizing preferential trading arrangements among LDCs and then discuss the economic problems.

Administrative and Political Problems

A strong unbiased administrative system is needed to develop generally acceptable policy options to encourage SST. These policies have to take account of the specific constraints which hinder SST. But strong secretariats have not developed in the case of many regional groupings because of the scarcity of administrative personnel. The importance of a strong secretariat is illustrated by the early experience of the establishment of the CARICOM (Axline, 1979). The secretariat was able to devise schemes which took care of some of the apprehensions of the less developed Windward and Leeward Islands. But a strong secretariat is obviously not sufficient. The secretariat for the Andean Group was very active in preparing various schemes to encourage cooperation among the countries. But because there was no agreement among the countries the schemes were not accepted (Puyana de Palacios, 1982).

This brings us to the political arrangements necessary for preferential trading arrangements to succeed. There has to be frequent political contact among the leaders of the member countries to resolve the issues that arise. The meetings between the leaders of the East African Community were quite successful in resolving many of the issues that arose (Hazelwood, 1975). But the military coup in Uganda led to a breakdown of the process of political consultation and finally the community collapsed.

Not only is it important that there be empathy among the political leaders, but there must also be basic similarity in the economic policies followed. Strong differences of opinion between Tanzania and Kenya about the role of private capital, particularly foreign capital (Hazelwood, 1975), and between Chile and the other members of the Andean group (Puyana de Palacios, 1982) contributed to the ultimate stagnation or breakdown of these schemes.

Apart from the requirement of a strong secretariat and adequate contact at the highest political level it is also important that day-to-day matters relating to the operation of the schemes be adequately tackled. The problem sometimes is that either the minister in charge of regional affairs does not have sufficient power so that decisions cannot be taken at regional meetings, or the minister is too important to spare the time to participate meaningfully in regional meetings.

Economic Constraints to SST

The major economic problem which has stymied attempts to foster SST has been that of a 'fair' distribution of the gains. The problem has been compounded in that the issue is not the distribution of the static gains from the regional trading arrangement but is rather a question of which countries have received the greatest stimulus to growth. The less developed members of the regional trading arrangement feel that the more developed members are gaining more. The problem arises partly because there does not exist an adequate method of calculating the impact of increased trade on growth. In the absence of such a method the slower growing country has the tendency to believe that the entire differential between its growth rate and that of another member country is due to the preferential trading arrangement. For instance, Tanzania felt that it was not gaining as much from the East African Community as was Kenya. But this was an entirely subjective judgement and it is difficult to see what it was based on. Intra-community trade increased in the case of Tanzania. Tanzania started exporting a number of manufactured products such as tyres, iron and steel tubes and pipes, fertilizer, clothing, radio receivers and cotton fabrics (Hazelwood, 1975). Exports of such products which were negligible in 1967 rose to 47 million Tanzanian shillings in 1973. Its trade deficit *vis-à-vis* Kenya was also reduced. While Uganda's exports of a number of agricultural products to the member countries decreased, its exports of more sophisticated manufactures, such as paper products, iron and steel products and tyres, increased (Hazelwood, 1975).

A number of measures have been adopted in the various schemes to give the less well developed members of the grouping a greater share of the benefits. One common measure is to allow the LDCs more time to reduce their tariffs or to allow them to maintain higher tariffs. But this has merely meant that the benefits to the more developed members have been reduced without necessarily increasing the benefits to the less developed who may still not be able to attract any industries. For instance, the experience of the less well developed countries in the Latin American Free Trade Area, CARICOM and the CACM was that delays in implementing tariff cuts hindered the attraction of new industries.

A problem that arises with preferential trading arrangements is that customs revenues are an important source of government revenue for many developing countries particularly the less well developed. For instance, in 1979 customs revenues accounted for about 13 per cent of government revenues for LDCs as a whole; they accounted for over 21 per cent of government revenues in the less developed LDCs.[18] A number of schemes have been devised to ameliorate the fiscal problems of the less well developed members including making explicit payments to the less well developed members to compensate them for the unequal distribution of the gains from the regional trading arrangement. The problem here is to find a basis for making the payments. Since the members are all underdeveloped and short of capital the paying country is unhappy while the receiving country feels that the payment does not compensate for the maldistribution of the gains from trade. The East African Community had an arrangement under which payments were to be made based on trade flows, since it was the trade flows which reflected the benefits. The payments helped in making the scheme acceptable to Tanzania and were adjusted in discussions between the heads of state. One cannot say whether this scheme of payments would have been able to maintain harmony in later years because one of the casualties of the lack of meetings after the coup in Uganda was that no further adjustments could be made. The West African Economic Community also has a provision whereby the less well developed members are partially compensated for their loss of customs revenue through distribution of the general customs revenue of the community, and the rest of these community funds are used for financing discriminatory devices to help the less developed members of the community.[19]

There have also been efforts to resolve the problem of the unequal gains from trade by allocating industries to different countries. This would, it was believed, help in establishing industries in the less well developed members of the regional groupings, an objective which was not achieved either by delayed implementation of tariff cuts or by compensatory transfer payments. But the allocation mechanism has not worked and this failure has slowed down the process of trade liberalization. The allocation scheme has failed mainly because most countries have wanted to establish the same range of industries. For instance, the Andean Group of countries could not reach agreement on the allocation of the different components of the automobile industry. The refusal of Venezuela to accept the regional assignment and its development of the A2 model supplied by Volkswagen resulted in Ecuador abandoning its own attempted collaboration for the model. The more homogeneous the group the more severe is this problem likely to be.[20] Where countries have been at different levels of development, the more advanced countries have not been willing to forsake the possibility of establishing any particular industry. Very often the problem has been aggravated by the existence of the same industry in a number of member countries with no country being willing to tolerate the possibility of elimination of the existing units in the interest of larger group efficiency. But there is no evidence to suggest that freer trade would lead to the elimination of an already established industry. Experience and the growth of intra-industry trade suggest that in such a case a regional trading arrangement is likely to lead to intra-industry specialization.

Reaching agreement on a regional trading arrangement together with an allocation mechanism has not, however, meant the end of difficulties. Allocating an industry to an LDC is not sufficient to lead to the establishment of an industry in a country in the absence of complementary factors, particularly of capital. The experience is important also in pointing to the limited role that trade can play in generating development. Freer trade by itself is not sufficient to generate industrialization. In a number of cases the regional trading arrangement has led to a considerable growth in trade: but the policy instruments for equalizing the benefits from trade have not operated as well.[21] In these circumstances, either SST must be extended to non-manufactures or some mechanism for encouraging industrialization in the LDCs must be devised. The problem with the former is that it might merely lead to a reproduction of the current division of labour between the North and the South among the Southern countries. The problem with the latter is the entire problem of development. In some of the regional schemes such as CARICOM and the East African Community a development bank was set up and part of its charter was to channel a disproportionate part of its fund for investment in the less developed members. But unless the regional scheme succeeds in attracting funds from non-regional members this would merely mean a diversion of scarce investible funds of the more developed members.[22] But international lenders have by and large been reluctant to lend to regional trading schemes.[23] Establishment of joint ventures with partners from different members has not been sufficiently tried for us to comment on its effects though such joint ventures have been considered an important component of regional arrangements such as CARICOM, the Arab Common Market and ASEAN.[24]

Apart from the inability of the preferential trading arrangements to equalize the growth effects of freer trade, the impact on trade among the member countries has been limited. Earlier analysis stressed the lack of complementarity among LDCs because they were mainly exporting the same primary commodities. But we believe that the concentration on cutting tariffs and the neglect of the important NTBs against trade among LDCs was largely responsible for the limited expansion of trade. The concentration on tariff reduction in the GSTP scheme that has been negotiated suggests that even if the agreement is ratified it may lead only to limited trade expansion among the participating LDCs.

In recent years the difficulties facing regional trading schemes have been aggravated by the BOP problems which many LDCs have experienced. BOP problems have often been approached by imposing QRs and in recent years these QRs have been extended to partner countries also. Jamaica and Guyana imposed QRs on imports from other CARICOM members in the mid-1970s with subsequent postponement of implementation or *de facto* cancellation of agreements already reached (Axline, 1979). The BOP problems in many CACM countries meant that imports from member countries were often not paid for, and such arrears constrained further growth of CACM trade even before the security problems became severe (Fuentes, 1988). Non-clearance of balances in the clearing bank arrangement under the Preferential Trade Area scheme in East and South Africa has created problems for intra-regional trade.[25]

BOP problems have also meant that tied aid has become more important for many LDCs in contrast to the earlier situation where, with Euro-dollar loans, the country could import from any source. The effect of tied aid can be greater than merely having to import certain project items from the aid-giving country. For instance, Tanzania started importing from China a number of products which it normally imported from Kenya after the Chinese started building the railway. Between 1969 and 1973 Tanzanian imports from Kenya of dentifrices declined from 3.2m shillings to 0.1m shillings, of toilet soap from 9.2m Shillings to 2.0m Shillings, of detergents from 8.2m Shillings to almost nothing, and of cement from 14.1m shillings to 2.5m shillings. Imports from China of dentifrices, toilet soap detergents and cement grew from negligible amounts in 1969 to 8.6m shillings, 10.1m shillings, 9.3m shillings and 14.2m shillings respectively in 1973 (Hazelwood, 1975). Rice exported by the USA under its PL 480 programme to countries in the CARICOM area has replaced rice exported by Guyana (Fuentes, 1988). Fuentes notes that this was the situation with respect to a number of agricultural commodities imported by the CACM countries.

SST AS A BARGAINING CHIP

The second oft-stated objective in encouraging SST is for it to act as a bargaining chip in global or sectoral North–South negotiations. We examine this possibility in this section and conclude that the prospects for using SST in this way are not very bright.

The possibility of using increased SST as a bargaining counter in global North–South negotiations can be investigated using the trade model developed at UNCTAD. Erzan, Laird and Yeats (1986) found that while increasing SST would lead to faster growth in the Southern countries, it would also lead to a worsening of the trade balance of most LDCs with the developed countries. This occurs because the increased production engendered in the LDCs requires larger investment, and the required capital goods are imported from the industrialized countries as both domestic production of capital goods and the prospects for importing capital goods from other LDCs are limited. As noted above, collective self-reliance among developing countries is the lowest for SITC category 7: namely, machinery and transport equipment. Because of the dependence of LDCs on the developed countries for capital goods imports, SST cannot relax the constraint to growth in many LDCs as the BOP problem has forced them to curtail imports of investment goods.

The other possibility of using SST as a bargaining tool is in sectoral negotiations. For instance, LDCs import textiles as well as export them and access for the textile exports of the developed countries could be made conditional on easier access for the textiles of LDCs in developed country markets. A similar possibility exists in the case of steel. However, when we examined such trade we found that it provided only a limited avenue for such reciprocal bargaining over access.[26] For instance, in SITC category 65 (textile yarn and clothing), the major importers are Hong Kong, Korea, Saudi Arabia, Singapore, the United Arab Emirates and Yugoslavia and the major exporters are Hong Kong, Korea, Singapore and Yugoslavia, although a number of developing countries are affected by the export restraints on textiles. Given the small number of importers and the overlap with the exporters it might seem easy to bargain for access, but part of the problem is that the imports of the major exporters are a relatively small part of world trade so that the major importers may not be willing to bargain. Only Hong Kong among the above exporters is a major importer, accounting for almost 10 per cent of world imports of SITC 65, and Hong Kong already follows a policy of relatively free imports. Furthermore, even in the case of the major exporters, only limited amounts of their imports are supplied by the developed market economies which are limiting their exports. For instance, only a third of Singapore's imports of SITC 65 items come from the developed market economies and the figure for Hong Kong is a quarter. In the case of apparel (SITC 84) the major importers among LDCs are Hong Kong, Singapore and Saudi Arabia, and again the situation seems more conducive to bilateral bargaining. In the case of steel the major exporters are Brazil, Korea and Yugoslavia, and the major importers are India, Iran, Korea, Saudi Arabia, Turkey and Yugoslavia. For negotiations a coalition of the importers would be required and it is not immediately clear what incentive can be given to countries such as India, Iran, Saudi Arabia and Turkey to form a coalition with the exporters. As in the earlier cases the imports of a number of the leading LDCs are small when compared to total world trade in SITC 67 and it is not clear that the countries restricting exports from LDCs can be induced to negotiate.[27]

We conclude from the above analysis that in the current situation we see little prospect of using SST as a bargaining counter in North–South negotiations at either the global or the sectoral level.

Notes

1. The theoretical basis for SST is reviewed in Ventura-Dias (1985).
2. A strong case against SST is made in Havrylyshyn (1988) and in Havrylyshyn and Wolf (1988), in particular.
3. For the traditional analysis of customs unions see, for instance, Lipsey (1960). For an application of the theory to developing countries see Balassa (1974), Dosser and Rivat Andic (1971) and Cooper and Massell (1965).
4. The difficulties of communication are stressed, for instance, on studies on Caribbean integration in Demas (1976) and Axline (1979). The study members themselves experienced the difficulties of travelling from one developing country to another because of the relative infrequency of flights.
5. For instance, most trade among members of the Economic Community of West Africa is among nearby partner countries. See Orimalade and Ubogri (1984).
6. See Helleiner (1976).
7. For an analysis of the distortions generated by exchange control regimes see Bhagwati (1978).
8. See Krueger (1978).
9. For the BOP adjustment measures undertaken by developing countries, the annual reports of any of the international organizations such as the IMF or UNCTAD could be consulted. For an example among the countries studied in this project the severe import compression can be seen in the case of Brazil in Abreu and Fritsch (1988).
10. For Brazil see Carlson (1982). See also Fuentes (1988) for the positive effect of CACM on manufactured exports.
11. Amsden (1980) also found no significant difference in capital intensities.
12. See UN Commission for Western Asia (1985).
13. See Stewart (1983).
14. Linder (1961) first stressed similarity of tastes based on similar income levels. Similarity of trade patterns has given rise to a large literature on intra-industry trade. See Greenaway and Tharakan (1986).
15. There are a large number of preferential trading arrangements among LDCs. Kolisevski and Stare (1984) note that there are some 43 such schemes. A number of studies analyse this experience.

These include El-Agraa (1982) and Vaitsos (1978). For a more recent evaluation see Singer, Hatti and Tandon (1988). For a survey of earlier Latin American experience see Wionczek (1966); for the Caribbean see Demas (1976) and Axline (1979); for CACM see Cline and Delgado (1978) and Fuentes (1988); for the Arab Common Market see UN Commission for Western Asia (1985).

16. The resolutions passed by developing countries expressing their desire to increase economic cooperation among themselves are collected in Office of the Chairman of the Group of 77 (1981, 1985).

17. Agarwal (1988b) contains an analysis of trends in SST up to 1980. Agarwal (1988a) updates the statistical work.

18. See Kolisevski and Stare (1984).

19. See Orimalade and Ubogri (1984).

20. For an attempt to form homogeneous groups of LDCs using component analysis see Owesenkum (1985) and Puyana de Palacios (1985).

21. As already referred to earlier there has been fresh questioning of the effect of liberalization on growth. For a survey of the issues see Agarwal (forthcoming).

22. For an analysis of such schemes see Hazelwood (1975) and Axline (1979).

23. Fuentes (1988), however, notes the confusion that can arise when there are too many different preferential schemes operating.

24. See Axline (1979) for CARICOM, UN Commission for Western Asia (1985) for West Asia and El-Agraa (1982) for ASEAN.

25. See Axline (1979), Fuentes (1988). In conversations officials in East Africa also stressed this aspect.

26. I would like to thank Sitaramani for the statistical work underlying this part of the chapter.

27. See Royer (1985).

References

Abreu, M. de P. and Fritsch, W. (1988) 'Obstacles to Brazilian Export Growth and the Present Multilateral Trade Negotiations', in J. Whalley (ed.) *The Small Among the Big* (London, Canada: CSIER, University of Western Ontario).

Agarwal, M. (1988a) 'Some Recent Developments in South–South Trade', CSIER Working Paper No. 8809C (London, Canada: CSIER, University of Western Ontario).

Agarwal, M. (1988b) 'South–South Trade: Its Role in Development', in Singer, Hatti and Tandon (1988).

Agarwal, M. (forthcoming) 'Trade and Development : A Review of the Issues', in *Essays in Honour of B. Datta*.

Amsden, A. (1980) 'The Industry Characteristics of Intra-Third World

Trade in Manufactures', *Economic Development and Cultural Change*, 29 (1), pp. 1–19.

Axline, W.A. (1979) *Caribbean Integration : The Politics of Integration* (London: Pinter).

Balassa, B. (1974) 'Economic Integration among Developing Countries', World Bank Staff Working Paper No. 186 (Washington, DC: World Bank).

Bhagwati, J. (1978) *Foreign Trade Regimes and Economic Development: Anatomy and Consequences of Exchange Control Regimes* (Cambridge, Mass: Ballinger).

Carlson, J. (ed.) (1982) *South–South Relations in a Changing World Order* (Uppsala: Scandinavian Institute of African Studies).

Cline, W.R. and E. Delgado (eds) (1978) *Economic Integration In Central America* (Washington, DC: Brookings Institution).

Cooper, C.A. and Massell, B.F. (1965) 'Towards a General Theory of Customs Union for Developing Countries', *Journal of Political Economy*, 75, pp. 461–76.

Demas, W.E. (1976) *Essays on Caribbean Integration*, (Mona, Jamaica: University of the West Indies).

Dosser, D.A. and Rivat Andic, S. (1971) *A Theory of Economic Integration among Developing Countries* (London: George Allen & Unwin).

El-Agraa, A.M. (ed.) (1982) *International Economic Integration* (New York: St. Martin's Press).

Erzan, R., Laird, S. and Yeats, A. (1986) 'On the Potential for Expanding South–South Trade through the Extension of Mutual Preferences', UNCTAD Discussion Paper No. 16 (Geneva: UNCTAD).

Fuentes, J. (1988) 'Negotiating Trade Preferences in Central America', in J. Whalley (ed.), *The Small Among the Big* (London, Canada: CSIER, University of Western Ontario).

Greenaway, D. and Tharakan, P.K.M. (eds) (1986) *Imperfect Competition and International Trade* (Brighton: Wheatsheaf).

Havrylyshyn, O. (ed.) (1988) *South–South or South–North Trade: Does the Direction of Developing Country Exports Matter?* (Washington, DC: World Bank).

Havrylyshyn, O. and Wolf, M. (1988) 'What have we Learned about South-South Trade', in O. Hawrylyshyn (1988).

Hazelwood, A. (1975) *Economic Integration : The East African Experience* (London: Heinemann).

Helleiner, G.K. (1976) *A World Divided: The LDCs in the International Economy* Cambridge University Press, Cambridge, UK.

Khanna, A. (1983) 'Testing for directionality of Exports: India's Exports of Manufactures in the 1970s', World Bank Working Paper No. 538 (Washington, DC: World Bank).

Kolisevski, M. and Stare, M. (1984) 'The Global System of Trade Preferences', (Ljubljana: Research Centre for Cooperation with Developing Countries).

Krueger, A.O. (1978) *Foreign Trade Regimes and Economic Development: Liberalization Attempts and Consequences* (Cambridge, Mass: Ballinger).

Lall, S., Ray, A.S. and Ghosh, S. (1985) 'The Determinants and Promotion of South–South Trade in Manufactured Products', paper presented to an UNCTAD seminar on South–South Trade : Obstacles to its Growth, Geneva, 26–9 June.

Linder, S. (1961) *An Essay on Trade and Transformation* (Stockholm: Almqvist and Wicksell).

Lipsey, R. (1960) 'The Theory of Customs Unions: A General Survey', *Economic Journal*, 70, pp. 496–513.

Office of the Chairman of the Group of 77 (1981) *Analytical Compendium of Decisions and Recommendations on ECDC/TCDC adopted at the Global Level, 1976–81* (Ljubljana: Research Centre for Cooperation with Developing Countries).

Office of the Chairman of the Group of 77 (1985) *Economic and Technical Cooperation Among Developing Countries* (Ljubljana: Research Centre for Cooperation with Developing Countries).

Orimalade, A. and Ubogri, R.E. (eds) (1984) *Trade and Development in Economic Community of West African States* (Delhi: Vikas).

Owesenkum, A. (1985) 'The Impact of Economic Differences among Developing Countries on South–South Trade – A Case Study of the Africa Region', paper prepared for an UNCTAD seminar on South–South Trade: Obstacles to its Growth, Geneva, 26–9 June.

Pack, H. and Westphal, L. (1986) 'Industrial Strategy and Technical Change', *Journal of Development Economics*, 22 (1), pp. 87–128.

Puyana de Palacios, A. (1982) *Economic Integration among Unequal Partners: The Case of the Andean Group* (New York: Pergamon).

Puyana de Palacios, A. (1985) 'The Impact of Economic Differences among Developing Countries on South–South Trade – A Case Study of the Latin American Region', paper prepared for an UNCTAD seminar on South–South Trade: Obstacles to its Growth, Geneva, 26–9 June.

Royer, J. (1985) 'South-South Trade in Iron and Steel Goods', paper prepared for an UNCTAD seminar on South–South Trade: Obstacles to its Growth, Geneva, 26–9 June.

Singer, H., Hatti, N. and Tandon, R. (eds) (1988) *Challenges of South–South Cooperation* (New Delhi: Ashish).

Stewart, F. (1983) 'Recent Theories of International Trade: Some Implications for the South', in H. Kierzkowski (ed.), *Monopolistic Competition and International Trade* (Oxford University Press).

Taylor, I. (1986) 'Economic Openness: Problems to Century's End', Working Paper prepared for WIDER, Helsinki, Finland.

UN Commission for Western Asia (1985) *Economic Integration in Western Asia* (London: Pinter).

Vaitsos, C. (1978) 'Crisis in Regional Economic Cooperation (Integration) among Developing Countries: A Survey', *World Development* 6 (6), pp. 719–69.

Ventura-Dias, V. (1985) 'The Theoretical Background for Analysis of South–South Trade', paper presented to an UNCTAD seminar on South–South Trade: Obstacles to its Growth, Geneva, 26–9 June.

Wionczek, M. (1966) *Latin American Economic Integration* (New York: Praeger).

11 The Structure of South–South Trade Preferences in the 1988 GSTP Agreement: Learning to say MFMFN

Robert E. Hudec

INTRODUCTION

In April of 1988, in Belgrade, the G-77 concluded the first stage of a long-term plan for SST preferences called the Global System of Trade Preferences, or GSTP.[1] Forty-six governments signed a trade agreement under which they exchanged preferential tariff concessions on over 1 300 tariff items. The trade impact of the concessions themselves is expected to be quite modest. The structural provisions of the GSTP Agreement, however, have a considerably greater significance.

The legal framework established by trade agreements tends to exert a decisive influence on the nature and effects of whatever trade liberalization is attempted under them. The GSTP Agreement will very likely have this kind of impact on the nature and effect of South–South trade liberalization over the next several decades. Even though its architects continue to insist that it is only a first step, it is the best evidence presently available of what SST liberalization will look like. For the moment, it is the GATT for SST.

This chapter examines the 1988 GSTP Agreement. It begins with a brief description of its evolution, starting with the 1971 GATT Protocol that established the first agreement on South–South tariff preferences. The main body of the chapter then examines the structure of the 1988 GSTP Agreement itself, comparing it to the traditional model of trade agreements represented by GATT. The chapter concludes by summarizing the GSTP Agreement's likely impact on SST liberalization.

Two acknowledgements are required at the outset. First, the author must acknowledge the considerable debt owed to the two UNCTAD studies by Mahmoud Abdel-Bari Hamza: his 1987 *Guidebook for the GSTP*,[2] and his earlier study on the 1971 GATT Protocol.[3] Both works are far and away the most comprehensive studies on their subject. No research in this area can begin without them.

Second, the author should acknowledge at this stage his personal view that GSTP is a bad idea.[4] It is not the purpose of this chapter, however, to argue that conviction. The goal, rather, is merely to perform a lawyer's analysis of how well this particular legal instrument performs the task it sets out to accomplish, in comparison with other trade agreements in the field, and to assess what sort of impact its particular legal characteristics are likely to have on the trade policy behaviour of its signatories. Perfect neutrality is obviously unattainable and, as the bit of whimsy in the title indicates, was not even attempted. The reader will simply have to judge the extent to which the author's views have coloured his legal analysis.

THE EVOLUTION OF GSTP

The ground-breaking for global South–South preferences took place in GATT. The first step was an agreement between India, Yugoslavia and the United Arab Republic, concluded in December 1967, providing for an exchange of tariff preferences between the three signatories.[5] The GATT Contracting Parties granted a waiver for the tripartite agreement[6] and then created a negotiating committee, under the Chairmanship of the Director-General, to conduct negotiations among developing countries generally.[7] After four years, the negotiations produced a trade agreement covering an exchange of tariff preferences between 16 developing countries.[8] The agreement was entitled 'Protocol Relating to Trade Negotiations among Developing Countries'.[9] In November of 1971, the GATT Contracting Parties adopted a decision waiving the MFN obligation of GATT Article I:1 to the extent necessary to permit participating countries to implement the preferences between themselves.[10]

The 1971 GATT Protocol was a very modest beginning. The preferential tariff concessions covered only about 740 tariff positions in total, with a 1972 trade value of about US$ 25 million.[11] The products on which concessions were granted tended to be traditional imports rather than products promising new trade, and the preference rates were often not a significant improvement on the existing MFN rates.[12] The trade agreement itself was similarly modest. It was brief, only six typewritten pages with 22 numbered paragraphs. Its obligations were very limited, focusing almost entirely on requiring governments to observe the concessions. With 13 of the 16 members being GATT contracting parties,[13] participants no doubt assumed that the basic ground rules for trade relations would be provided by the more comprehensive legal obligations of the GATT agreement.

The 1971 Protocol never took root. GATT did give it a more or less permanent legal status in its 1979 Enabling Clause decision, which contained a provision granting permanent legal authority for South–South preferences.[14] But even with its legal authority established, the Protocol lost the political support of the G-77. The definitive rupture occurred at a major meeting held in 1979 to review the Protocol, attended by both Protocol signatories and a large number of other developing countries. The breakdown occurred over the issue of whether non-members of the G-77, especially Israel, would be allowed to participate in South–South agreements. Following a debate on this issue, the G-77 recorded its dissatisfaction and stated that further South–South liberalization would henceforth be considered a matter within its own purview (rather than GATT's).[15]

At this point the action shifted to UNCTAD. The UNCTAD Secretariat had launched a study of South–South preferences a few years earlier with a paper presented to the 1976 UNCTAD IV conference in Nairobi calling for a 'global system of trade preferences.'[16] The proposal involved a worldwide preference system covering not only tariffs but all other trade measures as well. The proposal was developed further in a series of Secretariat papers, ending with a 1981 paper titled 'Outline of Possible Elements for the Initial Phase of the GSTP Negotiations'.[17] Political endorsement of the GSTP project occurred in a series of UNCTAD and G-77 meetings during the same period, ending with a decision by a G-77 ministerial meeting in 1982, in New York, declaring the GSTP negotiations to be open and creating a negotiating committee to manage them.[18]

A three-year lull followed the 1982 New York declaration. Progress was stalled by limitations on UN funding and other services due to the restricted membership of the G-77. These problems were eventually circumvented by creating a separate 'GSTP Project' funded by the UNDP, with UNCTAD as the executing agency. The negotiations were then revived at a G-77 ministerial meeting in New Delhi in July 1985. Following further working meetings, another ministerial meeting was held in Brasilia in May of the following year, and on

20 May 1986, 47 governments signed a Final Act adopting the texts of a GSTP trade agreement and other organic instruments for the negotiations.[19]

The Brasilia negotiating plan rejected the highly controlled negotiating scenario set out in the 1981 Outline drafted by the UNCTAD Secretariat.[20] In its place, it substituted a simpler plan calling for governments to negotiate concessions between themselves, using the typical GATT format of request lists and offer lists. The trade agreement in which the concessions were to be embodied bore a surprisingly close resemblance to the 1971 GATT Protocol.

The first round of GSTP negotiations was limited to preferential tariff concessions alone. It took almost two years. Finally, in April 1988 in Belgrade, 46 governments signed the GSTP trade agreement, together with the accompanying Schedules listing their individual tariff concessions.[21] Concessions on slightly more than 1 300 tariff positions were granted, not a very large number for the almost 50 countries who had negotiated. Statements accompanying the agreement did not claim that these tariff preferences would have any major trade impact, but instead stressed the fact that a difficult first step had at last been taken. The GSTP agreement was now 'up and running', and governments could now proceed, within its framework, to consider negotiations for a fuller and more meaningful set of preferential trade concessions.

As noted at the outset, the 1988 GSTP Agreement has a greater significance than the limited number of concessions actually negotiated at Belgrade. The Agreement establishes a legal framework which will exercise a decisive influence on future SST liberalization. It will influence the kind of commitments that will be made, as well as how effective they will be in determining government behaviour.

The best way to explain the structure of the GSTP Agreement is to compare it to GATT. The GSTP Agreement has some surprising similarities to GATT: similarities where one would have expected to see differences. Some of the major tenets of developing-country trade policy critical of GATT have had to give way to the realities of international negotiations. On the other hand, certain aspects of the GSTP Agreement do differ significantly from the GATT agreement, making it quite likely that, in the end, trade liberalization under GSTP will be quite different from GATT's approach to trade liberalization.

A BRIEF ANALYSIS OF THE GATT AGREEMENT

Setting aside special rules for developing countries, the basic function of the GATT agreement is to provide a legal framework within which governments can bargain with each other over reducing tariffs. GATT places no general ceiling on tariff rates. The process of trade liberalization is accomplished by negotiating individual 'concessions' that reduce and bind tariff rates at agreed levels. The process of negotiation depends on reciprocity. The incentive for governments to agree to lower tariffs is the prospect of valuable commercial opportunities from tariff reductions by other countries.

The dominant purpose of the legal framework created by the GATT trade agreement is to make certain that the other country's tariff reductions result in an effective reduction in barriers to trade. Tariff reductions have no commercial value by themselves. They have value only if (1) other trade barriers are held constant, and (2) no more favourable tariff treatment is given to any third country. Unless these two other conditions are assured, the country granting a tariff reduction can wipe out its commercial value at any time, either by erecting some other kind of trade barrier on the product in question, or by giving a still lower tariff to some third country. The basic function of a trade agreement is to prevent this sort of value-destroying circumvention.

The GATT agreement provides reasonably comprehensive protection against other trade barriers and against discrimination. Subject to many exceptions, the general plan is as follows. First, governments are required to concentrate all protectionist measures at the border (that is, they may use only measures that apply at the time goods enter through customs). Article III of GATT prohibits virtually all protective measures against foreign goods once they leave the customs shed and enter a country's internal commerce.[22]

Second, only one kind of protection is allowed at the border: the tariff (plus some service charges). All other non-tariff restrictions, and especially QRs, are prohibited. The key provision is GATT Article XI:1 which simply says, 'No prohibitions or restrictions other than duties, taxes or other charges . . . shall be instituted or maintained by any contracting party'.

Third, discrimination favouring third parties is prohibited by a MFN obligation which requires that any favour given to any other country must be given, immediately and unconditionally, to every GATT contracting party. The key provisions are Article I:1 for tariffs and, somewhat imperfectly, Article XIII for QRs.

Each of the three principles outlined above is subject to certain exceptions or escapes, but each exception or escape is limited by legal controls which confine it to defined circumstances, and for the most part require compensation.[23]

The use of rules specifically prohibiting various NTBs has turned out to be a particularly effective way of protecting tariff concessions. Rules which prohibit the measure itself are easier to enforce, because they do not depend on proving harmful effects (always a difficult chore in the complex world of international trade transactions). This is especially true for enforcement *ex ante* when governments are considering the measure, for at this time effects are never known.

GATT also sets up a second line of defence to protect the value of tariff concessions. Its legal prohibitions and limitations cover most of the explicit instruments of government trade policy, but many more remote kinds of government action can also impair the value of a tariff concession: for example, a new safety requirement that requires inspection during the manufacturing process by the government's own inspectors. It is impossible to undertake legal obligations prohibiting all such remote government measures, for governments cannot tie their hands in all the many areas where regulation can cause impairment. Instead, GATT deals with these more remote areas by a remedy known as 'non-violation nullification and impairment'. Article XXIII of GATT provides, in part, that if any government measure nullifies or impairs the value of a tariff concession, even a measure that is legally permitted, the injured party has a right to compensation for the lost benefit: either a new concession, or the right to take back one of its own concessions.[24]

The structure of the GATT trade agreement has one other important feature that must be underlined. The main legal obligations which specifically prohibit or limit NTBs and discrimination are obligations that apply to *all* products, not just to products subject to tariff concessions. This protection is really greater than is needed to protect the value of tariff concessions itself. It does, however, serve a very important function in facilitating the long-term process of reducing trade barriers.

Without these legal controls in place, a country would be free to implement and maintain a very wide variety of protective measures on any non-concession product, and in this continually changing situation negotiators would never know the existing level of protection on a product unless they could canvass the entire spectrum of possible measures: a task that is difficult for any government, and beyond the resources of many. If the level and character of existing protection cannot be measured, neither can the value of reducing any particular trade barrier. Unless the level of existing protection is simplified, therefore, governments simply cannot negotiate effectively over reductions in individual trade barriers, because they can never be sure that such concessions are in fact worthwhile trade opportunities. The only type of trade 'liberalization' that is possible in this blindfolded setting is a wholly different sort of commitment, one which involves greater rather than lesser government intervention. Negotiators who cannot rely on the value of reduced trade barriers will seek, instead, the security of quantitative access commitments: either commitments to import specific quantities, or some other kind of market sharing formulas.

The one case in which GATT's general rules have most clearly failed to perform this simplifying function is the exception that proves their value. GATT has utterly failed to regulate non-tariff protection on temperate agricultural products and, as a result, most producing countries have bewildering collections of trade barriers, market controls and production aids that defy calculation. In the Uruguay Round negotiations, governments have undertaken to restore order and to negotiate a reduction in these barriers. It has been generally recognized, however, that effective negotiations will be impossible unless governments can somehow work out some common measure of the protection now in place. Agricultural economists are trying to develop a common unit of measure, called a PSE, for this purpose. (This is what GATT's general rules have already done, for non-agricultural trade, by requiring governments to concentrate all protection in tariffs.) There have already been warnings that, without such a common measure, the agriculture negotiations of the Uruguay Round will be forced to turn to quantitative access commitments.

GATT's general rules involve a large price, of course. They require governments to surrender a substantial number of trade policy instruments, immediately and with respect to all trade. The 1947 GATT agreement diluted this commitment somewhat by allowing governments to retain trade barriers in force on the date of accession, provided that they were in fact required by 'mandatory' legislation. The key governments had relatively few such trade barriers, however, so that the general rules did in fact involve an effective commitment with regard to most products. This large price caused many governments difficulty, to the point where the general rules were almost abandoned in favour of a simple undertaking against nullifying concessions.[25] But in the end the general rules were insisted upon by the key governments, who correctly saw that they were a necessary foundation for any long-term commitment to reduce trade barriers by negotiation.

THE GSTP TRADE AGREEMENT

The form and structure of concessions

The GSTP Agreement provides that participating governments can make any of several different kinds of preferential concessions to other signatories. In addition to concessions on tariff rates, there can be concessions on 'para-tariffs' (mainly surcharges or other added taxes), concessions on 'non-tariff measures' (such as QRs), concessions on 'direct trade measures' which include long-term and middle-term purchase contracts, and concessions on 'sectoral agreements', which appear to involve a sort of multilateral industrial policy. The agreement mentions the possibility of several negotiating formats: product-by-product bilaterals, multilateral across-the-board concessions (for example, a uniform 10 per cent reduction of tariffs by everyone), and sectoral negotiations.[26]

The concessions granted by each GSTP signatory will be listed, as in GATT, in a separate 'schedule of concessions' containing a product-by-product list of the treatment promised by that signatory. The treatment can be described in any way suitable to the concession, and can be qualified in any manner agreeable to the negotiating parties. As in GATT, the schedules of every signatory will be appended to the agreement and become a part thereof.[27]

The GSTP Negotiating Process: Reciprocity Versus Non-reciprocity

One of the most important issues confronted in drafting the GSTP Agreement was the process by which governments would define the trade liberalization measures to be taken. GATT's process of reciprocal bargaining between individual countries was the obvious model, but GATT's 'reciprocity' model had been severely criticized by developing countries in various fora. Developing countries have long argued that both the obligations and the benefits of trade liberalization should be adjusted according to the level of development: namely, that poorer countries should pay less, and receive more. They had applied this so-called 'non-reciprocity' principle to trade liberalization between themselves as well. For example, in Part IV of GATT developing countries had supported a provision, Article XXXVII:4, which states:

> Less-developed contracting parties agree to take appropriate action in implementation of the provisions of Part IV for the benefit of the trade of other less-developed contracting parties, *in so far as such action is consistent with* their individual present and future development, financial and trade needs taking into account past trade developments as well as the trade interests of less-developed contracting parties as a whole. (emphasis added)

Logically applied, the non-reciprocity principle would call for a fundamentally different method of negotiation. Instead of individual countries bargaining with each other, the non-reciprocity principle would require some sort of centrally controlled process in which each country's contributions and benefits could be calibrated according to its ability and its needs. This new method was in fact proposed in the detailed negotiating plan developed by the UNCTAD Secretariat in the early 1980s.[28]

The GSTP Agreement rejected the elaborate management of the UNCTAD Secretariat design in favour of a simpler model which incorporated much of the GATT's reciprocal bargaining process. The Agreement did accept the 'principle' that GSTP must 'benefit equitably all participants, taking into account their respective levels of economic and industrial development, the pattern of their external trade and their trade policies and systems'.[29]

In terms of specific provisions, however, the Agreement made just one major commitment to the non-reciprocity principle: a special status for LDDCs. It permitted LDDCs to accede to the Agreement without having to grant any concessions themselves, and it also called upon other participating governments to grant special, non-reciprocal preferences to LDDCs alone.[30] For all other developing countries, the legal obligations of the GSTP Agreement ignore the non-reciprocity principle totally, and instead call for what appears to be GATT-type reciprocity. The provisions governing accession contain no indication that an individual government's contributions should in any way be dependent on its 'development needs.'[31] Moreover, the GSTP provisions governing subsequent modification or withdrawal of existing concessions go out of their way to ensure that governments will pay full compensation, incorporating large chunks of GATT legal text which state these reciprocity requirements in almost unseemly detail.[32]

The adoption of these GATT-like negotiating methods was a very important decision. How governments go about the process of SST liberalization will obviously have an enormous impact on the sort of trade liberalization they will agree to. Reciprocity-based negotiations will tend to give greater weight to the interests of the larger countries and, inevitably, less weight to objectives of distributive justice.

The decision appears to have been caused by practical considerations rather than a change of fundamental policy. The immediate problem was time. By May 1986, the GSTP negotiations had already been delayed for almost four years, and governments simply could not afford the added delay that would have been involved in trying to follow the elaborate UNCTAD design. In addition, even if time had not been a problem, it would have been extraordinarily difficult to make all the difficult decisions called for under the UNCTAD blueprint in a first-time negotiation, without any previously established institutional machinery to guide the process. The more prudent course was to start with a more limited agreement that would get the institution 'up and running', and then go on from there.

It is by no means clear, however, that the practical problems will disappear with time. It is one thing to elaborate convincing theories of distributive justice in debate, or as reasons for not doing something. It is another to get governments to follow them when they themselves are called upon to reduce trade barriers. The experience of developed countries has been that trade liberalization is a politically difficult process under any circumstances, and that reciprocity, whatever its economic or equitable validity, is essential to maintaining the necessary political support. The odds are that SST liberalization under the GSTP will prove to be no different.

The Basic Legal Protection of Concessions

Unlike GATT's general rules prohibiting various NTBs in all cases, the GSTP Agreement seeks to protect the value of concessions by means of just one general obligation. Article 10 of the GSTP agreement says:

> Subject to terms, conditions or qualifications . . . set out . . . in the schedules . . . , a participant *shall not* nullify or impair these concessions . . . through the application of any charge or measure restricting commerce other than those existing prior thereto, [except for border tax adjustments, service charges, AD or CVDs, BOP restriction, or safeguards measures.] (emphasis added)

GSTP Article 10 applies only with respect to the products on which concessions were granted. It thus leaves governments free to impose whatever new trade barriers they wish on non-concession products. Moreover, since Article 10 applies only with respect to new trade barriers imposed after the concession has been made, it leaves untouched all existing trade barriers affecting the concession product (except those dealt with in the concession, of course). Unlike the GATT exception for existing 'mandatory' barriers, the GSTP excepts all restrictions in force.

The scope of the obligation in Article 10 is even narrower than it looks. First, as will be discussed more fully below, the only types of government measures prohibited by Article 10 are 'any charge or measure restricting commerce', a term which does not seem to cover granting better treatment to third countries. Second, it is doubtful that these words really mean to prohibit 'any' government measure that has a restrictive effect on trade. The internal evidence of the agreement, together with common sense, indicates that the words refer to conventional trade policy measures which actually single out imports for less favourable treatment: the sort of measures prohibited by GATT Articles III and XI.[33]

Like GATT, the GSTP agreement backs up this main protective obligation with a second line of defence. Article 20 of the GSTP Agreement is essentially a copy of the GATT's entire nullification and impairment remedy, including the remedy for 'non-violation' nullification and impairment. Thus measures not in violation of Article 10 which none the less impair the value of concessions will entitle the injured country to compensation.

Articles 10 and 20 of the GSTP Agreement could be described as the absolute minimum legal protection needed to preserve the commercial value of concessions. They allow governments to retain the greatest possible freedom of action consistent with that objective.

In the short run, this minimalist legal structure may be a virtue in getting things moving. Many developing country governments, even many of those who belong to GATT, do not really have any established decision-making capacity for agreeing to reduce trade barriers, because in North–South trade relations they are seldom if ever called upon to do so. To participate in South–South negotiations, such governments will have to begin by developing the capacity to take negotiating decisions: setting up the necessary channels of information and communication, and allocating decision-making responsibility to particular officials. In starting up what will be a controversial process, the smaller the initial commitment, the easier it will be for governments to put the basic machinery in place.

In the long run, however, the GSTP Agreement's minimalist approach will have at least two potentially undesirable consequences. First, the minimalist type of obligation will be harder to enforce. By stating the prohibition in terms of a measure's impairing effect, rather than prohibiting the measure itself, the GSTP Agreement requires proving that the measure has in fact affected trade, which is always a difficult thing to do. An 'effects' standard is particularly ineffective at the time when governments are considering a measure, for at that time the effects are never known.[34]

Second, and considerably more important, by doing very little to prohibit or otherwise limit NTBs, the minimalist approach of the GSTP Agreement does nothing to help negotiators measure existing levels of protection, and thus makes it very difficult to measure the value of reducing any particular trade barrier. This is just the sort of situation that leads negotiators to eschew barrier-reducing concessions, in favour of more secure quantitative access commitments, such as purchase commitments or discriminatory quota shares. The safest way to deal in a market where government controls are unchecked is to ask that export sales be guaranteed by the government itself.

The long-term effects of inducing negotiators to seek such concessions will be to reinforce government controls on trade rather than to remove them. Concessions of this kind create a new interest group – exporters in other countries – that will support continuation of existing controls in order to keep its favoured position in the market.

This tendency is actually inherent in the entire preferential structure of the Agreement. Wherever preferential concessions are granted, the grantees will usually acquire an immediate interest in maintaining the larger restriction itself, be it tariff or quota or government monopoly. Preferential concessions on NTBs – preferential quota shares, preferential purchase agreements and so on – are especially likely to have this effect, for the greater the degree of government intervention, the more secure the commercial advantage offered by preferential treatment.

Control over Escape Clauses: More GATT-like than GATT

Although the GSTP Agreement gives only minimal legal protection against impairment of concessions by other trade measures, it draws a much harder line against escape provisions allowing the concession itself to be withdrawn. The Agreement allows all the normal GATT-type escapes: an 'open-season' escape, an escape when other members leave the agreement, and a safeguards escape.[35] But, as noted earlier, governments taking advantage of such escapes are required to maintain the balance of reciprocity.[36] Although GATT allows developing countries to plead 'development needs' in such cases,[37] no such exceptions are allowed in the GSTP.

A particularly interesting example of the GSTP Agreement's greater rigour toward escape provisions was its BOP escape, Article 14. Like GATT, the GSTP Agreement authorizes governments to restrict trade for BOP reasons, including, in principle, trade in products covered by GSTP concessions. Unlike GATT, however, the GSTP Agreement seeks to preserve the balance of reciprocity in these situations. Article 14 says that governments employing BOP restrictions 'shall endeavor . . . to [preserve], as much as possible, the value of negotiated [GSTP] concessions'. Moreover, governments imposing BOP restrictions are required to consult with trading partners about preserving the 'stability' of concessions and, if the other government is not satisfied, it may refer the matter to the governing Committee of Participants for further 'review' of an unspecified character.

The unusual character of the BOP exception in the GSTP Agreement is due to a common truth about BOP exceptions that is seldom recognized. A trade agreement cannot create meaningful legal obligations unless resort to BOP restrictions is rather severely limited. GATT had an unwritten limitation of this kind in the political commitment of its key developed-country members to attain full 'convertibility' as soon as possible in the post-war years, and to limit subsequent use to very brief periods. To be sure, GATT has no such implicit limitation with regard to developing country BOP restrictions, but GATT has long ago given up the idea of a reciprocal legal relationship with developing countries.

The GSTP Agreement obviously could not afford to accept the GATT's tolerant attitude toward developing country BOP restrictions. The more or less perpetual BOP problems suffered by most developing countries would have created a more or less perpetual escape from obligations, making it pointless to negotiate concessions in the first place, so some way had to be found to prevent BOP restrictions from having that effect. The way around the problem, it seems, was to make sure that the BOP restrictions did not affect GSTP concessions in the first place; in other words, that they be taken out of somebody else's trade.[38]

The GSTP approach to BOP restrictions is a good example of the GSTP's different policy on all these escape provisions. In GATT, developing countries had succeeded in establishing a number of justifications for enlarging escape provisions due to their 'development needs'. Even if these justifications were theoretically valid, developing countries simply could not afford to recognize them in the GSTP Agreement, for to do so would have destroyed the legal integrity of the Agreement.

GSTP Rules on Discrimination

It seems to be characteristic of recent legal instruments designed to assist developing countries that they involve multiple layers of discrimination. Usually, several different groups of countries are involved, each with its own specially favoured or disfavoured status *vis-à-vis* each of the other groups. There are, first, the 'insiders' who participate in the agreement; insiders are usually developing countries, and they are usually divided into at least two groups: LDDCs and others. Then there are the 'outsiders', who usually consist of at least three separate layers: LDDCs, other developing countries, and developed countries. Both insiders and outsiders often have to be subdivided further to take account of those countries who are members of regional groupings (customs unions or free trade areas), for they will usually be entitled to maintain further layers of discrimination between themselves.

An accurate description of developing country trade agreements normally requires a complex legal analysis of which groups or subgroups are entitled to better, equal or worse treatment at the hands of other groups or subgroups. With apologies for the wear and tear on the reader, the following is the author's analysis of the who-can-do-what-to-whom aspects of the GSTP Agreement.

Treatment of Other Insiders: MFFN and MFMFN

The 1988 GSTP Agreement contains two equal treatment provisions. First, Article 9(1) states a starting-point principle for all participants: except for special concessions to LDDCs, all concessions made in the GSTP agreement must be extended to every other participating country. Second, under Article 9(3), any special concession given to one LDDC participant must be given to every other LDDC participant.[39] Both of these equal treatment obligations apply only to a quite narrow group of trade measures, and even this narrow coverage is subject to several exceptions. Before detailing this coverage, however, we must deal with a threshold problem of terminology.

Preferential trade agreements with provisions such as Articles 9(1) and 9(3) create legal relationships involving, simultaneously, equal treatment of insiders and discrimination against outsiders. Writers have a tendency to label the non-discrimination side of this relationship – the equal-treatment-for-insiders obligation – as a species of MFN treatment. Writers then hyphenate the MFN concept, using terms such as GSTP-MFN, or LDDC-MFN, to indicate the discriminatory side of the relationship: that is, the fact that outsiders are not entitled to these benefits. Hyphenated MFN terms are troublesome, for when MFN means both non-discrimination and discrimination, only confusion can result.[40]

The better solution is for writers to reserve the term MFN for describing the sort of broad policy of non-discrimination that it is now generally understood to mean, and to use other more descriptive labels for the narrower sorts of hyphenated equal treatment common to preferential trade agreements. Not surprisingly, the author has a suggestion.

1. Let the obligation of equal treatment for all participants in a preferential trade agreement be called MFFN: that is, each participant in the preferential agreement should be called a 'favoured nation', and the right of equal treatment within that group should be described as being entitled to the same treatment as the Most Favoured Favoured Nation.
2. Let the obligation to treat all specially preferred participants equally (for example, the LDDCs in GSTP) be called MFMFN. That is, each recipient of special preferences should be called a *more* favoured nation,' and the right to equal treatment within that group should be described as being entitled to the same treatment as the Most Favoured More Favoured Nation.
3. And so on.

The particular virtues of this suggested terminology are its precision and its ability to accommodate multiple layers. Given that modern trade policy seems committed to employing progressively more and more discrimination, in more and more layers, writers simply must have a conceptual framework with this much descriptive power if they are to have any hope of keeping up with the world they are trying to describe.

Now, then, back to the GSTP agreement's own MFFN and MFMFN obligations. The first characteristic to be noted is their extremely limited scope. Unlike the GATT's MFN obligations,[41] which apply to *all* trade measures, on *all* trade between contracting parties, the MFFN and MFMFN obligations of the GSTP agreement apply only to the specific promise made in the concession: that is, the specific treatment promised for the specific product in question. The MFFN and MFMFN provisions do not require the removal of any other existing discrimination, and neither do they even prohibit new discrimination, though new discrimination on a concession product would probably give rise to a claim of nullification and impairment.[42]

The MFFN and MFMFN obligations are narrowed still further by other exceptions stated in Articles 9(2) and 9(3). Those sections provide that governments are not required to give either MFFN or MFMFN treatment on two types of concessions: so-called purchase agreements (which, one supposes, must necessarily be limited to certain buyers and sellers), and so-called sectoral agreements (which probably must also involve specific production arrangements between specific industries). The exception for these two types of concessions may be quite significant if it is true, as was suggested earlier, that

GSTP negotiators are likely to concentrate negotiating efforts on obtaining quantitative access commitments of this kind.

Closely read, the agreement would seem to require MFFN and MFMFN treatment for preferential concessions on quotas and other NTBs.[43] This is easier said than done, however. Quantitative controls are inherently discriminatory, and efforts to negotiate improvements in quota access (as opposed to dismantling them) inevitably accentuate these tendencies. The first problem is that there is no clear definition of what equal treatment means in the case of a QR.[44] To give GSTP participants equal treatment under a preferential quota, one would have to choose among several possible approaches, none of which is wholly satisfactory. One would be a first-come-first-served quota open only to GSTP participants: that is, a quota which would tend to favour more sophisticated exporters who can manage and finance the necessary timing and warehousing. Another kind of equality might be to auction licences limited to GSTP suppliers, a method which would tend to favour the low-price producers. Another would be to distribute GSTP-only licences to importers, a method which might place a premium on existing business relationships. Finally, a government employing country-specific quotas might simply offer a uniform percentage increase in the country quotas of GSTP members.

Even assuming some agreement on what equal treatment means in this context, there will be tremendous pressures to circumvent it. A government seeking to increase trade in a product under quota controls will almost always ask for an increase in the amount its own exporters are permitted to sell. The demanding government will usually not care how the other government meets this request. It will not object if the granting country follows the path of least resistance, meeting the request by reducing the share of other countries who have less bargaining leverage. Indeed, the demanding country will usually *prefer* that solution, for it will be easier for its own exporters to sell in the controlled market if imports from other suppliers are being reduced, or at least held constant.

In sum, it appears that a fair amount of discrimination between insiders will be permitted, MFFN and MFMFN obligations notwithstanding. And, once again, the long-term consequences of granting concessions on this basis will be to reinforce, rather than remove, the underlying trade controls. That is, wherever the GSTP agreement allows discriminatory concessions, it will be reinforcing the practice of discrimination itself, for it will be creating another interest group who would wish to maintain a commercial advantage based on that discrimination.

Treatment of Outsiders: The Legal Definition of Preferences

Preferences are not preferences unless they exclude some competitors. The purpose of the GSTP Agreement is explicitly to create preferences. One would think, therefore, that it must have some rule excluding outsiders. This is a novel legal concept, however, having no precedent in the GATT model of a trade agreement. Trying to express that idea in legal text apparently presented some quite tricky, even touchy, issues.

No provision of the GSTP agreement actually requires the exclusion of anyone. The draftsmen may have thought they were saying this when they said, in the first two 'Principles' of Article 3, '(a) The GSTP shall be reserved for the exclusive participation of developing countries members of the Group of 77; (b) The benefits of the GSTP shall accrue to the developing countries members of the Group of 77 who are participants'. In legal terms, however, neither of these provisions does the trick. The issue is not whether outsiders can be given membership in GSTP, or whether outsiders are entitled to the 'benefits' of the GSTP agreement. The issue is simply whether a GSTP participant can, if it wants to, give an outsider the same (or better) treatment than is provided for in its GSTP concessions. The only way to prohibit this is to say, in plain words, that participating governments *shall not* grant equal (or better) treatment to outsiders. This is never said.[45]

Looking at the issues involved in drafting such a provision, several problems emerge. First, one must identify which outsiders are off limits. Reading between the lines, one sees two groups of outsiders at issue here. The first are those G-77 members who have not yet (and may never) become participants in the GSTP. The policy of the GSTP is to encourage such countries to become members, but there has been a decision not to extend GSTP benefits to them until they negotiate accession. The situation with regard to these G-77 non-participants is arguably analogous to the situation GATT has faced from its inception. GATT also seeks to induce non-members to negotiate admission, but individual GATT contracting parties have for years extended GATT concessions to various non-members who have not bargained. GATT has tolerated this much weakening of the inducement to negotiate and so, most likely, would the GSTP participants. If there is ever a definition of preferences excluding outsiders, therefore, it would most likely have to exclude this more favoured class of outsiders.

The other group of outsiders are those countries who are not members of G-77, and for whom a permanent denial of GSTP benefits is pretty clearly wanted. As to these countries, the next issue is to decide just how much bad treatment will be required. The issue would have to be approached with caution. It would be extremely difficult, both legally and politically, to outlaw MFN reductions in tariffs (which impair the value of tariff preferences), or other GATT-consistent elimination of NTBs (which obviously impairs the value of NTB preferences). Paragraph 3(b) of the Enabling Clause expressly provides that the preferential treatment it authorizes 'shall not constitute an impediment to the reduction or elimination of tariffs and other restrictions to trade on a most-favoured-nation basis'.[46] They would no doubt take the same position with regard to NTB liberalization. But, if the GSTP Agreement allows participants to grant this rather broad kind of benefit to outsiders, on what ground will it prohibit more selective benefits, which would be less of an 'impairment'? The political crossfire on this issue may be one reason why the GSTP's drafters did not attempt a legal definition of preferences, and why they will probably continue to avoid a definition in the future.

Surprisingly, not only does the GSTP Agreement fail to prohibit equal treatment of outsiders, but it almost completely fails to prohibit *better* treatment of outsiders as well. This is a major failing of the Agreement. It will be remembered that one of the major threats to the value of a concession is the possibility that better treatment will be granted to some other country. GATT's legal protection of concessions meets this problem by establishing a broad MFN obligation which prevents contracting parties from ever granting more favourable treatment to outsiders. The GSTP legal structure has a serious gap here.

The only provisions in the GSTP agreement which could apply to more favourable treatment of third countries are (i) the Agreement's very general legal obligation prohibiting measures that impair concessions (Article 10), and (ii) its back-up provision establishing the non-violation nullification and impairment remedy requiring compensation for legal measures that impair concessions (Article 20). The prohibition of Article 10, however, is worded in a limiting manner that makes it inapplicable to such discrimination.

It says that a participating country 'shall not impair or nullify these concessions . . . through the application of any charge or measure restricting commerce'. It would strain this language to say that granting a lower tariff rate, or a larger quota, to a third country is a 'charge or measure restricting commerce'.

Thus the only provision that could possibly cover third-country discrimination would be the non-violation remedy of Article 20.[47] Governments would be entitled to compensation if they could show that such discrimination had impaired the value of a concession, even though the discrimination itself violated no GSTP obligations. (Note, incidentally, that even this remedy applies only to concession products; the GSTP agreement gives no remedy at all for discriminatory favours to outsiders on non-concession products.)

The reasons for this rather timid stand on impairment-by-discrimination are not known. In all probability, there were simply too many commercial arrangements involving some discriminatory relationship with outsiders. These no doubt included trade involving centrally planned economies, trade involving other forms of government-directed commerce and, above all, trade with partners in regional integration agreements. As the following section will explain, concerns about outsider discrimination become almost academic once the wholesale exception for discrimination in favour of regional partners is considered.

Treatment of partners in regional agreements

Article 18 of the 1988 GSTP Agreement contains an exception which expresses almost total deference to regional groupings involving developing countries. GSTP participants have no right to enjoy the benefits of regional preferences, including regional preferences made at any future time and neither, it would seem, do they even have any right to complain if such discrimination impairs existing concessions.[48]

The exception for regional groupings is exceptionally broad. There is no legal definition of 'grouping'. Presumably, any multilateral institution claiming to have an integrationist purpose would qualify, and any set of *ad hoc* regional preferences embraced by such an institution would be exempt from GSTP.[49] Particularly noteworthy in this regard is the fact that the exception extends to any and all future agreements.

Obviously, the government attitudes favouring the preservation of regional agreements are very strong. The reasons are political in part, for many developing country political leaders have invested considerable effort and prestige in these regional groupings. But there are also economic policy reasons. Apart from the limited success of the 1971 GATT Protocol, the only proven engines of SST liberalization thus far have been these regional agreements. The extreme deference to these agreements expresses an unwillingness to jeopardize these gains until the GSTP project proves itself capable of something better.

The exception for regional groupings is not the only gap in the GSTP Agreement's protection against discrimination, but it is legally the widest and economically the most significant. Discrimination in favour of regional partners is a well established trade practice. The absence of any limits on this discrimination is thus a greater threat to the value of concessions than the other gaps. It particularly threatens the value of tariff or para-tariff concessions, which can easily be undercut at any time by a more favourable preference given to a regional partner. In the end, the exception for regional groupings could well be yet another aspect of the GSTP Agreement that will influence governments to concentrate their negotiating efforts on obtaining quantitative access rights.

CONCLUDING OBSERVATIONS

One must begin by stressing once more that the 1988 GSTP Agreement is only a first stage, and that its generally minimalist character can be justified, at least in the short term, by the twin needs of speed and broad acceptability.

It is particularly important, in this regard, to recognize the special problem that SST agreements must face in building the proper decision-making capacities in participating governments. GATT has not provided very good training for its developing country members in the practice of trade negotiations, particularly in those aspects of negotiation which take place in national capitals. Governments outside the GATT have even less experience. This means that a truly global South–South agreement must be built slowly, beginning with the creation of the necessary decision-making capacity in capitals. The easier the first steps the better. This principle may even extend to a first round of concessions that is largely symbolic: a fair characterization, it would seem, of the Belgrade preferences.

All the same, it is not too early to begin thinking about the shape of the legal relationship one wants eventually to emerge in such an agreement. Analysing the long-term consequences of a minimalist trade agreement like the GSTP Agreement, in comparison to a fuller GATT-type agreement, tends to illuminate the choices.

Most of the long-term consequences of the minimalist approach can be summarized under a single principle: the more freedom governments have to employ trade controls, the greater the likelihood that trade negotiations will beget still more controls rather than fewer. Negotiators who must negotiate in a world where every kind of trade control is permitted will end up looking for quantitative concessions. Negotiators threatened by weak legal protection of concessions, and especially by the shadow of regional preferences, will be even more likely to insist on hard, firm quantitative commitments. And once government export policies begin to depend on such access commitments, the network of government trade controls will become even more entrenched. This is not to say that a programme of expanding trade is not possible under these conditions; it is just to say that it is a one-way street, toward progressively more comprehensive trade controls.

The analysis in this chapter suggests that, to avoid this one-way street, one needs a trade agreement which contains a certain critical mass of legal restraints on government trade policy. One needs enough legal restraints so that negotiators can assess the market opportunities created by reducing a particular barrier, and enough to make governments comfortable in relying on the value of such opportunities. It may not be necessary to copy the GATT code of behaviour as such, but it will be necessary to work toward a network of obligations that is as comprehensive and as stable, whatever the level of protection it accepts to start with.

Among developing countries in the late twentieth century, it will obviously be difficult to obtain this kind of critical mass. Giving up the existing degree of freedom in trade policy matters would be a major change for most governments. As difficult as that may be, however, the 1988 GSTP agreement contains signs that at least some change is possible. It is significant that the drafters of the GSTP agreement were able to reject, or at least rearrange, some principles of developing country trade policy that would have got in the way of a minimally effective agreement. It is significant that the non-reciprocity principle was put on a short leash. It is significant that the drafters at least began to rethink the inevitability of crippling

BOP restrictions. If it was possible to make these small changes in the policy status quo for the sake of an effective SST agreement, it should be possible to make others.

Notes

1. The final text of the 1988 GSTP Agreement is published in an un-dated GSTP document titled 'Ministerial Meeting of the Negotiating Committee of the Global System of Trade Preferences, Belgrade, 6–14 April 1988' and styled GSTP/MM/BELGRADE/3 (GE.88-50813). The 1988 text differs only slightly from the text negotiated at Brasilia in May 1986, which is published in two other undated GSTP documents: GSTP/MM/Brasilia, and GSTP/NC/7. For another copy of the 1986 texts, accompanied by a detailed and quite lucid explanation of its provisions, see Hamza (1987).
2. The formal title is 'Guidebook for the GSTP: The Global System of Trade Preferences Among Developing Countries – Origin, Dimensions, Negotiations and Prospects'. The study was made as part of the GSTP Project which is managing the GSTP negotiations, and which operates under the aegis of UNCTAD. The study carries an UNCTAD caption and is listed as document GSTP/NC/TP/2 (June, 1987). Its publication number is GE.87-51064.
3. 'Review of the Preferential Arrangements Established under the GATT Protocol Relating to Trade Negotiations among Developing Countries', UN Doc. TD/B/C.7/49 (27 October 1981).
4. The author's objections to the policy of GSTP are stated in Hudec (1987) pp. 210–15 and 228.
5. The agreement is reprinted in GATT Doc. L/2950/Add.1 (4 March 1968).
6. See GATT, Basic Instruments and Selected Documents (BISD), 16th Supp. (1969) p. 17.
7. See Hamza (1981) pp. 2–8.
8. Thirteen were GATT contracting parties: Brazil, Chile, Egypt (replacing the United Arab Republic), Greece, India, Israel, Republic of Korea, Pakistan, Peru, Spain, Turkey, Uganda and Yugoslavia. Mexico, the Philippines, and Tunisia were not GATT contracting parties at the beginning, but became contracting parties subsequently. Subsequent additions to membership were Bangladesh, Paraguay and Romania. Greece and, later, Spain withdrew upon their accession to the EEC.
9. The main text of the Protocol, together with its annex on rules of origin, is published in GATT, BISD, 18th Supp. (1972) pp. 11–18. The full text, including individual country schedules, is published in a separate, unnumbered and undated GATT pamphlet entitled 'Protocol Relating to Trade Negotiations Among Developing Countries.'

10. GATT, BISD, 18th Supp. (1972), p. 18.
11. See Hamza (1981) pp. 27-31, and Annex, p 2.
12. See Langhammer (1980). For a similar analysis, see Hamza (1981) pp. 26–33.
13. See note 8.
14. The Enabling Clause is just one part of a decision known as 'Differential and More Favorable Treatment, Reciprocity and Fuller Participation of Developing Countries'. The decision is printed in GATT, BISD, 26th Supp. (1980), pp. 203–5. It also appears in a new GATT publication titled 'The Texts of the Tokyo Round Agreements', GATT Sales No: GATT/1986-5, pp. 191–3. The key text on South–South preferences is paragraph 2(c) which provides that, notwithstanding Article I, governments may establish:

> (c) regional or global arrangements entered into amongst less-developed contracting parties for the mutual reduction or elimination of tariffs and, in accordance with criteria or conditions which may be prescribed by the Contracting Parties, for the mutual reduction or elimination of non-tariff measures, on products imported from one another.

15. The debate is described by Hamza (1981) pp. 23–4, citing GATT Docs. Spec (79) 28 (9 November 1979) and LDC/1 (21 December 1979). Hamza notes that, following the rupture, the title of the meeting was changed from 'Trade Negotiations among Developing Countries' to '*Ad hoc* Consultations among Countries Members of the Group of 77 and Others.'
16. UN Docs TD/192 and TD/192/Supp.2 (1976).
17. UN Doc. TD/B/C.7/47 (3 June 1981). Earlier chapters included TD/B/C.7/35 (10 October 1979) and -35/Add.1 (9 November, 1979: S&D treatment of LDDCs); see also TD/B/C.7/42 (22 July 1980: survey of issues). For a general account of these proposals and their development, see Ramcharan (1984) pp. 191-215.
18. 'Ministerial Declaration on the Global System of Trade Preferences among Developing Countries, adopted by the Ministers of Foreign Affairs of the Group of 77 on 8 October 1982', reproduced in UN Doc. A/37/544 (14 October 1982), Annexe II. For a complete account of the development of the political consensus supporting the GSTP negotiations, see Hamza (1987) pp. 6–13 and 27–31. See also *South–South Economic Cooperation: Problems and Prospects* (1987).
19. The text of the Brasilia documents are contained as an annex to Hamza (1987). These are also published as an undated document in a separate 'GSTP' series: GSTP/MM/BRASILIA, GSTP/NC/7.
20. For a description of the negotiating plan, see Ramcharan (1984).
21. See UNCTAD Press Release TAD/INF/1940 (14 April 1988). All but two of the 46 signatures were contingent on formal ratification. Two other governments had also negotiated concessions and indicated their intention to sign the agreement at a later date during the ratification process.

22.   The key provisions of Article III are paragraph 2 which requires national treatment in internal taxes, and paragraph 4 which requires national treatment in all other laws, rules and regulations. 'National treatment' means being treated no less favourably than goods of national origin: in short, no protection at all.

23.   For example, GATT Article IV excepts cinema 'screen quotas' from the prohibition against internal protective measures, but with four paragraphs of conditions and requirements. The prohibition against QRs is subject to several exceptions: Article XI:2(c) on agricultural price support programmes, Articles XII and XVIII-B on balance of payments restrictions, Article XIX on safeguard measures, and Article XXI on national security measures. All but Article XXI are subject to detailed conditions and procedures. Finally, the MFN obligation of Articles I and XIII also has limited exceptions: for example, the exemption for colonial preferences in Article I itself, and the complex exception for certain kinds of 'trade-creating' discrimination in Article XIV.

24.   The non-violation nullification and impairment provision is GATT Article XXIII:1(b).

25.   Initially, the GATT agreement was supposed to be nothing more than a 'provisional' trade agreement, quickly put together in the midst of the ITO negotiations to supply a legal framework for an early round of tariff negotiations that could not wait. Because of GATT's provisional character, a majority of participating governments supported a Norwegian proposal, UN Doc E/PC/W/272 (11 August 1947), that GATT contain only such obligations as were necessary to support the tariff concessions. As put most succinctly by the delegate of Australia:

> Mr. Chairman, I do not believe it is necessary to have anything in this agreement beyond, first of all, [an] undertaking to grant to the countries concerned the concessions embodied in the Schedules; secondly, an undertaking not to nullify or impair those concessions by indirect means; thirdly, an undertaking to listen to a complaint and consult if any other contracting country thinks that you have nullified or impaired a concession. (UN Doc. E/PC/T/TAC/PV/5 (meeting of 27 August 1947), p. 46).

The USA and a few other leading countries insisted on adopting the general trade policy rules as well, as part of what they expected in return for their own tariff concessions. The minority prevailed.

26.   The subjects and methods of negotiations are described in Articles 4 and 6 of the GSTP agreement, respectively.

27.   Schedules of concessions are provided for in Article 5.

28.   See note 17.

29.   GSTP Agreement, Article 3(c).

30.   Article 17 of the GSTP agreement contains the full set of special LDDC provisions. See also Article 9.

31.   Article 28 of the GSTP agreement on accession of members makes

no mention of 'development needs' or any other limitation on the need to negotiate concessions.

32. For example, Article 11 of the GSTP Agreement contains a somewhat garbled version of GATT Article XXVIII, which allows participating governments to withdraw existing concessions but requires that the balance of reciprocity must always be maintained: preferably with new concessions but, if not, with counter-withdrawals by other governments. In addition, Article 12 copies GATT Article XXVII, which provides that other participants may withdraw any concession initially negotiated with countries who later withdraw from the agreement. The GSTP Agreement also has a safeguards provision, Article 13, which is borrowed directly from GATT Article XIX, and which thus includes the GATT's requirement of reciprocity-protecting compensation whenever safeguard measures affect concession-products.

33. The most persuasive internal evidence is that Article 20 of the GSTP Agreement restates GATT's 'non-violation nullification and impairment' remedy, a remedy that would have been redundant if Article 10 had prohibited every nullifying measure.

34. The GATT's most notorious 'effects' test is the 'equitable share' rule of Article XVI:3, prohibiting countries from employing export subsidies on primary products which take more than an equitable share of the world market. It has been notoriously unsuccessful in regulating export subsidies.

35. GSTP Articles 11, 12 and 13 respectively.

36. See note 32 and accompanying text.

37. See the second paragraph of GATT Ad Article XXXVI:8, which applies the non-reciprocity principle to the compensation obligation under these and other GATT escape provisions.

38. One other way of dealing with the corrosive effect of BOP restrictions would be to adopt stricter substantive criteria governing when BOP restrictions can be employed. In this regard, the text of GSTP Article 14 contains some interesting signals. Although Article 14 recognizes the right to use BOP restrictions, it never once mentions the liberal criteria of GATT Article XVIII-B. The only legal text actually permitting BOP restrictions says: 'If a participant faces serious economic problems during the implementation of the GSTP, such participant shall be able to take measures to meet serious balance-of-payments difficulties.' Later on, the text of Article 14 makes reference to one of two criteria found in Article XVIII-B, but only the narrow one ('serious decline in monetary reserves'). No mention is made of the other, open-ended, XVIII-B criterion which permits a developing country to employ BOP restrictions whenever reserves are not 'adequate for implementation of its programme of economic development'. One has to wonder whether this is just hurried drafting, or an effort to begin writing different criteria for BOP restrictions in SST agreements.

39. Not to be technical about it, but it should be noted that nothing in the GSTP Agreement *prevents* a grantor country from extending a

    special LDDC concession to other non-LDDCs as well except that, if it does, Article 9(1) will at that point require that the concession be extended to all other non-LDDCs as well because the concession will no longer be an LDDC-only concession covered by the Article 9(3) exception to Article 9(1).

40.   It is true, of course, that the narrower GSTP-type discrimination is actually closer to the original meaning of the MFN concept: membership in a privileged few. But the usage of the past century or so has been to the contrary. For an analysis tracing the MFN clause back to these early roots, consult Nolde (1932).

41.   The two main GATT obligations are (i) Article I:1, which applies to duties and charges at the border and to every kind of internal measure covered by Article III, and (ii) Article XIII, which applies to QRs and other non-tariff restrictions. The obligations of both Articles apply to all trade, unbound as well as bound products.

42.   As discussed below, the Article 10 obligation prohibiting impairment does not apply to discriminatory measures, so there would be no legal prohibition against introducing other kinds of discrimination on the concession product. But there would be a non-violation nullification and impairment remedy in such a case. See text accompanying note 47.

43.   The only question in this regard is a term in Article 9(2) stating that the MFFN obligation also does not apply to 'agreement on non-tariff concessions'. This language is most likely a term of art referring to code-type 'agreements' containing general rules for certain kinds of NTBs, similar to the GATT Subsidies Code. Interestingly, this exception seems to put the GSTP Agreement in the same camp as GATT in using a 'conditional MFN' approach to such codes.

44.   For a more extended treatment of this part of the problem, see Hudec (forthcoming).

45.   The one legal restraint on granting similar treatment to developed country outsiders may be GATT. The Enabling Clause authority for South–South preferences (see note 14) extends only to preferential treatment of other developing countries. Extending the preferential treatment to selected developed countries as well is not permitted. Of course, the GATT remedy for that violation would be to require extending this favoured treatment to all other developing contracting parties.

46.   One of the underlying conditions of the 1971 waiver was the recognition that 'these arrangements should not impede the reduction of tariffs on a most-favoured-nation basis' (GATT, BISD, 18th Supp. (1972), p. 27).

47.   This conclusion finds some support in the negotiating history of this provision. In the 1971 GATT Protocol, from which this part of the legal design was also taken, there was a separate provision at the end of the Protocol, called a 'Declaration', which stated that granting lower tariff rates to fellow members of a developing country customs union or free trade area *shall not* give rise to a claim under

the nullification and impairment provision. The implication was that other forms of impairment-by-discrimination would have.
48. While the GSTP Agreement nowhere says that regional preferences do not 'impair' concessions, the 1971 GATT Protocol did (in a concluding 'Declaration'), and the GSTP Agreement's elaborate deference to regional groupings will almost certainly be read to require the same answer.
49. For a comparative analysis of the major regional agreements among developing nations, see Carl (1986).

References

Carl, B.M. (1986) *Economic Integration Among Developing Countries* (New York: Praeger).

Hamza, M.A.–B (1981) 'Review of the Preferential Arrangements Established under the GATT Protocol Relating to Trade Negotiations among Developing Countries', UN Doc. TD/B/C.7/49, 27 October.

Hamza, M.A.–B. (1987) 'Guidebook for the GSTP: The Global System of Trade Preferences among Developing Countries – Origin, Dimensions, Negotiations and Prospects' (Geneva: UNCTAD), June.

Hudec, R.E. (1987) *Developing Countries in the GATT Legal System* (London: Macmillan, for TPRC).

Hudec, R.E. (forthcoming) 'Tiger, Tiger in the House: A Critical Appraisal of the Case against Discriminatory Trade Measures', in M. Hilf and E.–U. Petersmann (eds), *The New GATT Round of Multilateral Trade Negotiations: Legal and Economic Problems* (New York: Kluwer).

Langhammer, R.J. (1980) 'Multilateral Trade Liberalization Among Developing Countries' *Journal of World Trade Law*, 14, pp. 508–15.

Nolde, Le Baron B. (1932) 'La Clause de la Nation la Plus Favorisée,' *Recueil des Cours*, 1.

Ramcharan, B.B. (1984) 'Equality and Discrimination in International Economic Law (XII): The Proposed Global System of Trade Preferences Among Developing Countries', *The Yearbook of International Affairs 1984* (London: Stevens & Sons).

South–South Economic Cooperation: Problems and Prospects (1987) (New Delhi: Radiant Publishers, for RIS).

12 Liberalizing Agricultural Trade: Some Perspectives for Developing Countries

H. Don B.H. Gunasekera, David Parsons and Michael G. Kirby

INTRODUCTION

In real terms, the prices for many agricultural commodities are at their lowest levels of the post-war years (Tyers and Anderson, 1987). Growth in consumer demand is weak, surplus stocks of a number of major agricultural commodities stand at unprecedentedly high levels, and production remains well above market requirements (IMF, 1987). The downturn in world import demand in the 1980s contributed to the problems. However, the extent of agricultural intervention policies and their general lack of flexibility, particularly in the United States, the EEC and Japan (which together dominate world agricultural trade), are largely responsible for this present situation in agriculture.

The main stated objectives of protection policies in major developed countries are to stabilize agricultural prices and to support farm incomes. However, evidence suggests that the support policies have neither offered long-term protection to farmers' incomes nor stabilized prices (Johnson and Sumner, 1976; Howarth, 1985; Schiff, 1985; World Bank, 1986). Winters (1987a) argues that this is because, in the long run, the benefits of price support accrue not to labour or capital but to those who were landowners at the time that farm policies were introduced or extended.

Support policies, however, involve transfers of income to agricultural producers from consumers and from taxpayers, and impose costs on the economy as a whole. The domestic costs of agricultural protection arise from misallocation of resources, within the agricultural sector as well as between agriculture and other sectors in the economy, induced by subsidized inputs and artificially high prices for protected agricultural commodities.

Winters (1987a), after surveying a number of partial and general equilibrium studies of the consequences of agricultural support policies in various OECD countries, identified several adverse effects.

238

He concluded that these policies increase food prices to OECD consumers, waste resources by overexpanding agricultural output in high cost areas and curtailing it in low cost areas, divert resources from manufacturing and services by reducing the competitiveness of these sectors of the economy, and may reduce aggregate employment.

The agricultural support policies of major developed countries have marked international consequences, affecting the level and variability of international prices and, as a consequence, the pattern of international trade in agricultural commodities.

The protectionist policies of major developed countries, including the widespread use of agricultural export assistance, can adversely affect other more efficient agricultural exporters by lowering world prices. In addition, the EEC and Japan rely significantly on variable import levies, quotas and other similar mechanisms to insulate domestic producers and consumers from world markets. Because the trade shares of these countries are relatively large, these trade barriers increase the volatility of international prices by isolating a substantial part of world consumption and production from international market forces. As a consequence of these price effects the volume of world agricultural exports is reduced, constraining the potential global gains from trade for both developed and developing countries.

Given this background to the current state of world agriculture, the purpose of this chapter is to highlight several issues of importance for international agricultural trade reform and to examine the developing country interest in liberalized agricultural trade.

The plan of this chapter is as follows. In the next section, a number of key issues which are relevant to reform of the current global agricultural trading environment are discussed. A brief survey of the potential impact on developing countries of agricultural trade liberalization and a discussion on developing country roles in agricultural trade reform are presented in the third section, while the final section provides some concluding remarks.

KEY ISSUES IN GLOBAL AGRICULTURAL TRADE

Need for Reform

As noted above, agricultural support policies have, in the longer run, failed to achieve their objectives. They have raised land values but have not raised farm incomes, especially those of smaller farmers. Significantly, there are also wider longer-run pressures facing agriculture which are not likely to be redressed by present policies. These pressures affect both the demand and the supply side and they require those engaged in agriculture to make continual structural changes.

On the demand side, most agricultural products, particularly food, are characterized by an important factor: they are basic necessities, with an income elasticity of demand less than unity. Consequently, as real per capita incomes increase in a growing economy, the demand for agricultural products grows more slowly than demand for many other products and consumers spend a declining proportion of income on agricultural products. Alongside these demand pressures are supply factors. Over many years, technological improvements in agriculture have yielded significant increases in productivity which in turn have led to an increase in supply of farm products.

The combination of these demand and supply forces has placed downward pressure on real agricultural prices and per capita incomes of existing farmers. As a result, agriculture's relative importance in an economy, in GDP and employment terms, tends to decline with economic growth. Farm incomes cannot keep pace with those in the rest of the economy, unless some marginal farmers leave the land or seek off-farm employment (Johnson, 1973, 1987).

The principal ingredient for reform of the agricultural trading environment is, therefore, fundamental change at the farm level and a policy environment which recognizes the need for such fundamental ongoing structural change in agriculture. The potential benefits from global agricultural trade cannot be fully realized until individual countries make these changes toward greater market orientation. However, given the problems confronting agricultural policy-makers at present, many issues must be addressed while this structural adjustment takes place. Some of these issues are likely to benefit from international cooperation.

Process of Reform

Towards a Multilateral Approach

For several reasons, a multilateral, multi-commodity approach to policy reform offers significant opportunities for longer term improvement (OECD, 1987). Because of the country and commodity interlinkages within the world agricultural system, a coordinated multilateral, multi-commodity approach would generate significantly greater benefits to the world community than can be achieved piecemeal. Furthermore, research suggests that because many of the changes in production, consumption, trade and world prices would be moderated under such an approach, the adjustment difficulties facing many producers would be lessened.

In addition, market-oriented policy changes are more likely to endure if a multilateral, multi-commodity approach is pursued. The complex interrelationships of agricultural activity and policy between countries and commodities may have the effect that a partial approach to policy change – either country- or commodity-specific – leads in some cases to further imbalances, exacerbating existing trade tensions. For example, without multilateral agreement, the danger of opportunistic action and retaliation by individual countries, as seen in the sometimes strained trading relationship between the USA and the EEC, is likely to persist. The confrontationist approach which has characterized the actions of these two groups is costly to them. Moreover, these actions further increase the market pressure placed on the low cost exporters and import-competing producers in developing and other countries.

Finally, treaties such as multilateral trade agreements can have substantial weight. The existence of an international understanding on standards of behaviour introduces a new element into the domestic policy-making process. A multilateral framework for agricultural reform may thus ease the political difficulty of domestic policy change.

The inclusion of agriculture in the new round of trade negotiations under GATT raises the possibility of reform within a multilateral, multi-commodity framework. However, in view of the diverse interests of the contracting countries, the negotiation of an accord on rules and disciplines affecting agricultural trade promises to be a formidable and time-consuming task.

Timing and Pattern of Trade Liberalization

Though there is widespread agreement on the benefits of trade liberalization, there is much less agreement on the best timing and phasing. One of the reasons for this is the difficulty of assessing the costs of adjustments resulting from trade liberalization in the major developed economies, where agricultural protection has become entrenched over many years. Behind the shield of protection, many farmers and associated service industries have avoided coping with the difficult process of adjustment that structural change in these economies would ordinarily demand. Protection has thus altered land and capital values and has influenced the expectations of a wide range of decision-makers about future profitability. Significant political commitment on the part of governments will therefore be required, since any liberalization would tend to threaten the established domestic political equilibrium.

Wolf (1986) argues that the extent to which economic agents are prepared to undergo structural adjustment will depend on the credibility and 'transparency' of the policy of liberalization. The less credible the policy – that is, the less committed a government is to going through with the necessary reforms – the higher the economic costs will tend to become before economic agents are convinced of the necessity to make the required changes in their activities and behaviour. Thus the liberalization process is likely to proceed more smoothly if it is credible, predictable and transparent, while not instantaneous. Economic agents usually need at least some time to adjust if the costs of adjustment are to be optimized.

The pattern of gradual reduction in protection is an important consideration in any approach to agricultural trade liberalization. It has been shown theoretically (Corden, 1974) that the economic costs of protection are more than proportional to its level, so that high protection creates proportionately more costs than low protection; and that a large intra- and intersectoral variation in protection levels is more costly than a more uniform pattern of protection. For these reasons, it is desirable to lower both the average level of protection and the variation.

Measurement of Agricultural Intervention

In view of the wide range and complexity of protective measures and support programmes in agriculture in various countries, trade negotiators and policy-makers may require comprehensive indicators of assistance to help them formulate and choose between possible reform policies. One important comprehensive indicator of industry assistance which has been the focus of recent attention is the PSE (OECD, 1987; US Department of Agriculture, 1987). This is a measure of the monetary amount that would be required to compensate agricultural producers for the removal of many forms of intervention affecting output, intermediate inputs and value-adding factors. PSEs are based on prices, production and trade under current policy and market conditions. When compared across countries or commodity markets, they show the relative importance of government intervention in different countries and markets in terms of its contribution to producer revenues. When compared over time, they show the extent of changes in government involvement in the agricultural sector. A comprehensive indicator of agricultural assistance, such as PSE, could thus be a useful measuring device in the context of multilateral trade negotiations and for monitoring the extent of policy changes.

One specific policy proposal for immediate action is to halt the escalation of subsidies, and progressively to reduce the gap – termed the 'price adjustment gap' by Miller (1986) – between administered internal prices and international market prices for farm products (Australian Government, 1987). According to Haszler and Parsons (1987), the price adjustment gap, though conceptually simple, accounts for some 80 per cent of the assistance that is covered by the PSE in OECD countries. A progressive reduction in this gap would allow international price signals to feed through to producers. This would tend to slow production in the major developed economies. At the same time there would be benefits on the demand side in the EEC and Japan, where consumers – as distinct from taxpayers – largely bear the cost of producer support. A reduction in the gap could reduce food prices and induce increased demand in these countries. At an international level, world prices for farm products would gradually rise as reduced supplies from the developed country exporters entered the world market. In this sense, the price adjustment gap would close from below as well as from above.

Effective Disposal of Stocks

The stability of agricultural trade is threatened by huge stockpiles of surplus commodities such as grain, sugar, dairy products and beef in the USA and the EEC. It is important that, in the short term, these stocks be quarantined by the countries whose domestic agricultural support policies have been responsible for their growth (Australian Government, 1987). Progress in removing international distortions in agricultural markets would be disrupted if there were fears that surpluses might be released in an undisciplined manner on to world markets. This can be avoided by releasing stocks gradually in the longer term, in accordance with success in reducing production.

Given these high stock levels and the need for a gradual reduction in internal prices where they are above world prices, direct supply controls may well be useful in the early stages of reform, particularly in countries unable to reduce their large price adjustment gaps quickly. More generally, however, supply controls are not likely to provide long-term solutions. Such controls face many practical problems: they are difficult to administer effectively; they can inflate costs faced by producers; and they tend to constrain the potential for efficiency gains which may arise through technological change. Supply controls and market management are therefore poor substitutes for the policy changes required to address the underlying causes of the problem: artificially high internal prices and associated trade restrictions.

Provision of Adjustment Assistance

If administered agricultural prices are reduced by a number of developed countries acting in concert and if stocks are successfully quarantined and managed, steady improvements in world market prices in the longer term can help to compensate producers for the reduction in subsidies and transfers. To ease the difficulties of adjustment for farmers in the interim – especially in countries with relatively high administered prices – policy-makers may choose to provide some farm income support. To minimize distortions, it should not be linked directly to farm output; preferably social welfare, adjustment assistance and direct income support policies should be used which will create minimal incentives to produce. This method has an additional advantage. By providing assistance in this form, governments must make explicit budget allocations for this purpose. The level of farm support can then be readily identified, and governments are thus publicly accountable to all sectors of the economy for their policy decisions. Over time, it is preferable that even these special support measures be progressively scaled down.

A more constructive alternative to protection, in the long term, is to prepare marginal farmers to make the transition from the farm. One key element of such a solution is to provide resources to raise their level of general education (Schultz, 1961). This should enable them to be more discerning about the decision to leave and the timing of that decision, and, more importantly, it should improve their non-farm job opportunities. Better education also has obvious benefits for the skills of those farmers who remain in agriculture.

DEVELOPING COUNTRIES AND AGRICULTURAL TRADE REFORM

Notwithstanding substantial structural changes in many developing countries during the past few decades, agriculture continues to be a dominant sector in a majority of developing economies. As a major source of income, employment and export earnings, the agricultural sector plays a vital role in these economies. Consequently, issues relevant to agriculture in the GATT negotiations are of considerable interest to many developing countries.

In previous rounds of multilateral trade negotiations, developing countries have taken a relatively passive role. Their limited participation was characterized by attempts to seek special and differential status within the GATT framework. Although they received such status, many developing countries have failed to reap any substantial benefits in the form of improved access to developed-country markets. However, the NICs, which have gained the most from S&D status, currently face market access problems arising from various NTBs, including VERs imposed by major developed countries (Hamilton and Whalley, 1987). Therefore, for developing countries, access to markets for both agricultural and manufacturing products is a crucial aim of the GATT negotiations. In the case of agricultural products, the key issues are tariff and non-tariff barriers on processed agricultural exports from developing countries and the subsidization of major food commodities by major developed countries.

Effects on Developing Countries of Liberalizing Agricultural Trade

As a result of the sizeable distortions in the agricultural sectors of many countries, both developed and developing, considerable net gains would be likely if protection were to be markedly reduced and agricultural trade were to be significantly liberalized. A number of recent studies have attempted to evaluate the various effects of agricultural trade liberalization in developed countries (for surveys of these studies, see World Bank, 1986 and Winters, 1987a). Although there are differences in the estimated effects of trade liberalization among these studies, the overall direction is clear. Liberalization of the agricultural policies of developed countries is expected to raise world market prices, to reduce world price variability and to stimulate growth in world agricultural trade.

Some of these studies have assessed the effects of trade liberalization specifically on developing economies (see Valdes, 1987, for a review of these studies). According to these studies, developing countries as a group are likely to benefit from trade liberalization in developed countries. However, the potential gains from liberalized trade are not likely to be evenly shared among all developing countries. In particular, low-income developing countries, such as those in Africa, are expected to suffer most from higher costs of food imports which are likely to result from such liberalization, particularly in cereals. However, a relatively small increase in export earnings from meats is likely to accrue to some of these countries. On the other hand, some of the middle-income developing countries such as those in Latin America could benefit substantially from liberalized trade in meats, particularly beef. The export revenue gains from trade liberalization in sugar are likely to be quite considerable for both low and middle-income developing countries (Valdes, 1987).

Most studies of the potential effects of agricultural trade liberalization on developing countries have concentrated on the temperate zone products, for which developing countries are typically net importers. However, Valdes and Zietz (1980) covered both temperate and tropical products in their study of the effect of trade liberalization in developed countries on developing countries. They estimated that developing countries' total export revenue would have risen by 11 per cent in 1977 as a result of trade liberalization by the OECD countries. Because protection in the OECD countries has increased since 1977, the benefits of liberalization would be substantially greater in the 1980s. While developing countries would have incurred some losses from higher prices of some temperate zone products, such losses would have been more than compensated for by the increases in export revenue if trade barriers on tropical products such as tobacco, roasted coffee, coffee extracts, cocoa derivatives and oilseeds were lowered or removed.

Tyers and Anderson (1987) and Parikh and Tims (1986) have added a new dimension to the agricultural trade liberalization literature by assessing the potential impact of a global trade liberalization scenario, including liberalization of developing country food trade. Although the broad picture which emerges from these two studies is similar to the one discussed above, the Tyers and Anderson (1987) study has provided an assessment of the likely impact of trade liberalization in the 1990s. Speculative though such assessments necessarily are, they provide a basis for estimating how much larger the potential welfare gains from liberalizing major temperate zone agricultural products might be under the current GATT round. Global trade liberalization is expected to raise net economic welfare considerably in the developing world in the 1990s, mainly due to the potentially large international price effects. According to Tyers and Anderson (1987), removal of agricultural protection in all developed and developing countries would raise food prices (weighted average for grains, livestock and dairy products and sugar) by 30 per cent in 1995. Among the developing countries, those in Asia and Latin America are likely to be the major beneficiaries.

Welfare analysis in Table 12.1 indicates that producers in developing countries gain while consumers lose as a result of liberalizing food markets in the major developed countries alone. Moreover, net economic welfare declines in many developing countries except for food exporting countries: Thailand, Cuba, Argentina, Brazil and other Latin American countries. This is because, in many developing countries, the consumer losses outweigh the producer benefits.

However, liberalizing food markets in both developed and developing countries is likely to raise the net economic welfare in a greater number of developing countries than liberalizing developed country food markets alone. This is because many developing countries have domestic policies which are biased against agriculture. Furthermore, liberalization of developed country markets for tropical agricultural commodities and related processed products, an aspect not covered in this simulation analysis, is likely to add substantially to the potential gains from agricultural trade reform to many developing countries.

The effects of liberalization on developing countries are likely to be diverse. Those developing countries that have a comparative advantage in producing food commodities are likely to benefit from their increased exports. For example, Argentina will benefit in wheat, Thailand in rice and sugar, the Philippines and Brazil in sugar and China in rice. On the other hand, rising world prices following liberalization are expected to reduce imports in many traditional food importing countries in the developing world, particularly in

Table 12.1 Welfare effects of liberalizing agricultural policies, 1995[1] (1985 US$ billion per year)

	Liberalization by USA EEC and Japan			Global Liberalization		
	Producer welfare	Consumer welfare	Net Economic welfare[2]	Producer welfare	Consumer welfare	Net Economic welfare[2]
Developed[3]	-104.6	154.4	45.0	-122.0	170.8	62.4
USA	0.6	2.5	3.0	9.0	1.2	8.3
EEC	-77.3	82.2	18.1	-68.1	75.3	22.5
Japan	-38.9	75.8	20.4	-38.9	77.4	22.0
Canada	3.1	-2.1	0.3	0.5	0.6	1.9
Australia	3.2	-1.6	1.5	3.8	-1.3	2.3
New Zealand	1.6	-0.6	1.0	1.7	-0.6	1.2
Developing	40.2	-41.8	-13.2	44.4	18.9	16.4
Asia	22.1	-22.2	-9.1	29.6	-6.0	8.0
Korea	0.4	-0.9	-0.9	-7.6	14.0	0.1
Taiwan	0.4	-0.5	-0.3	-1.3	1.4	0.1
China	7.5	-6.5	-0.6	33.0	-21.9	6.6
Indonesia	1.3	-1.1	-0.8	-1.4	3.6	2.1
Philippines	0.2	-0.2	-0.0	-1.1	1.4	0.3
Thailand	0.6	-0.6	0.2	1.7	-0.6	0.5
Bangladesh	0.8	-0.7	-0.6	1.0	1.4	-0.9
India	7.5	-8.1	-3.2	-2.8	-0.6	-2.2
Pakistan	1.7	-2.0	-1.3	3.1	-3.1	-1.2
Other Asia	1.7	-1.6	-1.6	5.0	-1.6	-1.5
Latin America	11.0	08.4	7.8	37.6	-20.0	13.4
Argentina	2.2	-2.1	1.9	9.2	-4.4	3.5
Brazil	4.0	-2.8	3.0	14.9	-8.8	4.7
Mexico	1.4	-1.2	-0.3	-1.2	0.6	0.3
Cuba	0.0	-0.0	0.4	2.3	-0.4	1.3
Other Latin America	3.4	-2.3	2.8	12.4	-6.9	3.6
Africa	7.1	-11.2	-11.9	-22.8	44.9	-5.0
Egypt	0.3	-0.5	-1.0	-1.4	4.5	0.5
Nigeria	0.6	-1.1	-1.2	-3.2	7.7	0.8
Sub-Saharan Africa	1.9	-3.0	-2.6	0.7	-0.3	-3.1
Other North African and Middle East	2.9	-4.7	-5.8	-18.8	32.8	-2.2

[1] Covers grains, sugar, livestock and dairy products.
[2] The change in net income is the sum of the changes in producer and consumer welfare plus the change in taxpayer cost and stock profits.
[3] Includes all industrial market economies.

Source: Gunasekera and Tyers (1987) and Tyers and Anderson (forthcoming).

Africa and some parts of Asia and Latin America. If rapid domestic farm production gains and the associated income gains in developing economies lead to trade-dependent drives to upgrade diets, then increasing demand for coarse grain imports can be expected in a number of rapidly growing countries.

Developing Country Roles in Agricultural Trade Reform

Any significant outcome of the multilateral trade negotiations in agriculture will depend on the extent to which the major trading countries – the USA, the EEC and Japan – can reach agreement on removing or reducing their domestic distortionary policies. In the absence of other influential power brokers, these major trading countries could reach bilateral agreements by largely ignoring the position of other trading countries, including those in the developing world. Such an outcome is likely to have adverse effects on the long-term interests of many developing and similarly affected developed countries, and for the GATT system as a whole.

In such a negotiating environment, the role that developing countries can play either individually or as a group is limited for several reasons. First, developing countries in general (except for countries such as Korea and Taiwan) have relatively low levels of agricultural protection. In fact, many developing countries tax the production or, more usually, exportation of non-staple agricultural products directly or have various domestic policies affecting prices, marketing and macroeconomic conditions that are biased against agriculture (World Bank, 1986). Therefore their contribution to the disarray in world agriculture is likely to be relatively small.

Second, developing countries differ widely in size, per capita income, production and trade orientation, international indebtedness and trade interests. They are not, therefore, a homogeneous group. This makes it difficult to form a single united front of all such nations that can negotiate and bargain effectively in multilateral trade fora.

Third, the above review of empirical evidence suggests that the potential benefits from removal or reduction of distortionary agricultural policies in major developed countries are unlikely to be evenly distributed among developing countries because of their heterogeneous characteristics. Therefore the interests of developing countries in agricultural trade reforms are by no means identical.

Nevertheless, there are several areas in which developing countries can make significant contributions to agricultural trade reform.

Supporting Issue-Specific Coalitions

Although developing country interests in agricultural trade vary, the overlap of interests between some developing countries and similarly affected developed countries (for example, Thailand and Australia) suggests the possibility of forming flexible coalitions which are issue-specific, given a willingness on the part of individual countries to form agreement across the developing/developed country division. An example of such a coalition is the Cairns Group of agricultural exporting nations (Australia, Argentina, Brazil, Canada, Chile, Colombia, Fiji, Hungary, Indonesia, Malaysia, New Zealand, the Philippines, Thailand and Uruguay). If the Cairns Group can act with sufficient cohesiveness then there is at least the possibility of it having some bargaining power as an important mediating force in negotiating agricultural trade reform within a multilateral framework.

Although the Cairns Group membership only covers a few developing countries which produce food commodities such as grains, livestock and dairy products and sugar, some of them are also major producers and exports of tropical agricultural commodities and related processed products. These include: Indonesia in rubber and coffee, Malaysia in rubber and palm oil, Brazil in coffee and cocoa, the Philippines in coconut oil and copra, Thailand in rubber and cassava, Colombia in coffee, and Nigeria in cocoa. Many developed countries have escalating tariffs accompanied by a wide range of NTBs on processed agricultural commodities exported by developing countries. These forms of trade barriers tend to erode the export revenue base of many developing countries and, in the longer term, to limit the possibility of economic development based on comparative advantage and on trade-oriented growth strategies. Although some agricultural exports from developing countries enjoy tariff concessions and exemptions in developed country markets under the GSP, the Lomé Convention and the US Caribbean Basin Initiative, the products concerned account for only about 7 per cent of developing countries' total exports (World Bank, 1986).

Therefore there is an overlap of interests among some developing country members of the Cairns Group and many other developing countries, particularly with regard to tropical agricultural commodities and related processed products. In this context, a plausible strategy for those developing countries which export tropical agricultural commodities and related products would be to support the Cairns Group directly or indirectly in international fora. This could add a new dimension to the developing country negotiating position in the current GATT round, while further enhancing the negotiating and bargaining strength of the Cairns Group.

Liberalizing Protectionist Regimes

The likelihood that developed countries would significantly liberalize their trade in the interests of developing countries without reciprocity is remote. With reciprocity the chances that they would do so are better. In such circumstances, reciprocal concessions to developed countries remain a viable option for developing countries, particularly those countries that have already made significant progress in economic development and that have promise of further growth in the future. Realistically, the degree of reciprocity in trade negotiations would have to take into account the level of economic development in each developing country. As a reciprocal concession developing countries could offer to liberalize and rationalize their own protectionist regimes.

In many developing countries manufacturing industries are highly protected. Generally such protection policies lower the relative incentives to agriculture and other export industries. This develops a bias against the exporting industries and thus reduces potential export growth. In particular, the rapidly growing developing countries such as Korea and Taiwan have relatively high levels of agricultural protection implemented through price support and both tariff and non-tariff barriers. Significantly, there are indications that a number of other middle-income countries are beginning to follow a similar pattern; examples include Mexico and Brazil (Ballenger, Dunmore and Lederer, 1987). Those developing countries that have relatively high levels of protection, either in manufacturing or in agriculture, could offer reciprocal concessions in multilateral trade negotiations.

Given the widespread use of NTBs, both in agriculture and in manufacturing, some doubts have been raised about the wider applicability of the concept of reciprocity. Importantly, its practical application requires some kind of valuation of the mutual concessions that negotiating countries could offer each other (Dell, 1986). However, Winters (1987b) has shown how previous GATT negotiating techniques on tariffs could be used to negotiate the removal of a subset of NTBs: the QRs. This involves the application of the 'principal supplier' rule whereby pairs of countries could negotiate over pairs of commodities for which each is the other's principal supplier. This is particularly relevant in the case of the developed and developing country link.

Improving Domestic Policy

Despite the progress made in agricultural development in the developing world, sector-specific taxes, subsidies and price controls in some countries continue to discriminate against agriculture to a considerable extent (Ray, 1986). In those developing countries where domestic policies discriminate against agriculture, rationalization could take a number of forms.

In countries where export crops are taxed to raise government revenue, the resulting disincentives to producers could be reduced by moderating such agricultural taxation, and giving higher priority to alternative ways of generating government revenue, such as broadly based value-added taxes.

Rather than relying upon price support schemes to safeguard producers and consumers from price fluctuations, developing countries could adopt alternative measures for reducing the risks faced by agricultural producers, traders and consumers. Such measures include agricultural diversification, greater development and use of capital markets, increased storage of agricultural commodities, and the sharing of risks through purchase and sales contracts. However, adoption of these measures requires greater dissemination of information about input and output prices, cropping patterns and crop choices, availability of storage facilities, access to credit facilities, and the availability of appropriate know-how and skilled manpower.

Agricultural producer subsidies, ranging from subsidized farm inputs to agricultural credit, are common in developing countries. However, the availability of subsidized inputs and credit is often limited by their budgetary cost, as well as by the inefficiencies and problems of distribution via public sector agencies (Ray, 1986). More careful targeting of input subsidies or credit is one way of reducing the budgetary cost of these subsidies.

Consumer price subsidies on imported food commodities are often used in developing countries to assist low income earners in urban areas. According to the World Bank (1986), however, consumer subsidies in developing countries tend to benefit middle- and upper-income earners rather than low-income earners. Their budgetary costs could be lowered by the adoption of cost-effective methods of improved targeting, such as restricting the subsidies to the poorest regions and lower-income groups and to items that are consumed predominantly by the target groups.

Failure to adjust exchange rates sufficiently in periods of rapid inflation and changing international economic circumstances has also been a major problem in many developing countries (Chhibber and Wilton, 1986). In those developing countries where agriculture is an important export sector, currency overvaluation has discriminated against the production of agricultural exports by allowing resources to move away from the tradable agriculture sector to other sectors. In countries where at the same time the import-competing sectors are protected, the disincentive to the export-oriented agricultural sector has been even greater. However, the importance of the exchange rate overvaluation problem differs considerably among countries. For instance, Cleaver (1985) argues that in sub-Saharan Africa exchange rate policies are not the most important factors affecting agricultural growth, having a relatively small influence compared with other factors such as farm input supply, agricultural investment and population growth.

International Management of Commodity Trade

In some developing countries, dependence on a few agricultural export commodities for foreign exchange earnings and uncertainty about the stability of long-term commodity prices have led to a search for means to modify the effect of unregulated commercial trade. The outcome of this search has been the various ICAs, commodity-oriented concessional financing arrangements and bilateral preferential trading agreements between importing and exporting countries. Through these schemes, participating countries have sought to limit the adverse effects of declining and volatile agricultural terms of trade on economic growth.

In agriculture, there are four ICAs still officially operating, covering cocoa, coffee, natural rubber and sugar. The primary objective of these agreements has been to increase export earnings for producers and stabilize markets for consumers, by stabilizing and/or raising export prices through production and export controls and buffer stock management. However, because of the difficulty of obtaining compliance by all producers, and the tendency of consumers to use substitutes for the commodities covered, effective implementation of ICAs is not easy. Evidence suggests that the long-run success of any of these agreements is unlikely (World Bank, 1986).

With the decline in the export earnings of many developing countries, there are calls for new initiatives to create additional world liquidity which could be used to make up export income losses, on the basis of the falls in commodity prices (Stanicic, 1985). However, according to the UN (1986), there is a need for international cooperation in assisting developing countries to diversify, in the long term, out of excessive dependence on a few commodities.

CONCLUSION

The world agricultural trading environment is characterized by major imbalances which have' increased in recent years. The real prices of agricultural commodities, especially temperate zone food products, are depressed while stocks of many of these commodities remain substantially above commercially-required levels.

Widespread agricultural support policies, especially in the EEC, the USA and Japan, have largely been responsible for the present predicament. However, it has been compounded by the downturn in import demand in the 1980s, which revealed the extent and the lack of flexibility of these interventionist policies.

Sustained reform of the agricultural trading environment depends on three fundamental elements. First, there is the need to replace existing farm support policies with more appropriate structural adjustment policies so that farmers can adapt to the long-run economic pressures facing agriculture. These changes to domestic policy in individual countries are likely to lead to more open and stable global agricultural trade. Second, in the interim, many of the immediate issues confronting trading countries can be addressed within a multilateral framework such as GATT. Third, improved agricultural markets and prospects of agricultural policy reform depend on the macroeconomic policy stance and conditions, whether in developed or developing countries.

Agriculture continues to play a dominant role in the economic performance of most developing countries. Thus agricultural policies, particularly in the major developed economies, have an important bearing on the growth and development prospects of developing countries. Although developing countries have taken a relatively passive role in previous GATT rounds, there is scope to influence the outcome of current negotiations on agriculture and other agenda items through supporting issue-specific coalitions and being more willing to contemplate reciprocal concessions, rather than continuing to concentrate on the pursuit of S&D treatment.

However, the potential benefits from agricultural trade reform are by no means evenly distributed across developing countries: the traditional developing country food exporters are likely to benefit, rapidly growing developing countries with high levels of agricultural protection are not expected to benefit unless their domestic polices are reformed, and those developing countries that are heavily dependent on food imports are likely to lose.

Nevertheless, an overall assessment of the potential effects on developing countries of trade liberalization needs to take into account not only agriculture, but a wider coverage of traded goods, including manufactures. Moreover, the potential growth and welfare effects of wider trade reform will depend on the extent to which these countries can liberalize their own trade regimes and the degree to which their sectoral and economy-wide policies are reformed.

References

Australian Government (1987) *Resolving the World Agricultural Crisis: An Australian Proposal* (Canberra: Australian Government Printing Service).

Ballenger, N., Dunmore, J. and Lederer, T. (1987) *Trade Liberalization in World Farm Markets*, Agriculture Information Bulletin No. 516 (Washington, DC: Economic Research Service, US Department of Agriculture).

Chibber, A. and Wilton, J. (1986) 'Macroeconomic Policies and Agricultural Performance in Developing Countries: How Macro-Policies can Produce a Bias against Agriculture', *Finance and Development*, 23 (3), pp. 6–9.

Cleaver, K. (1985) 'The Impact of Price and Exchange Rate Policies on Agriculture in Sub-Saharan Africa', World Bank Staff Working Paper No. 728 (Washington,DC: World Bank).

Corden, W.M. (1974) *Trade Policy and Economic Welfare* (Oxford: Clarendon Press).

Dell, E. (1986) 'Of Free Trade and Reciprocity', *The World Economy*, 9 (2), pp. 125–39.

Gunasekera, H.D.B.H. and Tyers, R. (1987) 'Distortions in International

Food Trade and their Impact on the ESCAP Region', background paper prepared for UN (1987) *Economic and Social Survey of Asia and the Pacific* (Bangkok: ESCAP).

Hamilton, C. and Whalley, J. (1987) 'Strategic Options for Developing Countries in the Global Trading System', paper presented at the Ford Foundation Conference on Trade Policy and the Developing World, Ottawa, 17–20 August.

Haszler, H. and Parsons, D. (1987) 'The Price Adjustment Gap and World Agricultural Policy Reform', *Quarterly Review of the Rural Economy*, 9 (2), pp. 177–88.

Howarth, R.W. (1985) *Farming for Farmers*, Hobart Paperback No. 20 (London: Institute of Economic Affairs).

IMF (1987) *World Economic Outlook* (Washington, DC: IMF) April.

Johnson, D.G. (1973) *World Agriculture in Disarray*, (London: Macmillan).

Johnson, D.G. (1987) 'Crisis in International Agricultural Trade', paper presented at the Conference on Economy-Wide Effects of Farm Support Policies (convened by the TPRC and Bureau of Agricultural Economics), Steyning, Sussex, England, 8–10 May.

Johnson, D.G. and Sumner, D. (1976) 'An Optimization Approach to Grain Reserves for Developing Countries', in *Analyses of Grain Reserves*, US Department of Agriculture Research Paper ERS-634 (Washington, DC: US Department of Agriculture).

Miller, G. (1986) *The Political Economy of International Agricultural Policy Reform* (Canberra: Australian Government Printing Service).

OECD (1987) *National Policies and Agricultural Trade* (Paris: OECD).

Parikh, K.S. and Tims, W. (1986) *From Hunger amidst Abundance to Abundance without Hunger* (Laxemburg, Austria: International Institute for Applied Systems Analysis).

Ray, A. (1986) 'Trade and Pricing Policies in World Agriculture', *Finance and Development*, 23 (2), pp. 2–5.

Schiff, M. (1985) *An Econometric Analysis of the World Wheat Market and Simulation of Alternative Policies, 1960–80*, Economic Research Service Report AGES 850827, (Washington, DC: US Department of Agriculture).

Schultz, T.W. (1961) 'A Policy to Redistribute Losses from Economic Progress', *Journal of Farm Economics*, 43 (3), pp. 554–65.

Stanicic, M. (1985) 'A New Approach to Compensation of Developing Countries' Export Earnings Losses', in *Primary Commodities: Challenge to Cooperation among Developing Countries, Conference Proceedings* (Zagreb: Institute of Developing Countries).

Tyers, R. and Anderson, K. (1987) 'Global Interactions and Trade Liberalization in Agriculture' in A. Ray and D. Gale Johnson (eds.) *Economic Policies and World Agriculture*, (Washington, DC: World Bank).

Tyers, R. and Anderson, K. (forthcoming) *Distortions in World Food Markets* (Cambridge University Press).

UN (1986) *World Economic Survey: 1986* (New York: UN).

US Department of Agriculture (1987) *Government Intervention in Agriculture: Measurement, Evaluation, and Implications for Trade Negotiations*,

Economic Research Service Staff Report No. AGES 861216 (Washington, DC: US Department of Agriculture).

Valdes, A. (1987) 'Agriculture in the Uruguay Round: Developing Country Interests', paper presented at the conference on GATT and the Developing World, East–West Center, Honolulu, 24–6 June.

Valdes, A. and Zietz, J. (1980) *Agricultural Protection in OECD Countries: Its Cost to Less Developed Countries*, International Food Policy Research Institute Research Report No. 21 (Washington, DC: IFPRI).

Winters, L.A. (1987a) 'Measuring the Economic Costs of Farm-Support Policies', paper presented at the Conference on Economy-Wide Effects of Farm Support Policies (convened by the TPRC and Bureau of Agricultural Economics), Steyning, Sussex, England, 8–10 May.

Winters, L.A. (1987b) 'Negotiating the Abolition of Non-Tariff Barriers', *Oxford Economic Papers*, 39 (3), pp. 465–80.

Wolf, M. (1986) 'Timing and Sequencing of Trade Liberalization in Developing Countries', *Asian Development Review*, 4 (2), pp. 1–24.

World Bank (1986) *World Development Report: 1986* (New York: Oxford University Press).

Index

Where abbreviations appear in subheadings, they are consistent with those used in the text.